T H E
IDEA FACTORY

T H E
IDEA FACTORY
LEARNING TO THINK AT MIT

PEPPER WHITE

A DUTTON BOOK

DUTTON
Published by the Penguin Group
Penguin Books USA Inc., 375 Hudson Street,
New York, New York 10014, U.S.A.
Penguin Books Ltd, 27 Wrights Lane,
London W8 5TZ, England
Penguin Books Australia Ltd, Ringwood,
Victoria, Australia
Penguin Books Canada Ltd, 10 Alcorn Avenue,
Toronto, Ontario, Canada M4V 3B2
Penguin Books (N.Z.) Ltd, 182–190 Wairau Road,
Auckland 10, New Zealand

Penguin Books Ltd, Registered Offices:
Harmondsworth, Middlesex, England

First published by Dutton, an imprint of New American Library, a
division of Penguin Books USA Inc.
Distributed in Canada by McClelland & Stewart Inc.

First Printing, September, 1991
10 9 8 7 6 5 4 3 2 1

 REGISTERED TRADEMARK—MARCA REGISTRADA

LIBRARY OF CONGRESS CATALOGING IN PUBLICATION DATA
White, Peregrine.
    The idea factory : learning to think at MIT / Pepper White.
      p. cm.
    ISBN 0-525-93347-6
    1. White, Peregrine. 2. Mechanical engineers—United States—
Biography. I. Title.
    TJ140.W45A3 1991
    621'.092—dc20
    [B]   91-10187
                                CIP

PRINTED IN THE UNITED STATES OF AMERICA
Set in Meridien
Designed by Leonard Telesca

*This book is dedicated to my mother
and to the memory of my father.*

Acknowledgments

Many people have helped and encouraged me along the way to this publication. From the beginning, in roughly chronological order since 1984, I wish to thank John Mattill, Liz Muther, Linda Simon, Aklilu Gebrewold, Carl Brandt, Bill Newlin, Bill Ijams, and the anonymous editor at Putnam who, in a rejection letter, told me to find a literary agent first if I ever wanted to publish this book.

Thanks also to the MIT professors and friends who reviewed sections of the manuscript; special thanks to Professor Elias P. Gyftopoulos for permission to use material from his course notes and textbook "Thermodynamics: Foundations and Applications" (Macmillan, 1991), and for his corrections to the manuscript.

And finally, warm thanks to Malaga Baldi, my literary agent, and to Alexia Dorszynski, my editor, who told me not to censor myself and who did not censor me.

C O N T E N T S

A Note to
the Reader

As is life itself, this book is a mixture of nonfiction and fiction. It is being marketed as nonfiction, since most of what happens in it is based on my best recollections of experiences I had as a graduate student at MIT. However, I was not wired for sound, and I did not take photographs of all the locations described herein. Thus, for example, the journal articles described in piles on Professor Mikic's chairs may have been, in fact, on Professor Rohsenow's chairs, or on someone else's chairs.

Names of key MIT professors have been retained, both to give due credit to the work they presented in the lectures I attended, and to present real people in the real institute. Dialogue or lecture material of these characters is often included in quotation marks to retain the narrative flow. However, as I mentioned above, I was not wired for sound; it was eight years ago, and the words I present are based on my memory and/or notes I took at the time. If my memory is at fault, I apologize. Those people whose real names are used are included in the book's index.

All other characters are composites. The names and physical characteristics have been changed to protect the innocent, and some of the scenes with these characters are purely fictitious. However, even the fictitious scenes are adapted from my real experiences at the institute.

Can we not bridge the chasm which thus makes for civil strife within the mind? The extremists on both sides say, no! The poet and the man of faith affirm that only through man's spirit, through intuitive understanding, can he touch the true reality. Those who have harder heads will toss this attitude aside as hopeless mysticism, irrational and false. Most men cannot decide on either course, and attempt to live a double life. The Hyde who holds discourse with science is a different man from the Jekyll of art or politics or religion. This divided allegiance is accepted as inevitable by many. . . . But such duality can hardly offer a sound basis for any satisfying life philosophy. At best it is demoralizing, at worst, perilous. . . .

—From Edward W. Sinnott, "Science and the Whole Man," centennial address, Sheffield Scientific School, Yale University, October 1947

Preface

The world of high technology is a mystery to most of us. Science seems to offer as much potential for danger as it did 100 years ago, and the mind of the technologist still eludes our understanding. The questions of whether science, technology, and the humanities are unbridgeable cultures; whether "objective" science necessarily results in dehumanization; whether morality has any component in scientific thinking—these are still unresolved issues. And nowhere are these issues more alive than at one of the world's foremost schools of engineering and science: MIT.

At MIT and similar schools, the resulting civil strife within the mind is an undeclared war. At MIT it manifests itself in various ways—in the "IHTFP" ("I hate this fucking place") written on the desks in lecture halls and bathroom walls and printed on T-shirts; in the annual "Institute Screw" contest, wherein a professor is singled out as the most inhuman; in the too-frequent occurrence of suicide.

The first professor I met told me that it didn't really matter what I learned there, but that MIT would teach me "how to think." In my last class, I studied artificial intelligence, the art of teaching computers how to think, how to solve problems. Between these two events, I learned how to model physical systems, how to design, how to invent.

I was taught objective, rational, logical modes of thinking. I learned intuitive thinking by doing research and by solving problems. And my heart was educated, for good or for bad.

This book is about the changes that take place in engineers as they learn to think. It explores the conflicts that result when engineers must suppress (or at least put on the back burner) their human, social sides in order to survive in the objective world of science and engineering.

What are the small steps that cumulatively form an engineer? How does an engineer learn to solve problems? How does he or she maintain relationships and friendships during the process? I've attempted to answer these questions here.

I'm glad I went to MIT; I'm not sure I would have been able to sell any of my other first-book ideas to a big New York publisher. Second, in my years at MIT, I was transformed from a fluff engineer into a real one. I spent some time in the company of greatness. And MIT really did make me smarter—which means that anyone can become smarter, by learning how to think.

A note on technical discussions: to show how an engineer learns to solve problems I've depicted my approaches to problems of varying degrees of difficulty. The main text includes the general sense of the problems to be solved and my approaches to them, and more discussion of technical material is presented in the Appendix and Chapter Notes. Figures that pertain to the technical discussions are placed on the upper part of the page on which each discussion begins.

MIT is a different place for everyone who goes there. But there exist invariants, and I hope I've hit on more than a few in what follows.

T H E
IDEA FACTORY

Prologue

Belgium
Saturday, May 9, 1981

The letter was getting wet and wrinkled in my pocket. I was thinking.

Leave Stephanie; go to MIT. Marry Stephanie; stay in Belgium. Put ocean between me and Stephanie; go to MIT. Marry Stephanie later; go to MIT.

"Dear Mr. White," the letter said. "We have not yet heard from you and would like to know if we should reserve a place for you in next fall's group for the Technology and Policy Program. Please let us know your decision at your earliest convenience."

This was their first letter and it didn't make sense. When you're accepted, you usually get a fat package with forms for housing and insurance. And funding.

Pop question tonight; call MIT Monday.

The peasants had had enough in 1794 and, during the French Revolution, they burned the abbey, all except the chimney and the columns now dormant amidst the trees. Peeled open, the chimney converged, the moss-covered gray stone narrowing gently upward.

It looked like a wind-tunnel stood on its end, like the wind-tunnels at the von Kármán Institute for Fluid Dynamics, the NATO center just south of Brussels where I'd been studying for the previous eight months. I wondered which monk had come up with the idea that the chimney's draft would be improved by the convergence.

The abbey, named Villers-la-Ville (five kilometers south of Genappe [twelve kilometers south of Waterloo (fourteen kilometers south of Brussels)]), dated from the twelfth century. The guide passed the chimney and pointed to the rectangular stone passage in the wall of the ruined refectory. "And what," he asked in French, "do you think this was for?"

I answered, "To heat the room with the smoke before it went to the chimney."

"Ah, oui, eh," he replied, "Monsieur must be un ingénieur."

Stephanie sat across from me that night in the Robin Hood Restaurant near Brussels's Place Louise.

"Oh," she said when I told her MIT had accepted me, "I'm very happy for you." But the look in her childlike brown eyes was sad, sad the same way that had made me fall in love with her when John Lennon died.

I couldn't break her heart.

"Is it that you would like me to marry?" I asked her in French.

She said, "That's 'Would you like to marry yourself with me?' " I helped her with her English; she helped me with my French.

"OK. Would you like to marry yourself with me?"

"Oui."

Oh mon Dieu, qu'est ce que j'ai fait?

Monday, May 11

"Hold the line please," the international operator said.

"Hello, TPP," said the woman's cheery voice from 4,000 miles away.

"Uh, yeah," I said. "This is Pepper White calling about the letter you sent me."

"Oh, gee," she said. "I don't know how to tell you this, but we made a big mistake here. Your file was put in the deferred acceptances filing cabinet by mistake, and it was supposed to be put in the deferred applications file. So you're not really admitted."

"Does that mean I'm rejected?"

"No, it means your file isn't complete. You need two more letters of recommendation."

"I'll see what I can do."

Brussels Airport
August 29, 1981

"I love you, too. . . . Be sure to write. . . . I'll see you at Christmas. . . . I'll miss you. . . ."

Above Cape Cod, Same Day

The pilot started the descent too late. Steeply downward the plane dropped.

I wanted to break into the cockpit, wake up the pilot, and say, "Pull back on the stick, you idiot; pull back on the stick!"

C H A P T E R

——— 1 ———

Logging On

Monday, August 31, 1981

I climbed the stairs from the Kendall Square subway stop, rounded the corner onto Ames Street, and began to feel the knot being tied in my stomach. Maybe I should have stayed in Belgium after all. The street was bounded by an old gray factory on the right and a drably functional red brick building on the left. The factory windows were half-open, and compressed air hissed and machines loudly punched holes in metal.

I remembered Mr. Hume and Mr. Ide in the physics movies from MIT that Mrs. DaRosa had shown my high school class. She had refused to write me a recommendation to MIT for college on the grounds that it wasn't human. Wait, she said, and go to a nice liberal arts school for college. Work hard, get good grades, and if you still want to, go to MIT for graduate school.

I went to Johns Hopkins. There, as I majored in environmental engineering, I studied art history, French, Italian, American cinema. I went on the Grand Tour. First six months in Milan and the environs, then my year at the von Kármán Institute. I felt rested, as if the broadening chapter of my life had been completed. Now it was time to focus and to work.

I turned right after the factory and went between it and the not-quite-as-drab beige concrete and glass building that came to a point. Farther along were the Bauhaus-style box of a swimming pool and temporary World War II buildings. I felt claustrophobic and yet protected. The windows at the Belgian monastery had faced inward also. The monastery had provided time and space for quiet reflection by a devotedly trained elite. I would become one of that present elite: a member of the intelligentsia.

I first heard of MIT growing up in the shadow of Duke University in Durham, North Carolina. Coming home from a business trip, my father brought me *The Great MIT Paper Airplane Book*— my favorite was the one that looked like a little helicopter and twirled down to the ground when I let it go. When I was eleven, my mother (a pianist), my father, my three older sisters, and I moved to Washington, D.C. He'd taken a job as a science writer with the National Academy of Sciences.

It was the first Earth Day (in 1971, I was thirteen) that sparked my interest in the environment. That interest lay dormant until I was trying to figure out where to apply for college and I saw that Johns Hopkins offered an Environmental Engineering degree. I started in that department, jumped over to physics, jumped back, and became interested in energy conservation as a way to help the environment. MIT's Technology and Policy Program (TPP) offered a generalist's approach to that type of issue; they accepted me and here I was.

On a small patch of grass between concrete and asphalt in the adjoining cloister an ROTC squad did their morning jumping jacks.

"And halt!" the leader ordered.

"Are we MOtivated?" he shouted.

"Yes, sir!" they breathed loudly.

"Are we Extreeeeeemly motivated?" he asked.

"Yes, sir!" they breathed again.

"Down for 20."

I admired their intensity. I wondered whether I'd ever be able to match it.

"This is Doctor White from MIT," I imagined my clients introducing me. "He's expensive, but he's good . . . and he's fast."

I asked the commander how to get to the TPP office, 1-138.

"Turn left at that building up there—that's Building 13; then go back up to the infinite corridor and turn right into Building 6.

Your second left from Building 7 lobby is Building 1; 1-138 should be about halfway to the Charles. At ease!" He spoke quickly, as if his tongue could not quite keep up with his brain. I imagined thousands like him within a quarter-mile.

"What's the infinite corridor?" I asked.

"It links all the main buildings, has glass doors on either end, and is about 319 paces long. On November 12 and January 31 the sun shines directly from one end of it to the other."

I found the infinite corridor and even though school was not yet in session the pedestrian cruising speed was just short of a jog. All eyes were fixed forward. Some nodded to friends or acquaintances but none stopped to chat.

There was a tug on the knot in my stomach. It was the same empty terror that had gripped me as a child waiting for the bus to take me to the first day of day camp.

I had a few minutes to kill, so I wandered from side to side, admiring the displays of past MIT greats. Vannebar Bush, a father of computers. Norbert Wiener, high school graduate at eleven, another father of computers and of modern theory of controlling devices like airplane automatic pilots. Karl Taylor Compton, noted physicist from earlier in the century, who was also president of MIT. Intelligence sparkled through the eyes of all the old black-and-whites of the late great masters.

The displays must be meant to inspire the present generation to work hard, to emulate their ancestors. But the first thing these walls seemed to tell me was "No matter how hard you work, you'll never be like these giants. Not only did they do nothing but work; they were gifted."

Outside it was heavily humid, the trees in Killian Court lushly green. Sponges transpiring into the heavy air. I waited near the Technology and Policy Office, alone at 8:30.

It was cool and dark inside. I looked through the corridor window across the Charles to the skyline of Back Bay.

After a few minutes, a guy from Brown named Jim Stuart arrived. He was there to get the pick of the desks. An office desk is the MIT equivalent of a library carrel, a home away from home where you can securely keep your books. Like me, Jim was also there to get in line for funding. If you don't have funding at least you should have a desk. My first friend.

"What was your major at Hopkins?" he asked.

"Environmental engineering," I said. "You know, wastewater

treatment, landfills, pollution control. How about you? What'd you major in?"

"Environmental sciences. Sort of the same kind of issues, but maybe with a little more chemistry."

He was articulate and had an Ivy League knowing look in his eyes. He'd picked TPP over Harvard's Kennedy School, another training ground for bureaucrats. As we talked, I began to wonder whether we had both been duped by the altruism of Professor Richard de Neufville, the "airport guy," whose computer programs for optimizing the flow of airplane traffic at airports had made his name big enough that he could start a program to train people to be bilingual: to speak the language of technology and to speak English.

I wondered whether we'd been fooled into a program that looked good only on paper. But, according to the brochure, the graduates went on to impressive positions at think tanks and high-powered consulting firms, and they were "engineers with a difference."

Karen Smith, the cheery voice from across the ocean, unlocked the office. Life in New England had flattened and compressed her southern accent but not her charm.

"So I guess y'all need keys to the student office," she said. "It's over in Building 20; you go through Building 13, take a right, and go under Building 26. Here's a chart of the desks that are left."

Of the twenty desks on the chart, only about 5 were unclaimed, and there were fifteen people entering the program. Jim and I had done well to be early.

"Is Professor de Neufville in today?" Jim asked. "I wanted to talk to him about funding."

"Yeah, I'd like to, too," I said.

She answered, "He's on sabbatical for the year. But here's a list of projects. You can also talk to people at the Sloan School of Management or in your base engineering department."

Each technology and policy student had to be affiliated with an engineering department. My affiliation was with mechanical engineering; I wanted to strengthen my fluid mechanics and environmental background. Also, I wanted to argue environmental and energy issues from a position of strength, with a degree from MIT.

"Oh, I almost forgot," Karen said. "You'll have three tests

before the term begins. The writing test is on Thursday; the test to qualify for the graduate economics course without taking an undergraduate course is next Tuesday; and you can take the swimming test whenever you want. No one can get a degree from MIT without knowing how to swim. And here're your course catalogs."

Jim and I walked back to Building 20, the World War II temporary building opposite the swimming pool. Three stories, gray, military. The TPP student office was on the third floor.

It had orange carpet, beige walls, and a brown couch. Pipes were exposed; lights were fluorescent. There were a hot plate and a refrigerator in the corner. This was home.

The Indian-looking guy talking on the phone when we walked in finished his conversation and introduced himself.

"My name's Amrit; what's yours?"

Jim and I each told him and while Jim was scoping out the free desks, I continued to talk to Amrit.

"What are you here to study?" Amrit asked.

"Energy conservation. I want to work on energy systems to help combat the greenhouse effect."

"Oh yes," he said. "I'm working on energy, too. I've just finished an energy model for my home country of Pakistan. I like energy. Energy is easy."

Right, I thought. What's a model? I couldn't ask him because I didn't want to sound dumb. His way of speaking indicated that he was bright, but it disturbed me that he thought that energy was easy. I didn't come here to learn fluff; I came to learn rigor, to learn how to save energy through good engineering and economic analysis. Amrit was friendly, but I couldn't help thinking that if he wanted to work on easy things he would land a cushy job at the UN in Geneva or New York, doing nothing for his country and riding on the coattails of his MIT credential.

Jim found a window seat, and I picked the one nearest the phone. It would soon be time to smile and dial for funding.

But first a look through the course catalog. It was as thick as the Boston phone book. I thumbed through it and found the section that had appealed to me about TPP. "The Technology and Policy Program produces 'engineers with a difference.' Through study of a broad mix of engineering, economics, systems analysis, and regulatory policy, graduates will be able to function in the technological and policy environments." It had sounded great two years back, but it bothered me that there wasn't any funding for its projects. Real engineering departments could solicit funding from Fortune 500 companies or from various government agencies. But there was no Department of Generalities, so TPP had few doors to knock on. If there wasn't anyone to fund graduate research, who would fund my paycheck when I finished? Besides, the von Kármán Institute had started me in a hard-core direction; TPP might be too soft. I asked Amrit for advice.

"So is it true that TPP produces engineers with a difference?" I asked him.

"Yes," he said. "The difference is that they can't get jobs." My doubts were intensifying. I continued to look through the catalog.

As at Seven-Eleven, there is freedom of choice at MIT. The departments specify the number of courses you have to take, but which you take is between you, your adviser, and the department graduate adviser.

Every MIT department has a number, as does every course. It helps you find your way through the catalog. Mechanical Engineering is "Course 2." The subdisciplines are signified by the next digit. Fluid mechanics is the 20 series, thermodynamics the 40 series, and heat transfer the 50 series. I noted potential courses.

2.25 Advanced Fluid Mechanics (A. Shapiro, K. Gemayel). "Surveys principal concepts and methods of fluid dynamics. Statics. Continuity, momentum, and energy relations for continuous fluids. Vorticity dynamics. Circulation. Dynamical similarity in fluid flows. Boundary layer theory, including separation and other examples of shear flow phenomena. Introduction to turbulence. Drag. Lift." Potential metaphors for the coming months.

2.451 General Thermodynamics I (Prerequisite: Permission of Instructor) (E. P. Gyftopoulos). "General foundations of thermodynamics valid for small and large systems, and equilibrium and nonequilibrium states. Definitions of state, property, work, energy, entropy, thermodynamic potential, and interactions other than work (nonwork, heat, mass transfer). Applications to properties of materials, bulk flow, energy conversion, chemical equilibrium, combustion, and industrial manufacturing." Sounds like this one should help my energy conservation skills, I thought. Maybe Gyftopoulos has funding, too. I put a star by it.

2.55 Advanced Heat Transfer (W. Rohsenow). "Develops similarity between heat, momentum, and mass transfer in forced and buoyancy-driven flows. Covers fundamental modes of heat transfer: diffusion, internal and external forced and natural convection, boiling, condensation, and radiative heat transfer. Flow instabilities and heat transfer augmentation techniques. Extends heat transfer results to analagous convective mass transfer processes." This could help in designing a heat exchanger to recycle waste heat from a chemical process, or in designing a solar collector. I put a star by it, too.

Fluids had interested me since my canoe tripping days, when the waves and wind and rain in the middle of the lake seemed at once chaotic and orderly. I wanted to see, to feel the order. My first heat transfer experience was as a child with a hard-boiled egg. After it had boiled for twenty minutes, I poured water over it. It cooled down for a second, then heated up again. Why?

"I'm gonna go get my athletic card and take the swimming test," Jim said. "Either of you guys want to come?"

"Oh, yes," Amrit said. "I've got a squash game with my friend Dilip at 9:30. I'd be happy to walk over there with you."

"I think I'll hang out here," I said. "I want to start contacting the people on the project list Karen gave us."

Smile and dial. Tuition for the first term is $3,700. If it takes me six terms counting summers to get out of here, and tuition goes up at, say the inflation rate plus 3 points, how much will I owe if I don't find some sugar daddy to pay my way through? Oh, and don't forget living expenses at another $5,000 or so a year. And it's not like med school or B school or law school where I'll be making 60K+ when I get out of here and can pay off any debts in a year or two. The $1,000 I borrowed at 15 percent from my parents and each of three friends is as much debt as I ever want to bear.

Big smile. Feel the corners of that mouth extend across the face. Deep breath. Pick up the phone.

"Hello, is Professor Mikic there?"

"That's Mick-ish," the Slavic voice on the other end said. "What can I do for you?"

"Uh, my name is, uh, Pepper White, and I'm in the, uh, Technology and Policy Program, and I saw that you, uh, have a research project in phase change materials. I was wondering whether I, uh, could come and talk to you about it." My knees were shaking.

"You don't want to waste your time with me," he said. "I don't have any money."

"Maybe I could talk to you about my classes. I think I need some guidance."

"As you wish. How's eleven o'clock?"

"That sounds fine. Thank you, sir."

Call number two. "Professor Robert Pyndike, Economics Department (Sloan School). Thesis project: Computer modeling of global oil pricing. Determination of supply and demand curves, compilation of econometric data, and sensitivity analysis. Half-time research assistanceship."

It sounded good. Maybe I'll do that and go work for an OPEC sheik for $100K. OPEC's in Vienna. I like Vienna.

"Hello, Professor Pyndike, I'd like to make an appointment to talk to you about your oil pricing research."

"Talk to my secretary and make an appointment. I'll be out until next Tuesday."

"OK. Thanks."

"Professor Leon Glicksman. Experimental and theoretical study of outgassing of freon in foam refrigerator insulation. Development of computer models to predict experimental results, construction of test apparatus, and refinement of models."

His answering machine said he'd be back next Tuesday. I didn't leave a message after the tone.

Mikic's office was in Building 3. Across the hall I stopped to look at the display case with photos posted and things made out of oatmeal boxes, rubber bands, and string. Must have been some kind of contest.

His office was professorly. Piles of journal articles on the table next to his desk. A blackboard opposite where he sat. A wall of full bookcases behind him. His window overlooked the humid trees of Killian Court. His young assistant, about my age in gym shorts and a T-shirt, was typing at a computer terminal near the blackboard.

Mikic offered me one of the black MIT captain's chairs, the kind that alumni have in their dens, the one that didn't have a stack of journal articles on it. The piles were neat. I had the feeling that I could ask him about anything in heat transfer and he could go to the right pile and pull just the right article out of the middle of it.

He was about fifty, trim, with most of his hair, wearing a white short-sleeve button-down shirt, no tie. The top button was unbuttoned. He had a friendly, intelligent smile.

"So, what can I do for you, Mr. . . ."

"White. I did some work on phase change materials in Belgium, so I thought that experience might be useful for your project."

"Well, I'm sorry, but I already have given that project to that fellow sitting over there." The guy at the terminal was looking smart, typing fast. I wanted to look smart and type fast in my mentor's office, too.

Mikic asked, "What do you want to do when you get out of here?"

"I want to be an energy expert."

"Well, that's very good. That's a good topic now. Be careful, though. When you finish oil might be back down to $15 a barrel and everyone will forget about energy conservation. It doesn't really matter what you study here. We teach you to think. We make you into a professional. Then you can do whatever you want."

"Could you help me pick out my classes for the term? I've starred some that look interesting to me, like fluids, thermo, and heat transfer. I was thinking about taking five or six this term including some TPP courses since I don't have funding yet. Then I'll be ahead of the game."

"Start with five, then drop two," he said briskly. "And make sure you get A's in the real engineering classes. Most of us don't give much credit to A's in that soft policy stuff. We hire people who can make it in the hard courses."

Mikic continued, "You know it's a courageous thing you're doing, coming here without any money. I did the same thing twenty-five years ago. I flew here and had money for one term and a plane ticket home to Yugoslavia. If I didn't make it in the first semester it would have been 'back home to Tito.' I worked harder than most in that first term, and I got A's in all my classes. Now I'm a tenured professor. Who knows? Maybe the same will happen to you."

"I hope so," I said as I rose to leave.

"Good luck now. If you ever need any help, please drop by."

If Mikic was academe, Gyftopoulos was industry. I needed his permission to take General Thermodynamics I. His desk and chairs were teak; a single pad of paper was on the center and a small stack of correspondence to his left. While he was on the phone I glanced at the annual report from Thermo Electron that I had picked up from the reception area. Net revenues of $17 million on $270 million in sales. On the page where the directors were pictured, Gyftopoulos had a passport-size photo, looking wise and wealthy. In the mental marathon that is MIT, he was a gold medalist.

Gyftopoulos was pushing sixty, a little overweight but he carried it well. He had salt-and-pepper gray hair and a receding hairline that had stopped well short of baldness. His shirt had no pockets, but on the left chest was a neatly monogrammed E.P.G. He smoked a cigarette he had taken from the silver cigarette case next to the pad.

"I'd like to take your general thermodynamics class, sir," I said.

"That's fine." His accent sounded like he'd learned English from a Brit in Athens. "What kind of background do you have in thermodynamics?"

"Well, I took a course at Hopkins with Professor Schwarz, and I've also taken several fluid mechanics and heat and mass transfer classes that touch on it."

"Did you get A's in those classes?" he asked directly.

"Yes, I did. I'd really like to take your class. I'm especially interested in the energy conservation aspects of thermodynamics."

"Do you have any background in energy conservation?"

"I did an energy conservation study of a factory while I was in Italy. I found that if they would pay a guy to go around and fix the leaks in the compressed air system they could save $25,000 per year."

"That's very interesting," he answered, "and it's good that you noted that they would have to pay the guy to achieve the savings. There is always a trade-off of capital, labor, and energy. You're welcome to register for the course. I shall look forward to seeing you at the first lecture."

It felt good to have his approval.

"Thank you, sir. Is there any book I can read to get a head start on the material?"

"No, it's best that you wait until the first class. We will be handing out course notes then. Gian Paolo Beretta and I are working on a text that we believe will not make the mistakes that are commonly found in thermodynamics texts. If you read any other material perhaps it might confuse you."

Friday the TPP orientation meeting was in the Miller Room, the lounge on the second floor of Building 1. I finally met all the other students in one place. They were all bright enough, but most seemed to lack the focus and direction I expected of people at MIT. Some had survived a year or more, though, and I hungered for their confidence.

One of the other rookies was Michael Picardi, who'd just earned his physics degree from Williams College the previous May. His senior thesis was on "Relativistic Effects in Black Holes."

"Why aren't you going to physics graduate school?" I asked him.

"Because I'm not a Korean genius and I want to have a life," he said. "I agonized over it a while, but sometimes you just have to go with your gut. I'm going to do mechanical engineering and energy conservation. It seems a little nearer-term than physics. Fusion isn't going to be feasible for forty years at best, and I want to do something useful now."

"Gee, you sound just like me," I said. "Only I bailed out of physics in my junior year at Hopkins. I still remember the problem. 'Find the electrostatic potential at the geometric center of an infinitely long cylinder of uniform charge.' Then I took up fluid mechanics as sort of a compromise. At least you can see the fluids. How can you see an electric field?"

"I know what you mean," he said. "Maybe we'll take some classes together."

Pyndike's office
Tuesday, September 8

"You're in that TPP program, aren't you? You must be more interested in a topic dealing more with technology. I'm really looking for someone with a more straight economics and policy slant."

That afternoon in Glicksman's office. "You're in that TPP program, right? You must be more interested in a topic dealing more with policy and that kind of stuff. I'm really looking for someone with a straight mechanical direction."

Wednesday, I met with my TPP adviser, David Marks. A civil engineering professor, he figured out how to manage water flows in river basins with several dams as his specialty. Jerry Cohon, my freshman faculty adviser at Hopkins, had been Marks's first Ph.D. student.

"What I want out of TPP is a sound engineering background and some economics so I can figure out cost-effectiveness of energy conservation programs," I said.

"You should get out of TPP then. Go straight to Course 2— get your degree in mechanical engineering. You seem to know what you want out of this place. We try to let talented people who know what they want achieve it here; we try to stay out of their way. But if you're at all uncertain, you'll be in for a rough time. By the way, you'll know we've got you when you call the men's room by its number."

The last hoop of my transition from TPP to real mechanical engineering was the meeting with Warren Rohsenow, graduate adviser for mechanical engineering students. I still didn't know the full circumstances of how I was admitted, and I was a little scared that trying to leave TPP would uncover the error they may have made in letting me in.

Rohsenow, leaning back in his chair and cleaning his pipe, looked through my file and said matter-of-factly, "You're already in this department."

Phew.

Now the bad news. Rohsenow continued: "The hooker is, since you didn't take mechanical engineering in college, you'll have to take all the department's undergraduate core courses: two-oh-one Statics, two-oh-two System Dynamics and Controls, two-ninety-four Dynamics, two-thirty-one Strength of Materials, and two seventy Design. That's the deal; take it or leave it."

My term of indentured servitude had just doubled. "I'd still like to start with the graduate courses in my strong areas," I said. "I think it'll help me find funding."

"Well." Puff puff. "It sounds kind of bass ackwards if you ask me but it's your decision. You need six graduate courses for your master's so it'll be good to get three of them out of the way."

"Thank you for your signature," I said. "It looks like you'll be teaching heat transfer, so I guess I'll see you in class."

"Right. See you in class."

C H A P T E R

2

Class

Thursday, September 10, 1981

9:23 A.M. Room 3-214, on the second floor at the end of the hall, on the corner of the building with a view of the river. A hint of fall was in the air. The 100 hard wooden movie theatre chairs on the level floor of the 30-by-40-foot classroom each had a little desk surface that swung up from the arm of the chair. I picked one on the second row just left of center. Close enough to see the blackboard, far enough not to get called on first if that's what they do here.

Professor Ascher Shapiro arranged his notes for two twenty-five, Advanced Fluid Mechanics, on the table on the slightly elevated wooden platform in front of the three blackboards. He looked close to retirement age, with longish gray hair around the sides of the bald spot. He wore light brown corduroys, a green turtleneck, and small silver-rimmed half-spectacles that he looked through only when looking down at his notes.

The hundred or so desks filled around me as 9:30 approached. My fellow students were in their mid- to late twenties. Many Americans, but at least a third were foreigners. Greeks, Koreans, Iranians, Indians, French, Chinese conversed in their native tongues. There were about five women.

At 9:28 Shapiro began drawing diagrams, and at 9:30 he quietly said, "I'd like to begin now." He had a slight New York accent. Thirty seconds later all the conversations had stopped.

"Before we get started, I'd like to go over some housekeeping details for the class. There will be two quizzes during the term and a final exam. At the end of class we will be handing out a set of problems for you to work on during the term. These will not be for handing in or count toward your grade. However, we strongly recommend that you do them. It is essential for your mastery of the material that you do problems. And by doing problems, I don't mean mimicking a worked-out solution from a handbook—I mean that you need to pioneer your way through the solution yourself; blaze your own trail, find the dead ends, backtrack, and move on. There will be two tutorial sessions every Friday. You can come to these to ask Professor Gemayel for help finding solutions. Also, we want to encourage you to take good notes from the lectures. At the end of the term you will have the option of submitting your lecture notebook. If it is well done and you are on the borderline between one grade and another, you will receive the higher grade."

I guess we're big boys and girls now and don't get forced into doing homework. I'll write fast, though, and copy over my notes after every class. The brownie points might come in handy.

"Now for the lecture," Shapiro continued. "Fluid mechanics is a branch of mechanics. Mechanics may be defined as the study of motions, forces, and bodies, and the relationships between the motions of bodies that are brought about by forces. The subject of fluid mechanics is very broad, including hydraulics, plasmas such as those in a hydrogen fusion reactor, gas dynamics, physical oceanography, magnetohydrodynamics, and fluid control systems. This particular course is advanced, approaching the fundamentals with what is hoped to be a greater degree of insight and sophistication than you may have experienced before."

He spoke as one having authority. The twenty-seven times he must have presented the identical lecture since the early 1950s had polished the presentation style, cut it down to a flawless gem of wisdom. I wrote, scribbled as fast as I could, briefly wishing that I knew how to take shorthand; I didn't want to miss a facet.

Shapiro explained density. He started by drawing little chunks of fluid. They were little circles on the blackboard, with a little line from the center to the edge of each circle. "We have a continuum model; that is, we model the effects of the molecular motion as an average instead of looking at each molecule. The continuum is a total fiction which attempts to model the real. The connection between the continuum and the real is that the continuum properties should represent appropriate averages of the real material. With density, we assign density values to a point. We give density a value at each point in our continuum field as a function of space and time. This is the giant intellectual leap made by . . ."

I didn't catch the name. I'll raise my hand and ask. No, I'll leave a blank in my notes and ask later. It would be nice if I knew what he meant by a model.

His lecture brought me back to my physics days. I had sort of wimped out on physics, and here the same kind of abstract concepts that applied to fluids were coming back to haunt me. But I enjoy fluids. If you understand them, you can have an idea why a tornado does what it does, why the wind blows from the ocean in the day and to the ocean at night. I'll be able to see more than clouds in my coffee.

He elegantly continued, covering fluid statics—what happens when the fluid is standing still. This is what civil engineers worry about when they build dams. The deeper the water, the higher the pressure. The higher the pressure, the bigger the force on the dam. The bigger the force, the thicker the concrete. Otherwise the water pressure would cause the dam to burst. There were no questions from the students, only rapt attention and fast writing. When the bell rang just before 11:00, I had filled eighteen sheets of paper with notes. It felt like an information overload, but at least I had until Tuesday to digest the material before the next lecture.

Shapiro finished by saying, "I want to reiterate the importance of doing problems. Through working problems on your own, you will find that there is an enormous difference between learning and being taught. Professor Gemayel will be handing out the problem packets." The one hundred of us went to the front, crowding around like options traders in a pit as Gemayel handed out the half-inch-thick packets.

While I waited my turn I saw near the door a guy who looked familiar. "Excuse me," I said. "Did you go to Johns Hopkins?"

"Yeah, but I transfered to MIT for my junior and senior years. My name's Matt Armstrong."

I remembered the acute questions he had asked in physics class freshman year. Matt had been a "Simpy" (for SMPY, Study of Mathematically Precocious Youth); in seventh grade he took the SAT math test and scored 700 on it, the highest of any seventh grader in Baltimore. That score qualified him to study math at the college level through high school. I had the feeling Matt might be on the other side of the bell curve from me in this class. Math talent notwithstanding, he was a nice guy. In the fall of 1975 he had had shoulder-length hair, but it was short now.

"What have you been doing since you graduated?" I asked as we walked down the hall toward the infinite corridor.

"I worked the past two years out at a high-tech company on Route 128, developing a high-efficiency water heater. I should be getting a patent on it soon. In fact, I have to go out there this afternoon to sign some papers."

Patent. This guy has a patent.

He asked, "Do you have a class now?"

"Yeah. Two four five one."

"Hey, that's great. I'm taking two four five one, too. Maybe we can find a couple of seats together."

On the infinite corridor the air was more electric, the walking pace slightly faster than it had been before classes started. Still no eye contact. I had the feeling these people didn't waste time.

Gyftopoulos's lecture hall had the same movie chair desks, only the rows went up as you went back in the room. Matt and I found two in the fourth row.

A lot of the students were the same ones as in Fluids. Maybe there were a few more Americans in this class. Again, mostly men, with four or five women. There weren't many particularly good-looking people of either gender, but there was a universal look of embattled concentration in the eyes. A lot of the guys looked like they only shaved every other day.

Gyftopoulos chatted at the front of the class with a guy about my age who had a light brown mustache and a small beard on his chin alone. All the younger guy needed was a monocle and the right clothes and he could have been in a "Spy" cartoon. A couple of minutes after 11:00 Gyftopoulos called the class to order. He smiled and nodded my way when he saw me in the fourth row.

"First I want to go over a few housekeeping details," he said. "Homework will be assigned every week, due at the lecture the following week. Also there will be one or two two-hour quizzes during the term, plus a final examination. Your grade will be based

30 percent on homework, 30 percent on quizzes, and 40 percent on the final examination."

It was nice how both he and Shapiro called the two-hour tests quizzes. Perhaps it was institute policy to mellow-speak them down from midterm examination or test; a quiz is what you take for ten minutes in high school. At least I was comforted by the grading and counting of the problem sets. I figured if I could just hang in with those, I should be able to do respectably in the class.

Gyftopoulos continued, "Gian Paolo Beretta will be helping me teach the class; he will also be available to assist you with any questions you may have. And of course you are always welcome to come to my office to ask questions."

Beretta must be brilliant, I thought. If he's teaching he must already have his Ph.D., which isn't bad for a twenty-four-year-old.

"Since there are no texts available that teach what we shall be presenting here, you will be required to purchase a set of class notes that Gian Paolo and I have put together. Please remain seated while we count the number of sets to reproduce."

Gian Paolo started counting, as did I. Matt looked up and down, to the left and the right, and by the time Gian Paolo was on the second row Matt said out loud, "Seventy-six."

"Good. Thank you," Gyftopoulos said, not questioning the number that Matt had stated with such conviction.

I asked Matt quietly, "How'd you count so fast?"

"Each row has 14 chairs. There are 6 rows—that's 84—and there're 8 empty seats. That's 76."

Well, I guess we know who's going to get an A in this class.

Again Gyftopoulos: "I want you to feel free to ask any questions during the lecture also. I will not be calling on students as a regular practice, but I may from time to time ask someone to help with a derivation."

Not quite as bad as the Socratic method, but I should keep up with the reading and problem sets here. Usually engineering classes are one-way data transfer; you try to keep up with the lecture's logic flow, but only the professor has to think fast when questioned. But Gyftopoulos would challenge us, and maybe challenge me.

"Now for the lecture," Gyftopoulos went on. "The course title again is 'General Thermodynamics.' *General* refers to several aspects of the approach to the course. First of all, the exposition is of an approach that is valid for all systems, regardless of their size. Second, the results will be valid for all states and conditions of our systems. Third, the approach suggests that thermodynamics is not a closed field, but rather includes many areas that are open for discussion and new analysis. *Thermodynamics* in the title refers to a study of the properties of matter and the changes in properties of matter which occur; thus the interactions of different parts of matter. The science of thermodynamics is more general than mechanics in that it can describe hot and cold bodies, an area that the science of mechanics is incapable of describing. In addition, mechanics cannot deal with the concept of entropy."

Right. What's a state? What's a system? What is entropy? I kept writing, scribbling fast.

"Now for some basic concepts," Gyftopoulos continued. "As in any scientific approach, we shall concentrate on a small part of the universe, a system. A system needs at least two things: (a) the amount of matter in the system—its mass—and (b) constraints or external parameters—i.e., you must define the system boundary. Now how do we analyze systems? There are two possibilities. First at one instant in time, and second as a function of time.

"At one instant in time, the state or condition of the system is a powerful concept in analyzing the system. If you know the system and its state, you can calculate everything you want to know for the one instant of time. *State* is a set of numbers or parameters that allow us to calculate properties."

Right. What's a property?

"Second, the function-of-time analysis relies on the equation of motion to describe the transition from one state to another."

Gyftopoulos talked in similar abstract terms for another hour. Matt listened attentively and wrote a perfectly neat set of notes while I scribbled away, following bits and pieces of the line of reasoning but wondering where this all fit into my aspiration to be an energy czar. I would copy over the notes later.

"Thank you for your attention. Please pick up a copy of next week's problem set and the copy of an article I've written."

The article was entitled "Thermodynamics, Principles of." It was reprinted from *Encyclopaedia Britannica*.

I asked Matt as we left the classroom, "Say there, Matt, do you know of any desks anywhere? I quit the Technology and Policy

Program just before classes started and they want my desk back."

"So you punted TPP? Sounds like a good move. There's a desk in my office that's available. Why don't you talk to Charlotte Evans, the department secretary, and see if you can get a key? I'd hate to see you wandering around the institute with a shopping cart full of books. By the way, do you play soccer? We're putting a team together for intramurals. It's called the Calorics. We've got a practice tonight at 6:30."

"Yeah, that sounds great. I played a little bit in Europe. Sounds like a good way to meet some people, too. Maybe get some funding. Do you have an R.A.?"

"I'm working on outgassing of fluorocarbons for foam refrigerator insulation for Glicksman. He just hired me about a week ago. How about you?"

"I'm glad that at least that research assistanceship went to a nice guy. He turned me down for it. I'm still looking. If you hear of anything, maybe you can let me know. What are you doing for lunch?" I asked.

"I'm going up to Harvard Square to meet my wife, Claudia. Maybe the three of us can get together some time."

Gee, this guy's got it all. R.A., brains, wife Claudia. He probably even has an apartment with a level floor. Which reminds me I should give Stephanie a call. But first lunch at Walker.

It's not fun to eat by yourself, but it's tolerable if you have the notes from your classes to look over. It seemed like about half the tables were occupied by parties of one, so it didn't bother me so much to be alone. Besides, there would be soccer and company that evening.

I spent the next half hour sick in the men's room. It's tolerable if you have the notes from your classes to look over. What is it? I wondered. Am I stressed out already? I should really be at my desk copying over these notes. What's the story here? I've got to get going.

It took three hours to copy over the notes from Shapiro's class. It was painstaking, but his words were fresh and I wrote every one I could remember. It was as if I'd met Moses and he'd dictated the Ten Commandments. It was also something I knew I could do. The problems that he'd handed out were another story. I dared not crack the packet until I'd finished the transcribing job. Complete one task at a time, the easiest ones first.

The train was leaving the station. It was going slowly but would soon pick up speed. Now I could walk or trot beside it, but sooner or later I would have to get on board or I would lose it.

Soccer was a welcome relief. I'd bumped into and recruited Michael Picardi; he wanted to play goalie. I had a decent shot with my left foot, so I volunteered to play left wing.

The soccer team was from the Heat Transfer Lab, hence the name Caloric, after the archaic caloric theory of heat transmission. Carlos Lopez (thesis topic: steam flow in piping in nuclear power plants) from Mexico would play left halfback. Dave Orlowski (thesis topic: computer simulation of heat conduction in semiconductor crystal growth) was the coach and center forward; he was about to finish his Ph.D. Hamid Reza worked on quantum thermodynamics for Gyftopoulos and played right fullback. Robin Thomas was another theoretical computer type. Ted Bain was from England and was working for Gemayel on boiling in a moving fluid. Norm Jason had an R.A. in fluidized bed coal combustion and was patenting the safety ladder he'd designed for his senior project at Michigan. I felt like I'd joined an instant fraternity. They were friendly and smart, and they accepted me.

The institute looks lovely from the playing fields in the afternoon sun. The two domes line up beside each other with the high-rise Green Building behind them both in the distance—a dense pack of knowledge.

It felt like fall. It felt like high school. It felt like things were going to be all right when I played soccer.

I called Stephanie.

»Allo,« she said.

"Salut, cherie, it's moi, Pepper."

»Oh, Peppeur, how are yoouu?«

"Fine, thanks, but things are becoming hectic. Say listen, Stephanie, I've been meaning to . . ."

»I juste sent you a care package. Some Godiva chocolates and some biscuits from the Italian bakery we go to.«

"Oh, wow. Thanks. Say, I . . . uh."

»Je t'aime, Peppeur.«

"I love you, too."

Back to Building 20. I had my TPP desk for at least a few more days, plus the key to the office and therefore access to the couch for staying over nights. Gyftopoulos's lecture notes took only two hours to copy, including my break to get cheese and peanut butter crackers and a cup of tea with extra cream and extra sugar from the vending machine down the hall. That left some time to crack into the *Encyclopaedia Britannica* article on thermodynamics.

It started with Galileo and the first thermometer that he invented. Gee, those Renaissance guys did everything. Then in the Age of Reason, Black invented the caloric theory after which my soccer team was named, and finally Monsieur Carnot came along and invented the theory for the steam engine that James Watt invented. Then Clausius perfected the concept of entropy, although he never really defined it. It made interesting reading but it wouldn't help on the problem set.

Ah yes, the problem set. No time like the present to get started. It was neatly typed. Problem 1 looked like a piece of cake. "A room contains 10 barrels of oil and adequate air for the complete combustion of the oil. Upon burning, this oil can transfer a maximum of 6 million btu/barrel to systems in the environment. a. If the combustion occurs without any energy transfer to the environment, what is the change in total mass of the contents of the room?"

Piece of cake. The room is closed, I guess, like a closed system, so there won't be any change in mass. I mean where's it going to come from? Or go to?

Next part of question a. "What is the change in mass between the oil-air mixture and the products of combustion if the maximum energy is transferred to the environment?"

Answer: Same thing. What difference does it make? Mass is still conserved.

"b. If a uranium 235 fission can yield a transferrable energy of 200 million electron-volts per fission, how many grams of U-235 are the energy equivalent of 10 barrels of oil?"

Say what? He didn't say anything about U-235 in the lecture. What business does he have pulling that out on the problem set? Then I remembered that he was also a nuclear engineering professor, and the class was also a nuclear engineering class. And I remembered that this was MIT. The point of this problem must be to show us what a piddly amount of uranium takes the place of a huge amount of oil. This is basically an exercise in converting the energy values from electron-volts, what physicists measure energy in, to British thermal units (Btus), what engineers measure energy in.

I cranked through the conversion factors and it came out to just less than a gram, or close to the weight of several grains of salt. Nuclear power. Safe, clean, reliable.

$$OIL:$$
$$(10 \ BARRELS) \times$$
$$(42 \ GALLONS/BARREL) \times$$
$$(150,000 \ Btu/GALLON) =$$
$$63,000,000 \ Btu$$
$$(6.3 \times 10^7 \ Btu)$$

$$URANIUM:$$
$$(6.3 \times 10^7 \ Btu) \times$$
$$(1055.1 \ JOULES/Btu) \times$$
$$(1 \ MeV / 1.6 \times 10^{-13} J) \div$$
$$(200 \ MeV / FISSION) =$$
$$2.08 \times 10^{21} \ ATOMS$$

$$NUMBER \ OF \ GRAMS:$$
$$(2.08 \times 10^{21} \ ATOMS) \times$$
$$(1 \ MOLE / 6.022 \times 10^{23} \ ATOMS) \times$$
$$(235 \ g / MOLE) =$$
$$\boxed{0.812 \ GRAMS \ OF \ URANIUM}$$

Problem 2 looked a little harder and it was already 10:30 so I hopped on my bike for home, a four-bedroom apartment on the first floor of a sagging triple-decker in Allston. You could skateboard down the hallway from the front to the back without pushing, but at $80 a month the price was right. My bed was a mattress that Jim Stuart and I had roped onto his old Impala and had driven from the used furniture store in Somerville. The flowery little table lamp was the cheapest one at the MIT furniture exchange. I hoped my standard of living was bottoming out.

I stopped in at the neighborhood Seven-Eleven for a late-night snack of a honey bun and a pint of chocolate milk. Highly caloric, but I'd earned it with my labors of the day. My reflection stared back from the glass on the inside of the Seven-Eleven door; its hair was standing straight up from running my hand through it doing my work, and it looked tired. I wondered whether I'd go bald.

At the kitchen table my roommate's cat purred against my ankle.

"Get away from me, cat. I don't want to be bothered now," I said softly so as not to wake anyone. "I just want to read the funnies in my *Globe* here and enjoy my honey bun and chocolate milk." I nudged the cat away but it came back.

"Purrrpurrr," it said, nestling on the front of my shin.

"I'm warning you. You want to take a ride, you're going to take a ride."

"Purrrrpurrrr."

"How can I pay attention to the *Wizard of Id* with you there?"

I lofted the cat gently, a couple of feet—well, maybe more— so it slid on its claws on the gray linoleum floor another couple of inches after landing. It came back again, so I guess I didn't hurt it.

"Purrpurrrr."

Friday, September 11

There were only twenty students in Rohsenow's class. Some were in their thirties, special students coming in from General Electric in Lynn to get their master's degrees part-time. A couple were in the navy, in the master's program that they follow; the intent is to give them some mental firepower to deal with the defense industry consultants, who have high-powered degrees from places like MIT. The rest were in their mid-twenties like me.

Two fifty-five. Advanced Heat Transfer. I'd done a background check on Rohsenow in the library and found that he had founded and owned Dynatech, an R&D firm in Cambridge. Dynatech employed about 950 employees and had annual sales of $51 million. Rohsenow was in his sixties now and had received his Ph.D. at Yale just after the war. His specialty was the science of boiling water. If you know what causes boiling, you can figure out how big to make the tubes the water goes through in your nuclear power plant. The more you know about the boiling, the smaller you can make the tubes and still sleep at night. If the tubes are smaller, the power plant is less expensive, and therefore viable.

Rohsenow wore a light blue tweed jacket, darker blue double-knit slacks, white shirt, and blue tie. He was bald with a little brown hair around the edges and wore glasses that seemed not quite strong enough; before he started the class, he tilted them forward and squinted to see the clock at the back of the room.

"Well, I guess it's time to get started," he said, setting his pipe on the table by his notes. "First I'd like to go over some housekeeping details. We've put together a package of problems for you to do. We don't grade them because we'd rather have that time available for you to ask questions." (Or for your lucrative consulting jobs, I thought.) "The solutions for each problem will be posted on the board outside the classroom, so you can go there and check your own work. Jamie Mohammed here will be the teaching assistant; once a week he'll conduct a tutorial where you can ask him questions about the assignments."

"Oh, and about grades," he continued. "Jamie and I get together at the end of the term and we discuss whether or not you have a nice personality. If you do we give you an A."

There was nervous laughter. He spoke slowly, deliberately, with a soft, deep voice and pauses at the punch lines.

"Actually, we give two quizzes, each an hour long, and a final quiz, three hours long. If you do better on the hour quizzes, we weight them more heavily. If you do better on the final, we say, 'Hooray, he finally got it,' and we weight it more heavily. If you don't do well on either, well, there's always business school."

More nervous laughter.

"Now about the course material for the day." He picked up his pipe and tried to light it.

"There's a couple of ways to do any problem. You can do it the fast way, and get an answer that's accurate within 20 percent, or you can do it by computer, take two weeks setting it up, and get an answer that's accurate within 2 percent."

"Now you guys," accent on the you, pause, "want to be the boss. I'll show you the fast way. You'll do that in five minutes, and then pull it out of your sleeve when your assistant comes to ask you a question. You'll look at the graph he came up with and say to him, 'It should go this way, not that way,' and he'll think you're smart. . . . Reminds me of a story. Rickover told it to me. You know, Admiral Hyman Rickover, father of the nuclear navy. He had this young guy working for him. The kid was all bright-eyed and bushy-tailed, straight out of Annapolis. Rickover gets him to design this heat exchanger to heat water with exhaust from the ship's smokestack. Since I'd taught it to him, Hyman had the trick I'm about to show you up his sleeve. He knew the heat exchanger should be about, say, as big as this room."

Rohsenow puffed on his pipe a couple of times and waved his arm around to indicate the size of the room.

"So the kid goes off with his computer and comes back a week later and tells Rickover the heat exchanger should be about as big as the whole ship. Ha ha ha," he chortled.

"The kid's an admiral himself now. But don't worry; I taught him the trick, too."

That night I plowed through some more thermo homework, alone in the TPP office. This isn't like what I'd read and heard about business or law school, I thought. We're all taking our individual courses, mostly on our own. We have to learn by searching our own knowledge, by reasoning, by looking things up in books.

At 11:30 I looked out the window at the plume from the power plant's smokestack. The stack converged gently upward. The plume bent over slightly and made a billowing white-orange arc across the high-crime-lit sky of East Cambridge. I wanted to know everything about that arc, how to make less of it.

I unrolled the olive drab sleeping bag onto the office couch, grabbed a chair cushion for a pillow, and tuned to the Latin music on WBUR on the clock radio. A train of oil tank cars pulled by a diesel locomotive rolled by slowly, close enough to shake the building; the Main Street grade crossing bell ding ding dinged. The train stopped at the power plant.

I wondered how Stephanie was.

CHAPTER

3

Break

Tuesday 10/6/81
Dear Ma + Pa,
Sorry for not writing for so long. I'm writing now very fast. Classes continue to move at fast pace. First test a week from Friday. I talked to my heat transfer prof for two hours on friday got some good Ideas by asking him lots of specific questions on lecture mat'l . . . including a few he didn't know how to answer. I also brought to his attention a typo that had been in his book for twenty years.

I sold my track bike for $180 so now I definitely can make it through this term sans probleme. We played soccer again, winning 1–0. Lots of fun; I feel like I'm getting into reasonable shape.

Routine is now get up at 6:30, ride in along Charles River to MIT, great sunrises now, see crews rowing up the Chas. at that hour. Nice view of downtown Boston, with sun coming through buildings, light very orange in distance. Then read then big breakfast at dining hall. Then study or write letters (this is about the first time). Then classes then study. I leave at about 10:00 P.M. after lunch in dining hall. Dinner = vending machines in Building. Learning very much, striving to master concepts.

One prof has consulting firm in energy conservation so maybe job possibility in offing.

Gotta go.
Love, Pepper

TPP Office. 8:00 A.M.
Saturday, September 12
Thermo, Problem 3

"An important task in everyday life is the pumping of water from underground wells. Among other methods, this can be carried out either by human effort or by a machine. We wish to compare the energy costs of these two methods of pumping 10,000 gallons from a depth of 300 feet. Assume that a person is fed with eggs.

"An egg provides 80 kilogram-calories (kcal) (a.k.a. calories to the layperson) of energy and costs about $1.20 per dozen. The human body transforms caloric food into muscle power with an efficiency of about 25 percent, by using a pedal-powered apparatus similar to a stationary bicycle.

"A gasoline engine transforms fuel into motive power with an efficiency of about 25 percent. Gasoline can make available about 20,000 Btu/pound-mass and is priced at about $3.00 per gallon (in most places except the United States).

"a. Find the energy cost of each of these two methods of pumping the water."

Answer. This is still right out of high school. If they stay like this I'll have no problems. Just calculate the amount of energy required to raise the 10,000 gallons of water the 300 feet. Then figure out the number of eggs required, taking into account the energy content of each egg and the efficiency of egg conversion. (405 eggs.) Ditto for the gasoline. (1.10 gallons.) I'd rather eat four hundred eggs than drink a gallon of gasoline.

"b. By considering other foodstuffs and including in your approximate calculations both capital and labor costs, which of the two ways of pumping water would you recommend? Express your considerations and recommendations in a paragraph or so."

This again is easy, I thought. Figure about 50 hours for the quarter-horsepower person; at $4 an hour that's about $200 for the person. Add to that the $40 or so for the eggs, and you have $240. I'll figure the bicycle apparatus and the engine would cost about the same. Then it comes to about 73 times as expensive for the human as for the pump.

Halfway through Problem 4 Michael Picardi came into the office. "Do you want to go see the 'Sky Art' exhibit?" he asked.

"Sure. What's the 'Sky Art' exhibit?" I answered.

"They're displaying various airborne sculptures in the quadrangle by the student center. Various artists from around New England are exhibiting their work. If we go now, we can catch the launch of the 'Sky Jellyfish.' "

"Sounds interesting. Let's go," I said.

The artist prepared the sky-jellyfish for launch. He enlisted Michael, me, and five others to hold onto the ends of the sky-tentacles, while he inflated the bowl-shaped body with helium. The thing expanded to about the size of a backyard swimming pool in Levittown. It was all made of silver and red Mylar, the tough plastic they wrap satellites with.

"Can you believe they call this art?" I said to Michael.

"Pay attention," Michael said. "It's almost time for launch."

The artist said, "Now I'm going to finish inflating this and then we'll have the countdown from five. When we get to zero, everyone let go of what they're holding."

"Five, four, three, two, one," we all chanted in unison.

"Lift-off," said the guy wearing the NASA T-shirt.

At T plus 15 seconds I said to Michael, "I'll be doggoned. It *does* look like a jellyfish. Just look at the way the tentacles and the body are floating and oscillating. The guy must have calculated all that stuff, the thickness of the Mylar, the mixture of helium and air in the body, the length and width of the tentacles."

"Yeah, either that or he's lucky. Let's just hope all that Mylar doesn't bring down a 'sky-jumbo-jet,' " Michael said. "Say, are you hungry? Would you like to join me for a falafel?"

"Sure. I haven't had a falafel since I was in Istanbul two months ago."

"You went to Istanbul? Did you see Hagia Sofia, the church dedicated to wisdom?"

"Yes. It was beautiful."

Michael continued, "I'll never forget the slides my Art History professor showed. 'Note how they hid the means of support of the dome,' he said. 'Note the shimmering pencils of light dancing beneath the ceiling's soaring verticality.' Did the pencils of light really shimmer?"

"Yes, they shimmered all right. And you know the amazing thing about it? How long do you think it took to build it?"

"Fifty years, a hundred years?"

"Try a year and a half. They did it with the wonder material of the fifth century: brick. It was the largest church in the world when they finished it."

The soccer game was at 8:30 Sunday morning on field C, beyond the tennis bubble. They schedule the intramural games for Sunday morning. That leaves Sunday afternoon and evening free for work.

Intramurals are big at MIT—they're one of the few instances of group activity. Teams represent the various groups, the support structures. Some shirts had the Greek letters of fraternities embossed onto them, others the names of labs or graduate departments, and some the names of countries—Greece, Turkey, Chile, Korea, any country that's on our side and has an industrial base.

The guys on our team who'd been at MIT for several years had faded red shirts with faded yellow *Caloric* written on the chest. Into the latter years, fourth, fifth, sixth, seventh, of their Ph.D. research, they hadn't as a rule aged as gracefully as professional athletes in their late twenties. Several had started or finished losing their hair. Over half wore glasses; potbellies were common. I wondered whether MIT would do the same to me.

The fifteen of us stood on the sidelines of field C while the Aquanauts finished their game with the Dixie Chickens. The four intramural divisions, A-, B-, C-, and D-league, are named after the grades you get in your classes. A-league is the best, composed mostly of foreigners; B-league is foreigners plus some of the jockier frats; C is mostly lab teams and frats with lower concentrations of foreigners. D-league is for dorms.

Our opponent was TEP, a frat from across the river. Once we started, we fought hard and passed well. TEP, as undergraduates, had not forgotten how to run. I felt in the middle of the two groups—not as vigorous as the frat boys but certainly more so than many of the Calorics.

It was clear and windy and in the second half the wind was going our way. Robin, the left halfback, gave me a tap of a pass while I was 30 yards out from the goal and I chipped the ball with my left foot. Up, up, and away it went, the wind carrying it toward the goal, the far corner—but it hit the top of the crossbar, went past the end line, and TEP kicked a goal kick. Oh well, maybe next time.

In the end we were still ahead by 1–0 from the goal Carlos had scored in the first half. We all put our hands in a circle and shouted together, "Rah, rah, rah, TEP!" to salute our vanquished opponents.

Several of us picked up our bicycles and walked toward the Lobdell cafeteria for breakfast. I locked mine near the sign that read, HANDICAPPED RAMP: NO BICYCLE PARKING; there were three other bikes on the railing, so I figured it was all right. Even though it was Sunday morning I didn't want to waste time looking for another place to leave the bike.

I said to Carlos, "That was a good shot. You seem to have played soccer before."

"Yes, well, I played a little at university in Mexico," he said. He was husky like me and had dark hair about the length John Lennon's was in 1965.

I asked him how long he'd been at MIT, whether he'd found funding, whether he knew any professors who had money.

"I came here last spring," he said, "on a scholarship from the Mexican government. As long as I do well enough to stay here I have a student visa. My thesis subject is a study of erosion in steam piping by water droplets in pipe elbows. You know something? Last spring was the toughest time I've had in my life. I had a hard time believing I belonged here; I thought maybe my being admitted was a fluke. And the whole time I am thinking that everybody in my classes must be smarter than I am. If everyone is smarter than I am, that means no matter how well I do on the test, I'll be below average. If I'm below average, I'll get C's and I'll be back in Mexico City. Do you know what I'm saying?"

"Yes, I think I know what you're saying," I answered. "Let's talk about something else."

We joined the self-congratulation of the guys at the other end of the table, the play-by-play of the game in review. We agreed on the need to go after the ball more both on offense and on defense.

My eyes wandered across Massachusetts Avenue to the two great domes, the trees nearing the end of their green season, and the Ionic columns of Building 7. Building 7 blocked the view of the Green Building, so I could just see the weather sphere on the roof, and the ladder with a strobe light on top. The cornice on Building 7 bore the inscription "Massachussetts Institute of Technology. William Barton Rogers, Founder." The *u*'s looked like *v*'s because the Romans didn't invent *u*'s.

I didn't know whether I could do research with my teammates, or score A's in classes we might take together, but at least in soccer, I was in the right league.

Monday morning. The saga of the desk. Charlotte Evans was the Mechanical Engineering secretary. She was in her late thirties—blonde, attractive, and aging gracefully, like Lauren Bacall. Her accent was from Quincy or maybe Stoneham.

Her office was the antechamber to Rohsenow's. She knew the department and its rules as well as or better than Rohsenow or any of the other professors. It was Charlotte Evans to whom I would have to make my request for a key. She had a rubber stamp with Rohsenow's signature on it and the authority to use it for the lesser issues. It was up to her to decide what was a lesser issue, so she had almost as much power as Rohsenow himself.

"I'm a friend of Matt Armstrong," I said, standing before the seat of judgment, "and I don't have an R.A. yet, but Matt said there's an extra desk in his office. I've just left Technology and Policy, so I'm kind of in no-man's-land in the desk department."

"First you need this," she said briskly, pulling out a stapled set of xeroxes. "This is a list of all the ongoing research projects. You should look through the list and find out who's got the most money in the area closest to what you're interested in. These guys are always closing on deals with their industry contacts and their buddies at the Department of Defense or Energy. Sometimes they need help right away, and if you keep hounding them, eventually you'll be in the right place at the right time and you'll get funding. Also, keep an eye on the department newsletter; sometimes they post their openings there." Her confidence and strength were comforting, almost motherly.

"Now there's something else I should tell you," she continued. "The professors here can be jerks. But remember that just because they've made it through more hoops than you have, that doesn't make them better people." She took two orange index cards out of the little green metal file box and typed my name on each; she stamped Rohsenow's signature on the bottom.

"Fill these out with the room number and the numbers on the lock and take them to the key office on the fourth floor of Building E-51. If anyone there or in the lab gives you any trouble, tell them to come talk to me."

It was good to have a powerful person on my side.

———

Monday afternoon I went to Allen Greene's first lecture on Energy Engineering. From its description in the catalog, this course was right on the money for what I wanted out of MIT.

He started his lecture with an example. "Suppose that the country wants to go into gasohol, a mixture of corn-derived alcohol and gasoline, in a big way. If it did, what would be needed? You'd need fuel for the tractor to plant and harvest the corn. You'd need an investment in tractors. And you'd need an investment in refineries for the alcohol production. Each of these production factors has an internal and an external economic impact. For example, the price of other grains may go up as the fields that would have otherwise been planted with them are made unavailable. That's a microeconomic phenomenon, and we can model it.

"Similarly, we can model the processes within the various subsystems, using efficiencies of the various components and costs of those components. Heavy investments in equipment may drive up prices in certain materials. We can model that as well. Then we can take all the models that we've constructed, link them, and test them for sensitivities to various parameters. Then we as decision makers can make value assessments to determine where our research and development funding should go—we can determine what are the key rate-limiting problems."

Right. It would really help to know what a model is.

It was good, though, to hear such a practically oriented lecture. Greene had a sort of middlewestern down-to-earthiness about him, a real-world slant that must have been partly due to his stint as vice president for research and development at Union Carbide.

After the lecture, I went up to the podium to ask him for advice about the class. I said, "I'm really interested in what you're teaching, but I've got three other classes this term that are a full load. What would you think of my signing up for your class, auditing the lectures, and taking an incomplete. Then I could devote all of January to doing a project for the class work."

"That doesn't really sound honest," he answered.

"You're welcome to audit the class, although it might be a waste of time if you're not doing the homework. Why don't you come back to my office in January, and we can talk about your doing an independent study project under my direction in the spring term."

"That sounds good," I said. "I'll drop your class now and come back to talk to you in a few months."

Tuesday, October 6

I needed help on Problem 4 of Problem Set 3 in Thermo. I'd had 48 out of 60 correct on Problem Set 1 (I'd checked my answers with Matt, and he'd tipped me off to 15 points worth of errors; I made the correction during Gyftopoulos's lecture). I'd done Problem Set 2 without help from Matt and had 36 out of 50. It would be a good idea to get as close as possible to 100 percent on the problem set points since they constituted 15 percent of the grade. Each ate up about fifteen to twenty hours, but the quizzes would involve more acute time pressure and I might choke on them. The problem sets could be gift points.

Gyftopoulos had said his office door was always open, so I decided to take him up on it. He seemed kindly, like Professor Walker at Hopkins. Professor Walker taught freshman physics and encouraged students to come to his office and ask any question they wanted to. No question was too dumb for him. I expected the same with Gyftopoulos.

But this was graduate school. And it was MIT.

It was quarter to four and the clouds made it seem more like dusk. It was beginning to be cold outside. His secretary knocked on the window in his door and Gyftopoulos motioned me in. He finished recording a letter to a colleague at Oxford. "And I'm looking forward to seeing you at the Nuclear Thermodynamics Conference in Marseilles in January. Sincerely, Elias."

I sat in the teak chair in front of his teak desk. He asked, "How are you finding MIT so far, Pepper?"

"I'm finding the work challenging, especially in your course. I'm spending a lot of time on the problem sets, fifteen or twenty hours."

"That's good. One of the reasons I have the problem sets graded is to encourage students to work on my class more than on their others. I feel that mastery of the fundamentals of thermodynamics is essential for a good engineer. Now, what specifically can I do for you today?" he asked.

"Well, I'm having a little trouble with the problem with the three blocks of metal at three different temperatures. This is the one where you ask that if you move heat from one to another in the most efficient way possible, what is the maximum temperature one of the blocks can reach. I don't really know where to start with this and I wondered whether you could help," I said.

I hoped he would just give me a clue or two as to how to set up the problem. For example, he might tell me first to take the two lower-temperature blocks and cool one and heat the other, then do the same thing with the one that was first hottest and the one that I just heated up. Or there might be some other trick to the problem. I just wanted a hint.

"It is not an easy problem," Gyftopoulos said. "In fact, my colleague, Professor Clarke at Oxford, has just submitted a paper with a solution to that problem in it to the *Journal of Thermodynamics*. I agree with his solution; I'm interested to see whether anyone in the class comes up with what he arrived at."

Great, I thought. Did Professor Clarke have four other problems due the same week?

Gyftopoulos continued, "Why don't you go to the blackboard, Pepper. I'd like to ask you a few questions. They may lead you in the right direction."

Uh-oh. I thought the Socratic method was reserved for law school and business school. All I wanted was a hint, not an impromptu oral exam.

As I picked up a piece of chalk from the dusty aluminum tray, he asked, "Please define for me available energy."

Say what? That's from three weeks ago. The test isn't for three weeks. He can't expect me to have reviewed that from my notes to the second lecture. Help. Get me out of here.

I answered, "The available energy is the energy that is . . . available to do useful work." All I remembered was that several pages of the class notes were devoted to the concept. I'd read them once and had intended to get Matt or Beretta or Gyftopoulos to explain them to me before the midterm.

Gyftopoulos would not let up. "I need a more rigorous definition than that," he said.

I drew an upside-down horseshoe on the board, for the capital Greek letter omega. The last letter. I tried to remember the equation with the inequality that Gyftopoulos had written on the board at the beginning of the third lecture.

It began to come back. Omega minus omega-sub-zero is greater than or equal to T-sub-zero multiplied by S minus S-sub-zero.

"What does S refer to?" he probed.

An easy one. "Entropy."

"Please define entropy."

A hard one. "Entropy is well, it's, uh, well, it has to do with randomness and, uh, the system's ability to do work and sort of how hot it is."

He wasn't smiling anymore. "You're obviously not prepared for this session," he said sternly. "I'm a very busy man, and if you are not prepared and you do not have your questions well-formulated, please do not come here again."

Don't cry, I thought. Big boys don't cry. He'll never look at me the same if I cry. I'm so tired, though. It's getting darker outside. I'm in debt. I don't know what to do about Stephanie.

The tears and sobs welled up from my body to my head and out my eyes, mouth, and nose.

"If . . . if . . . if." I couldn't say it.

If I knew how to formulate the question, I could answer it without you.

"Now, now, there's no need for that," he said a little more compassionately. "Go and wash yourself and sit down for a few minutes. Then we can go over the problem."

I walked past Beretta and the secretary in the waiting area. I tried to avoid eye contact. They didn't seem disturbed by my red face. Maybe they'd seen scenes like this before.

I washed the salt from my eyes and sat in one of the stalls with my blue jeans still on and the door closed. I took some deep breaths. I went back to pick up my notebook from his office.

Gian Paolo was sitting in the other teak chair, talking to Gyftopoulos. Gian Paolo handed me a sketch of the beginning of the problem, and the two of them explained how to start.

They shot Sadat today. As the bullets ripped apart his body he stood, as always, at attention, chest out, defiant.

Thursday, October 8. 9:00 P.M.

T minus sixteen hours to the first quiz in Rohsenow's class. It will be the first indicator of whether or not I belong at MIT. The way to study is to read through the notes, read through the textbook, but that is just fertilizer. The way to prepare for the test is to do problems, even though there is no graded homework.

It would be nice if there were a solution manual to the problems, in the back of the chapter. Then I could try the problem, get stuck, look for a hint in the solution that someone else had worked out, get stuck again, look for another hint, and so on. That's how I'd gotten through my undergrad classes.

Look at enough similar problems and you begin to see patterns. Know the patterns and you have something to put on the paper. Then at least you can get partial credit points, when the grader gives you 3 out of 10 for putting down a relevant formula, 3 for making an attempt at plugging the specific parameters of the problem into the formula, and 4 more points if you get . . . the answer.

Here at MIT there were fewer patterns. Every problem seemed to have 100 steps, and each step seemed to have a subtlety to it that made Jamie's ability to solve them seem arbitrary, magic, or a gift from above. Time to try another one.

"Extra Problem 7. Find the temperature 2 feet from the leading edge of a flat plate that is infinitely wide, infinitely long, and has a uniform flow of water going over it. The heat flux to the plate is uniform, at 4,000 Btu per square foot.

Right. I wondered why anyone would care about a flat plate that was infinitely long and infinitely wide. The biggest plate I'd ever seen was round and underneath a 20-inch pizza. This problem seemed almost as obscure as the infinitely long cylinder of uniform charge that made me into a nonphysicist.

I started my attempt. Step 1. Draw picture.

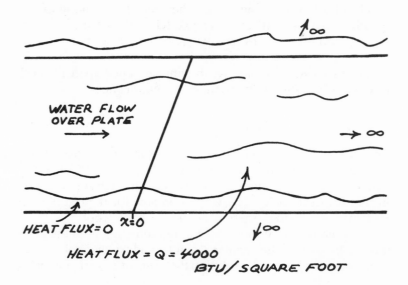

What would give you uniform heat flux anyway? If the heat flux is uniform, why isn't the temperature uniform? Ack-ack, as Bill the Cat would say.

Step 2. Look for similar sample problem in book. There isn't one that's even close.

Step 3. Look through four different heat transfer books on office mate's shelf. Rohsenow said yesterday that we could bring to the test any book we wanted to. "The only thing you can't bring," he said with a wink, "is a consultant." There's nothing in them, either.

Step 4. Look through class notes, then office mate's class notes from previous year's lecture. Another dead end.

Step 5. Think about what's going on in the problem. Refer to the picture. Redraw the picture.

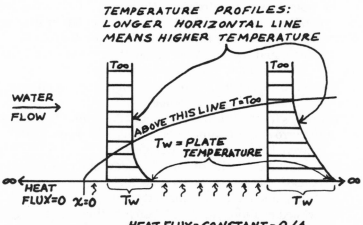

TEMPERATURE PROFILES:
LONGER HORIZONTAL LINE
MEANS HIGHER TEMPERATURE

T_∞ T_∞

WATER
FLOW →

ABOVE THIS LINE T=T_∞

T_w = PLATE TEMPERATURE

∞ ← HEAT FLUX=0 $x=0$ T_w T_w → ∞

HEAT FLUX = CONSTANT = Q/A

Maybe the point of the two infinities is to simplify the problem so you don't have to worry about what happens at edges. This will enable the problem to be solved as if things vary in two directions only, i.e., in a plane.

I still wondered what would produce a uniform heat flux and why it mattered. Then I saw the article about the Seabrook nuclear plant on the front page of Matt's *Globe*. Atoms splitting underneath the plate might appear to be a uniform heat flow.

Water or some other coolant would have to flow over the top of the plate. Otherwise the plate, no matter what it was made of, would melt. The China syndrome in class Two fifty-five.

If the water is coming from the left, and the plate is really really hot, hotter than the water, then the water will be coolest at the left end of the plate, and more of it will get hotter farther and farther away from the plate. The hotter the water is, the less it can cool the plate. Ergo, the plate gets hotter as you go downstream.

The trick they have to get right at the nuke plant is to make sure the plate isn't so long that its temperature goes above the melting point of what it's made of. Who would want to eat a tomato as big as a beach ball?

But wait. *Rohsenow* is they. If I can figure out how to do this problem, *I* am they.

As I started setting up the formula, Eddy the janitor knocked on the door and came in to empty the wastebasket. Eddy had an uncanny resemblance to Monsieur Nicaise, the technician who built parts of my experiment in the heat transfer lab in Belgium. It seemed a little like the resemblance that the Scarecrow, the Cowardly Lion, and the Tin Man had to Aunty Em's farmhands in *The Wizard of Oz*. Eddy was born in Sicily.

"How's it going, Peppy? You're here kind of late, aren't you?" My name sounds like Peppy in Italian.

"It's only eleven. The night is young," I said. "I've got my first test tomorrow and I want to be as prepared as possible."

He answered, "Don't get too wrapped up in your work. Have some fun sometimes. Some of these graduate students just work for five years—then maybe at the end their experiment doesn't work and they don't get their master's or Ph.D. They must feel like they wasted all those years and there's nothing left to live for. Some of my janitor colleagues have found these students hanging from the pipe in the offices they're supposed to clean up. It ruins their shift. Don't let it happen to you."

It's true. I'd heard about MIT's suicide problem from people who knew people who went here, but I'd shoved the knowledge aside and forgotten about it. I wondered who I knew, or didn't yet know, who might not survive. Or whether it was me.

"I'll try to keep things in perspective," I assured him. "Do you know any offices around that have couches in them? I don't want to waste the time it'll take to ride my bike home tonight and back in tomorrow morning."

"Sure. There's one just down the hall. Just find me in Building 5."

"OK. For now I want a change of scenery. I'm going to the student center library for a couple of hours," I said.

The student center library is open twenty-four hours a day. It's on the fifth floor of the student center. The tables are brown veneer; the chairs are Naugahyde. This is where the power tools go in the middle of the night. It is also where some MIT students live. Some little alcoves are pretty dark, and underneath the chairs or in a cubbyhole somewhere they keep their toothbrushes and razors. At least the ones who brush their teeth and shave do. The trick to sleeping here is to put two of the lounge chairs across from each other and lean on the arm of one with your legs on the seat of the other.

The student center library is on the fifth floor, but there isn't a view of the playing fields. There are windows, but they look onto a concrete sidewalk and exterior wall. This is to prevent you from lobbing one of the Naugahyde chairs through the window and following it after your eighth consecutive all-nighter.

I found an empty chair at a table across from an Oriental student who was reading a textbook entitled *Semiconductor Physics*. He tapped his foot on the chair leg in a semirandom rhythm, once or twice a second. At the same time he twirled his pen like a baton from his little finger to his thumb and back again every ten foot taps.

It made it difficult to concentrate. "Excuse me, would you mind stopping that?" I asked him.

"Stopping what?"

"Never mind." I went to another table and studied until 1:30. I knew it was time to stop when I realized I had been looking at one sheet of Rohsenow's lecture notes for fifteen minutes. Looking at it as if it were a sheet of Chinese writing that meant nothing to me, just marks on a page. I was asleep with my eyes open.

2:00 A.M.

I asked another janitor whether he'd seen Eddy.

"He's at lunch." I guess if you work the 10:00 to 6:30 shift, 2:00 A.M. would be lunchtime. I went toward my office and found Eddy pulling a mop and scrub bucket out of the hall closet. He opened the door to the office with the early American couch. I took two lab jackets off the hook on the inside of the door and used them as blankets for my nap.

At 6:15 Eddy knocked on the door again. "Here, Peppy, I made you a cappucino. Just like my mama makes. A little espresso and a lot of sugar and milk. Now you get going again in your studying and do well on that test."

At 2:00 P.M. the test began in the classroom with the twenty of us using our little deskettes from the chair arms to write in our bluebooks. Rohsenow was at a Dynatech directors' meeting and Jamie left the room for most of the test. Professionals do not cheat. Problem 1 was surprisingly easy and took twenty minutes. Problem 2 was a little like the one I'd done last night, so at least I had something to put on the paper. Not yet torpedoed, my head was still above water.

8:00 P.M. October 9

Another Friday night and I don't got nobody. Ain't got no money 'cause I don't get paid.

It was getting colder outside. The deco desk lamp with built-in ashtray warmed my face and my hands. The only lamp, it made a pool of soft light on the writing tablet on the desk's dark green blotter. The fluorescent light above buzzed too much.

"Friday, October 9, 1981
Dear Stephanie,
    . . . As you know, my father, now over seventy, has had some health problems. Maybe part of why I asked you was to please him, to be married while he was still with us. I didn't want to hurt you. I hope you will someday find it in your heart to forgive me. . . ."

Thunk, echoed the mailbox in the Building 7 lobby. Par avion, to Brussels.

CHAPTER

——————— 4 ———————

Midterm

Columbus Day was clear, windy, and warm with Indian summer sun, and the Charles was full of sailboats. Jim Stuart and I watched them from the middle of Memorial Drive while we waited for the 10,000 women to pass in the Bonnie Belle race.

They passed at all speeds. They were American—free thinkers, every one of them.

Thursday, October 15

I sat next to Mary Patterson in the third row in Gyftopoulos's class. She wore faded jeans and a black T-shirt with a skull on the front. The skull had the stars and stripes of the American flag on it and "Sport Death" written in big letters beneath. The teeth were shaped faintly like letters, and they spelled "Only life can kill you."

"That's an interesting T-shirt," I said. "Where'd you get it?"

"I was in Senior House as an undergrad. This is the dorm logo."

"Was there a contest and that won?"

"I don't know the full history," she said. "I think somebody swiped the skull off the cover of some book by Hunter Thompson. As for the 'Sport Death,' I don't know if anyone knows where that started."

"Senior House sounds like a fun place. Did you go to MIT?" I asked her.

"Yeah, I graduated in '78. I've worked at Dynatech for the past three years. But it seemed that if I wanted to be a big wheel in research and development I needed at least a master's and preferably a Ph.D. Otherwise I could get stuck running coffee."

I asked her how she liked Dynatech.

She answered, "It's really good. They give all the engineers private offices—well, okay, none of them has windows but it's better than the 'pigpens' that some of my friends who got jobs in aerospace work in. And the work is really interesting."

"What's a pigpen?"

"That's what the engineers who work in those big open offices with rows and rows of desks call them. There's no privacy, and it's really hard to concentrate. The trick there is to shine enough so you get one of the outside offices with a door," she said.

I hadn't yet worked in a real job, so this was disturbing news.

I said to her, "I wonder whether it's too late to transfer to law school." She laughed. "By the way," I added, "I like your ring. Where'd you get it?"

"This is my brass rat," she said. It was a signet ring, with a beaver, the MIT mascot, as the signet. "That reminds me, now that I'm back in school here, I have to turn the ring around so the signet's against my palm when I make a fist."

"Why's that?" I asked.

"When you're here, the beaver uses you as a toilet. After you get your degree, you're one with the beaver, so you turn the ring around and you and the beaver use the rest of the world as a toilet," she said.

I could see the validity of at least the first part of the metaphor. Mary had the same confidence that the TPP people had, but she was smarter. Four years of undergrad work here probably does that to a person. Her confidence scared me a little, but there was also a gentleness in her eyes. I hoped we would become friends.

Gyftopoulos started the lecture of the day. Up until now the presentation was completely foreign. He and Beretta had presented their own language of thermodynamics, including new terms like "available energy," "stable equilibrium state," and "perpetual motion machines of the first and second kind." Today the lecture— on Maxwell's relations—was similar to one I'd heard at Hopkins.

Maxwell's relations were invented or discovered by James

Clerk Maxwell, the nineteenth-century British physicist who also invented or discovered Maxwell's equation for the relationship between electric and magnetic fields. Those nineteenth-century guys did everything. After Watt's engine, after Carnot's theory, after Clausius's entropy, Maxwell came along with relations that enable you to take measurable quantities like temperature, pressure, and volume and figure out the magnitude of the more abstract quantities, like energy and entropy.

And so today's lecture presented Maxwell's relations. They were all partial derivatives. Since, for example, entropy, whatever that is, is a function of temperature and pressure, a very small change in entropy can be thought of as the sum of a small change in temperature's effect on entropy and a small change in pressure's effect on entropy. Simple enough. But when you then look at the same analysis for energy, and another thing they call enthalpy, and when they shoot all this at you in an hour and a half, it quickly becomes soup. There are so many equations in your notes that it's nearly impossible to know what the important ones are, what the intermediate steps are, and how they all fit together. It all goes so fast and it's hard enough just to write the stuff down, much less comprehend anything and follow the reasoning.

Mary's notes were perfectly neat, like Matt's, uncluttered and useful. She even had time to draw little leafed plants in the margins.

At the end of the lecture, Gyftopoulos made a final note. "What I've just presented is exactly what you will see in a physical chemistry class, or a physics class in thermodynamics. This is scientific knowledge. What you will find, though, in the real world is that the scientific knowledge is the easy part. At least it is logically consistent and invariant. What you will have to do as engineers is make assumptions about the systems you are designing. Making assumptions that enable you to produce something that works while being consistent with the scientific principles can be very difficult."

I wondered what he meant.

"By the way," he continued, "the first quiz will be October 29, two weeks from today."

I said to Mary, "That date rings a bell with me, but I can't place it, like it's the date of some historic event."

"Try Black Thursday 1929, the stock market crash."

"You've got a great memory. Are you doing anything for lunch?" I asked.

"I'm getting my car inspected," she replied in a nonrejecting tone. "Maybe some other time."

Friday afternoon I went to the fluids tutorial. This was conducted on the second floor of Building 1, by Kamel Gemayel, from Lebanon. At a tutorial, you ask questions about how to do problems. It's also your chance to make the professor look stupid, which is only fair since they have so many chances to make you look stupid. Gemayel was a nice guy, though, so nobody wanted to make him look stupid.

Building 1 adjoins Memorial Drive and the classroom's window looked right onto leaf level of the trees along each side of the drive. It was a blue sky afternoon through the window and the leaves were brilliantly golden and the wind blew on the Charles as it had on Monday, only cooler. Fall was fully with us, with little chance for more warm weather. The waves made me think back to my canoe-tripping days.

Gemayel presented problem C-32. Oil and water were between two plates, and a wave of the water moved down the length of the plates. Naturally the plates were infinitely long. The problem asked you to relate the wave speed to the density of the oil and the water and the height of the wave. He went through the derivation of the solution from his notes. It wasn't a wave on a lake, but it was a start.

The Libyan nuclear engineering student next to me asked Gemayel to do problem C-33; it asked us to calculate the frequency of oscillation of a ship of a given size in waves of given sizes. This was a new problem, added this year, so Gemayel didn't have a written solution. In fact, he'd never looked at the problem before.

He hemmed and he hawwed for five minutes, going around in some circles, and then he finally said, "Did anyone here do this problem?" The Korean sitting in front of me got up and wrote the solution.

It was comforting to see that a professor wasn't omniscient, but it was equally discomforting to see that the Korean, who would be on my bell curve, was smarter than the professor.

Rohsenow made us wait until after the class to hand back the heat transfer tests. The first thing he did was draw the bell curve, with a number line from 0 to 20. He drew the x's before he spoke:

One x at 7, two at 9, four at 10, none at 11, two at 12, four at 13, six at 14, and another eight between 15 and 20.

"The data came out pretty much the way Jamie and I expected," Rohsenow said. "Now if you're here, or to the right, that's good," he said, pointing to the 14. "If you're to the left of here, well maybe you should do some more problems or think about dropping."

With 3,400 hard-borrowed dollars invested in tuition, dropping a course is not an option.

The blue books were all sitting on the front table. After the lecture we pushed to the table, rummaging through the pile in turn to find our own.

I hoped the grades weren't put on the front cover, but they were. Mine was 14—I made class average. I remembered in elementary school the verbal version of grades: "A, excellent, B, good, C, average, D, poor." Average had always seemed a bad thing back when I was smart. But here I just breathed a big sigh of relief. Average meant B.

I bumped into Mary on the way out of the class. She was at the door of her office, offering words of encouragement to an undergrad who was taking two twenty, the undergrad version of Fluids. Mary had a teaching assistanceship, which meant she graded problem sets and helped the students with any questions they might have. She, like any good TA, did more teaching than the professors. She did not bite her students' heads off for not understanding. And there was almost always someone at her office, so she must have known her stuff.

"Did your car pass the inspection?" I asked.

"Sure did. Not bad for a '77 Chevette. I didn't even have to pour any money into it. I'm about to go down to the Friday night beer blast. Care to come along?"

"That sounds like fun." We went downstairs to the lounge between Mikic's office and Charlotte Evans's office. The area was packed with people: circles of gray-haired professors talking to one another, circles of graduate students talking to one another and to their advisers, the assistant professors. And there was the occasional undergraduate. The atmosphere was wired, but in a friendly way.

"Hey, soccer star," Carlos said to me.

"Moi?"

"Yeah, you. How's it going?"

"Fine, thanks. How about you?"

"Good. Say, you met Jim Stuart? He's in that Technology Policy program," Carlos said as Jim walked up to us.

"Of course he has," Jim said. "Everyone knows Pepper."

Professor Mikic walked up to Mary and gave her a light pat on the shoulder. "It's good to see you back here," he said.

He looked at me and said, "I am Mary's mentor. She has been one of the students I am most proud of. And how are things going with you?"

"I'm surviving, so far anyway," Mary said.

We exchanged further pleasantries and headed for the refreshment table. Mary pointed out a blond-haired guy with a mustache. "That's Peter Huber. He started here as a freshman the same time I did. He had his Ph.D. by the time he was twenty-three, and he's now an assistant professor and he goes to Harvard Law School full time. I hear he's already gotten an offer to clerk for Justice O'Connor in the Supreme Court."

"OK, but how's his golf game?"

"He doesn't play golf. I don't think he plays, period. I don't know anybody more focused and directed than he."

"Who's the white-haired guy over there with the beard, talking to Shapiro?" I asked.

"That's 'Maharaji Hank' Paynter. He's the resident controls genius. He kept all the sewers in Boston from backing up once when he did some emergency consulting at the treatment plant in the harbor. A pipe had broken or a valve had stuck and the whole place was out of control. He took out a portable computer he'd developed and simulated the system on it and told them what valves to open, what valves to close, and how fast to do it."

We mingled until the crowd started to thin out, and I asked her whether she had plans for dinner.

"No," she said. "How'd you like to go up Chuck River?"

"Excuse me?"

"You know, up the Charles to rub elbows with the Harveys. We can go to Café Pamplona, order espresso, and talk about Descartes and Sartre."

"Sure," I said, and we walked to her car. I asked her more questions. "I can account for the past seven years between Dynatech and MIT. Where'd you grow up?"

"I went to high school and most of elementary school in Dobbs

Ferry, north of the City. My parents were really excited about the Soviet Union, so I went to first and second grade there."

"Amazing," I said. "Do you realize that means you were in Russia when I ate the Hershey bars that my mother had hidden under the ping-pong table that was going to be my family's fallout shelter? What was it like?" I asked.

"It was no big deal, really; I mean I didn't have much to compare it with. It was great for my Russian, though; I'll tell you that much."

The door on the passenger side of her blue '77 Chevette didn't open from the outside, so she had to reach over to let me in.

"They don't make 'em like they used to," she said.

"Yeah, that's 'cause there's too many B-school bozos running things in Detroit. It's really annoying that those people are going to be our bosses, and they don't know anything."

"Yeah, I know what you mean," she said. "But maybe we'll get some power some day and be able to change things."

We drove to Harvard Square, up Mass. Ave through Central Square, past Jack's Nightclub and the Orson Wells theater. We talked more about Russia, Wall Street, Gyftopoulos, and his home in Sudbury. At times there was a tone of irony in Mary's voice, as if her intelligence were a burden—a burden because she couldn't be fooled.

"Ah, a parking space," she said gleefully. "And only three blocks from the square."

"You know, my father went there for both college and law school," I said, pointing across the street at the big old brick building with ivy growing up the side. "Remember that guy in *The Paper Chase*, the one who was fourth-generation Harvard and Harvard Law? I would have been third generation."

"So why didn't you go there?" she asked as we walked left onto Bow Street.

"I didn't want to get in there because of my genes. I wanted to go somewhere that was more merit-oriented. Besides, you look at Harvard, it's the fruit of industry. MIT *is* industry. And you know the funny thing; I think my father agrees with me."

"Well, you're right about MIT. Here's the café."

It was a little downstairs room hardly bigger than my bedroom; we sat at one of the small round tables. There were several berets and tweed. Vivaldi's *Four Seasons* was playing on the café stereo.

"Summer," Mary said.

"Excuse me?" I said.

"That's which season this is. You can tell because it's the most upbeat."

"Gee, and I thought I was doing well to recognize it was one of the *Four Seasons,*" I answered.

We ordered our dinner and continued to talk. "So give me some more dirt on Gyftopoulos," I said. "How'd he do so well?"

"Well, he and his buddy Hatsopoulos were both graduate students here back in the '50s. After they finished their Ph.D.s they needed newer challenges, so they started applying for government grants for contract research. They also did a lot of work for the Natural Gas Research Institute. So they developed a reasonable cash flow from that and started investing some of the excess in product development. One thing led to another, and now Thermo's in the Fortune 1000."

"How many millions do you think Gyftopoulos is worth?" I asked.

"I don't know. He's probably set for life, though."

"Gee. I wonder what keeps him going," I said.

"These guys aren't in it for the money, once they make it," Mary said. "Then it becomes a matter of how much of an influence they can have in the world. And I think Gyftopoulos genuinely loves teaching and being at MIT. It must be fun to be one of the kings of the mountain."

"Yeah. He's the kind of guy we all would like to be like," I said. "Not to change the subject, but what was your social life like here when you were an undergrad?"

"Well, basically it was nonexistent until the first warm day in the spring. Then when I would study in the library, guys would come up to me one after the other and say, 'Uhh, hi. Uhhh, what are you, uhhh, reading?' The same thing happened to a lot of my friends."

"How about the profs? How were they?"

"Some were okay, others were jerks. You've got to remember that a lot of these guys are MIT cubed—you know, B.S., M.S., Ph.D. They never matured socially in high school. They came here and did nothing but work for the second half of their lives. They finally relax when they've got tenure. They see a nice young woman like me and they don't know what to do—if they have any power over you, like they're your thesis adviser, some stupid sexist comment is bound to come out sometime. Three years ago I cut my hair short to try to look less attractive and ward off the comments and you know what one of my professors said? He said, 'Oh, Mary, you look so punk sexy.' But other than that it was fine."

We finished the vegetarian meal, went to see *Chariots of Fire*, and Mary drove me home.

"Let's drop by the Seven-Eleven," I said. "I'll get some tea bags, milk, and sugar, and something from the Hostess rack."

We sat at my kitchen table and talked some more. It was good not to spend Friday night by myself. It was good to know that there were other women in the world besides Stephanie. It was good to talk with Mary.

"Oh, what a nice cat," Mary said as my roommate's cat jumped up onto her lap and purred.

"Yeah, it's nice to have the cat around," I lied. "It belongs to my roommate."

"Oh, I think the water's ready," Mary said as the kettle started to rumble.

I spilled some hot water on the floor when I brought the cups to the table.

"No problem," I said. "I'll just wipe it up with a paper towel." The hot water left a white spot on the otherwise dirt-gray floor. "Uh, I've been meaning to do some cleaning," I said.

"Don't worry about it," she said, letting me off the hook.

She was beautiful in a way that had nothing to do with the layout of her face. We didn't kiss goodnight, didn't touch. She was my friend.

Tuesday, October 20

Gyftopoulos did his own tutorials, with Beretta sitting in the front row of the small classroom to help with any questions that Gyftopoulos hadn't heard before. The room had recently been redone with indirect lighting, and at the end of the day it felt almost homey. Gyftopoulos wore his cashmere sweater and before we started begging for hints for how to do that week's problem set, he tried his hand at stand-up comedy.

"You know, we've been starting to talk about chemical reaction, for which we use the symbol nu. Well, that reminds me of the time I was giving my first lecture back in 1954. I was young and, I have to admit, I was a little nervous. After talking about an hour and a half and writing the Greek letter over and over again on the board, one of the students said, 'Excuse me professor. . . . What's new?' "

I laughed dutifully. Several people hissed.

Gyftopoulos then fielded questions. The guy wearing the army uniform who sat in the second row raised his hand quickly, in a rigid military motion. He asked a question about the problem set that had been handed out that morning, due in two weeks.

"I don't think we need to look at those yet," he said. "Let's focus on the problem set that's due next week. Your eagerness, though, reminds me of a little story. It seems that there was a sergeant who received a telegram that one of his soldiers' mother had died. He didn't know how to bring it up to the soldier, whose name happened to be Schultz. So he had all his men line up, and he said, 'Everyone who has a mom step forward.' As the men stepped forward, he said, 'Not so fast, Schultz.' "

Everyone laughed at that one.

"Well, enough of the fun and games. Let's get back to work," he said. "Are there any other questions?"

"Pro-Fesser?" the guy with wire-rimmed glasses and a bushy mustache said.

"Yes, Lewis."

"Could you go over the problem on cogeneration on the last problem set?"

"Certainly. Do you have a copy of the problem statement?"

Lewis unclipped it from his binder. Gyftopoulos put his cigarette down and went to the blackboard. The chemical engineer sitting next to me whispered, "I don't know about you, but it makes me nervous that he smokes. I'd rather that a nuclear engineer was a little more risk-averse."

"At least they're filter cigarettes," I whispered back.

Gyftopoulos started his explanation. "As you know, cogeneration is the simultaneous generation of electricity and useful heat with one engine, typically a diesel engine or a gas turbine. What we want to do is to minimize the overall use of fuel to protect the environment. We realize that there have to be smokestacks with products of combustion, or as some would say, 'products of pollution,' but if we design systems with a match between needs for electricity and heat either for industrial processes or for heating of homes, we can minimize the products of pollution. And by the way, let me emphasize one point to you. If in your future careers you become involved in the energy industry, you will see that there is a tremendous amount of money to be made. But you must never forget that as an engineer you must not think of the money, but rather how you can benefit society."

Gyftopoulos continued the explanation of the problem. Other questions continued for the rest of the hour. There were occasional wisecracks from the students, never left without a rebuttal from Gyftopoulos. The atmosphere was collegial, nonthreatening, human.

That night Mary, Matt, Carlos, and I met in Carlos's office to go over some fluids problems. Matt suggested the way to proceed. For a given problem, one of us would draw the problem statement on the blackboard and start the solution. The rest of us would help whoever was doing the problem if he or she came to a dead end. "Let's start with some of these problems with the Bernoulli equation," Matt said. "Do you want to give one a shot, Mary?"

"Sure," she said. "Here's one that I worked on last night— problem D-28. It's a carburetor. But first everyone understands the Bernoulli equation, right?"

Matt and Carlos nodded and I shook my head. "I understand the derivation Shapiro did in class, how the Bernoulli equation falls out of the Navier-Stokes equations, but I don't fully understand it physically."

"Yeah, it is kind of a toughie," she said. "Just imagine Bernoulli sitting in his cousin's jewelry shop on the Ponte Vecchio in Florence. He's looking down at the Arno trying to figure out what to put in his next research proposal for the Medici Foundation. He's looking at two rocks in the middle of the river, and he notices that the water speeds up between them. He has a seminal idea for fundable research. 'If I draw a line following the path of the stream through the rocks, and then imagine a little tube of fluid going along that line, the energy of that little tube has to be constant along that line.' Got it?"

I nodded up and down. "I understand that much, but I still don't have the physical meaning down. I mean, you'd think if the fluid sped up it would have more energy, just like a car has more kinetic energy the faster it goes," I said.

Mary continued, "But the kinetic energy has to come from somewhere. And it comes from the energy stored in the static pressure of the fluid. Think of it like this: the little tube is a little spring that's compressed, and there's a whole bunch of these little compressed springs moving along parallel to each other. The only way they're all going to make it through the rocks is to loosen up a little bit. For this little spring, loosening up means that the front of the spring moves away from the back of the spring. All the other springs do the same thing and the water goes through the rocks, *senza problema.* When a compressed spring expands, it has less energy stored in it. The amount of decrease in pressure energy is equal to the increase in kinetic or speed energy."

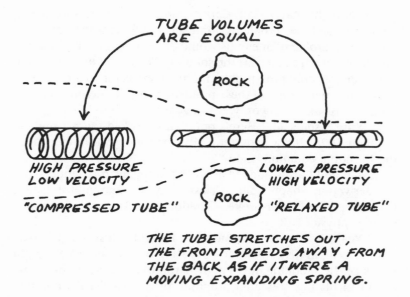

TUBE VOLUMES
ARE EQUAL

ROCK

HIGH PRESSURE
LOW VELOCITY

"COMPRESSED TUBE"

LOWER PRESSURE
HIGH VELOCITY

ROCK   "RELAXED TUBE"

THE TUBE STRETCHES OUT,
THE FRONT SPEEDS AWAY FROM
THE BACK AS IF IT WERE A
MOVING EXPANDING SPRING.

"OK. I'll buy that," I answered. "But Shapiro said today that it only applied to incompressible flows. If the flow is incompressible, how can the pressure go up and down?"

Carlos jumped in on that one. "Incompressible just means that the volume doesn't change when you apply the pressure. It's like if you put a weight on some water, the volume doesn't change but the pressure goes up. Come to think of it, it's like being a student here. They put lots of pressure on us but our volume doesn't change."

Not if we can help it.

Mary went back to the problem. "It's a carburetor," she reiterated.

"They want to know how much air has to go through how small a tube to bring in a specified amount of fluid from the holes around the outside of the tube. Now instead of water going through a couple of rocks in the Arno, we have air going through the tube. When its static pressure goes down below atmospheric, it sucks in fuel that's at atmospheric pressure. The faster the air goes in the tube, the lower the pressure will be, and the more fuel it will pull in."

She went on to set up the equations and derive the fuel flow rate as related to the geometry of the problem. I had seen fluid mechanics before, but the problems here were different. Before the concepts were abstract—here they were tangible. Many of the geometries and the problems in Shapiro's class were real devices. I remembered Rohsenow's telling me that a physicist derives equations for a phenomenon and says "Hooray," and an engineer starts with the equations the physicist derives and then tries to build something that works.

"There," Mary said as she circled the answer on the bottom of the chalkboard. "Next?"

"Can someone explain why the tea leaves end up in the center of the cup?" I asked. "Ever since I saw the *Peanuts* cartoon where Peppermint Patty asks that, I've wanted to know the answer."

"I can help out on that one," Matt said. "It was in one of those films Shapiro produced; I saw it when I took undergrad fluids. It's what they call a secondary flow. When you stir the tea, the liquid goes around in circles, like horses on a merry-go-round. The mystery is that you might expect the tea leaves to go to the outside of the teacup because of centrifugal force, just like when you're on a fast merry-go-round. But they don't—they end up in the center. Let me draw it on the board."

He drew a vertical cylinder with a circular arrow above it to indicate rotation. I wondered whether I'd ever be as smart as Matt and Mary. It seemed almost unfair to let people with MIT undergrad educations loose in classes with people with lesser backgrounds.

"If you imagine a little chunk of fluid at any height in the cylinder, sort of like a rectangular horse on the merry-go-round, it'll have pressure pushing on it from the side closer to the center

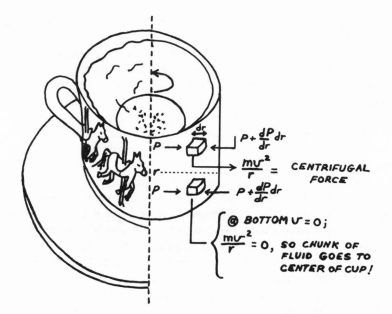

$$P + \frac{dP}{dr}dr$$

$$\frac{mv^2}{r} = \text{CENTRIFUGAL FORCE}$$

$$P + \frac{dP}{dr}dr$$

@ BOTTOM $v = 0$;

$\frac{mv^2}{r} = 0$, SO CHUNK OF FLUID GOES TO CENTER OF CUP!

and pressure pushing on it from the side closer to the outside of the merry-go-round. The pressure on the outside has to be greater than the pressure on the inside, to balance the centrifugal force of the chunk of fluid. On the bottom of the cylinder, the pressure at a given distance from the center is the same as it is at the top of the cylinder. But the tea and the tea leaves, too, go slower at the bottom because of the friction caused by the bottom of the cup. You know that, just like when you're on the merry-go-round, the slower you go, the less centrifugal force you have. So if you still have more pressure on the outside than on the inside, and less centrifugal force, you, the chunk of tea plus leaves, are going to move to the center of the cup. In fact, some of the tea is always circulating, up the center of the cup, across the top, down the side, and back to the center along the bottom."

I said, "Thanks. I think I've got it. Anybody else have any questions they want to go over?"

Carlos said, "There's this fire hose problem from section B. 'If a fire hose is delivering 800 gallons per minute to a fire, horizontally, and a fireman can provide a horizontal force of 125 pounds, how many firemen will it take to prevent the fire hose from flailing around like a wild snake?"

"I think I can solve that one," I said. "It's a momentum theorum problem. You just have to figure out how much momentum is going out of the fire hose and how fast. That equals the force."

I wrote on the board. First I calculated how fast the water was leaving the hose, on the basis of the size of the nozzle. 100 feet per second, or about 70 miles an hour. That was the easy part, the part that any eighth grader can do. In Japan. Below that I calculated how many pounds of water were leaving the hose each second (about 100 pounds).

Then I converted both numbers to the metric system and multiplied them together. This gave me the force, in newtons, named for Sir Isaac. Then I converted it back to pounds and had the answer—2.8 firemen.

My colleagues applauded my solution, and Mary added, "That reminds me of what my freshman adviser said during my first week here. 'Getting an education at MIT is like getting a drink of water from a fire hose.' "

CHAPTER

5

Funding

November 2

Monday at three o'clock I went in to talk to Tom Bligh. Tom Bligh was the Mechanical Engineering department's resident energy conservation, solar, and alternative energy guru. Originally a British South African, he'd paid his dues as assistant professor at the University of Minnesota. There he'd made a name for himself in underground buildings (buildings so designed need less fuel to heat and cool because of the insulating value and stable temperature of the ground). He'd also developed a system to make ice in the winter and then melt it in the summer for air-conditioning.

MIT recruited him as an associate professor; he had several ongoing projects with the Department of Energy—grants from the Carter era, when the government funded those kinds of things.

Bligh's office was on the fourth floor of Building 3, down the hall from that of Woodie Flowers, who taught a course called "How Things Work." A little farther down the hall was Warren Seering, the robotics whiz who raised his consulting fees by $10 an hour every month in an effort to slow business.

The fourth floor housed the design section of the department. These were the inventors, the truly creative. While many at the institute had one foot in science, the other in engineering, and two hands in the government's pockets, the fourth floor would rent itself out to product developers for thousands of dollars an hour just to shout ideas back and forth to one another.

In the display case next to Bligh's office was a student project from the year before—a music stand with an automatic page turner. In the waiting room outside Bligh's office was a poster that read, "If you love something let it go. If it comes back to you it's yours. If it doesn't it never was." It was the first time I'd seen that poster, so it meant something to me; it reminded me of Stephanie.

"Hello, Professor," I said. "I'd like to apply for a Lindbergh Fellowship for $15,000 and I'd like to know whether you'd be interested in being my faculty sponsor. The general area is alternative energy, and I've got an idea for a project."

"Please, call me Tom," he said. His office had a skylight. Papers and models were everywhere. He had brown hair, a beard, and glasses and was about forty.

He continued, "Well, if you can stomach applying for a grant in memory of a fascist, I'd be happy to help you."

"Why was he a fascist?" I asked.

"He was very pro-German in World War II, very much against U.S. involvement. Plenty of books have been written about it," he said.

"All I know is he was a technologist and aviator. That's all I need to think about when I apply for this grant. I need the money."

"All right, then, what's your idea?" Bligh asked.

"Well, it's an idea I got from a friend of mine in Belgium last year. You know how it gets really cold and windy in Kansas and Nebraska in the winter? Why not have a windmill that drives a heat pump directly to heat the house or the barn? The windier it gets, the more power will be available from the windmill to drive the heat pump, so the cooling effect of the wind will be negated by the increased heat that's pumped," I said.

"Hold on a minute while I call my patent attorney," he joked, then went back to being serious. "Can you explain to me how a heat pump works?"

It was a friendly cross-examination, so I answered honestly. "Not really. All I know is that it's sort of like an air conditioner in reverse. I could figure that out after I get the grant."

"That's the spirit," he said with irony, but also the wisdom of a successful time manager. "Let's put an outline together now, then you can come back in a week or so with a fleshed-out version. What do you propose to investigate?" he asked.

"First, I'd take the windmill as an off-the-shelf item. Maybe you could even use one they use to pump water and attach a conversion kit to a different gear mechanism. Then I'd look at the power curves for the windmill and the performance curves for the heat pump at different temperatures, and then I'd recommend different size-matching strategies. Finally, I'd put together some economic analysis, figure out the payback over a conventional oil-fired heating system."

"There are your four sections. See you in a week."

November 5

Charlotte Evans's packet listed Joe Smith as a specialist in cryogenics, the study of the very cold, and cogeneration, the small power plants in Gyftopoulos's problem sets. I didn't have much interest in the very cold, but cogeneration seemed to be a great way to keep the polar ice caps from melting.

Joe Smith, tenured professor, had his office off to one side, near the high-voltage magnet laboratory. He, a mechanical engineer, kept the electrical engineers' magnet cold enough to do tests in superconductivity. His window overlooked MIT's steam heat generating plant.

"What can I do for you, son?" he asked in a fatherly manner, with a southern accent.

"Well, I'm interested in energy conservation, cogeneration, heat recovery, insulation, solar energy—anything that saves energy. I saw that you do work in cogeneration," I said.

"Yes I do, but right now I don't have any money in it," he said, leaning back in his chair, his feet up on the desk and hands clasped behind his head. "If you can come up with some funding in that area on your own, though, I'd be happy to be your adviser." He reminded me of a southern plantation owner.

"Just a little piece of advice, son," he added. "When you work on energy, pretend you're running a mining operation. Focus your efforts on finding and extracting the most out of the concentrated areas of what you're mining. Don't worry about recovering anything from the slag heap. You'll spend more time and energy than you'll ever get out of it."

I remembered watching a TV show in high school. The master at the monastery talked in riddles like that, too. When I understand what he means, I can leave.

November 16

The yellow glossy brochure spoke glowingly about the patriotism of the rental car magnate—how his hard work and determination, plus the freedom of the marketplace, had enabled him to build a fortune. Now he wanted to repay the country by providing free rides to talented science and engineering students.

The brochure noted, "A strong technical workforce is essential for a strong defense, to maintain technological superiority over our adversaries. Individuals committed to these principles are invited to apply for the fellowship. The fellowship includes tuition, an allowance for books and supplies, and a stipend of $800 per month, free of taxes."

My application had been reviewed and my interview was scheduled for ten in the morning at Draper. Draper Laboratories' logo had a series of circles and a bull's-eye point inside the D. Since their main product involved aiming things, the bull's eye made sense. The lobby had models of the inertial guidance systems developed at Draper. These gyroscopes allow airplanes to operate under automatic pilot. They let men walk on the moon. And they enable intercontinental ballistic missiles to fly thousands of miles and land within hundreds of feet of target.

The guard—greased black hair, rayon shirt, polyester tie, and double-knit jacket covering a bulging shoulder holster—telephoned Dr. Jackson. Dr. Jackson arrived and signed me in; then we both took the elevator to the fourth floor. The new building, built in 1976, was sleek and white with glass that wrapped continuously around each of the eight floors. The visitor's badge I clipped to my brown tweed jacket stuck forward a little. The conference room had a window, with a view across Broadway and up Hampshire Street into Somerville. Most of the doors on the hallway were closed, with punch code locks.

The only question of the interview concerned energy. The two engineering doctors wanted me to tell them how I would extract power from the flow of a river. Not at a waterfall, or a dam, or a reservoir with a pipe going to a turbine 3,000 feet down the mountain like I'd seen in Switzerland, but from a river gently meandering along.

"Well," I answered, "I suppose you could put a pipe in the middle of the river and put a turbine at the downstream end of the pipe."

"How would you calculate the power output? Would the angle between the pipe and the water surface make a difference?"

Good questions. I wanted to ask whether I could leave and get back to them in a couple of hours. Instead I verbally fumbled for several minutes, until one of them said, "I think we've heard enough. Thank you for interviewing with us."

Outside was a group of several demonstrators, and a short, thin-bearded, white-haired man holding a stick with a globe on it. It looked like a giant blue and green Tootsie Pop.

The others' homemade banner—felt letters on a white sheet—said, "To disarm requires wisdom, love, and mercy."

Cambridge liberals, I thought. Why don't these people do something productive for the economy?

One of them offered me a green sheet of paper. I looked around to see whether there were any video cameras pointing in my direction, then accepted.

The leaflet read, "Every Monday since 1979, a nonviolent vigil has taken place at Draper. Fully conscious of our personal failures in the practice of nonviolent love, we continue to choose to witness to the truth of the way of nonviolent love as the way to peace. We vow to express this truth in our silent witness, our leaflets, tax resistance, service to the poor, direct actions, and in serving time in jail."

I wondered what they meant by direct action. I wondered whether these people considered themselves real Americans, what sense they had of the need for defense. Maybe they were little Soviet-funded gnats trying to undermine the commitment of Draper's engineers and scientists. Or maybe, just maybe, they were right. I remembered that my ancestors had left a secure, well-defended island (England) to sail off the edge of the world and make friends with the Indians.

I met Jim Stuart at the student center coffee shop and told him about the interview. "You probably won't get it," he said. "I heard those only go to straight-A undergraduates. Besides, I'm not sure you'd want it. They say there're no strings attached, but they really push you into defense work. They encourage you to have high-paying summer jobs at defense labs, and then that's the only thing you know. A friend of a guy from my lab had one of those and didn't know what was happening until it was too late. I think he ended up in a mental hospital."

Tuesday, November 17

Frederick Weare had advertised in the department newsletter: "Research Assistantship available. High-pressure application to fracture in geological structures. Sponsor: Mobil." Translation: Weare crushed rocks for a living.

Weare, rumor had it, rode his bicycle to and from his apartment fifteen miles away in Needham every day. Rumor also had it that his wife had recently divorced him because she never saw him anymore.

My appointment was at the end of the day in Weare's lab in the basement of Building 3. The lab had several black tabletops with samples of oil-laden rock on them, and bits and pieces of electronic circuitry and several oscilloscopes, miniature green TV screens in fancy boxes with lots of knobs on front.

Weare was young and quite slim, with blond hair and a mustache. His eyes looked a little tired. He spoke with a slight accent, as if he'd been overseas somewhere for an extended period, but I couldn't place it. Maybe he was originally from Ireland.

"What's your expertise?" he asked me early in the interview.

I didn't know I was supposed to have expertise already; I thought I had come to MIT to get it.

"Uh, well, I've done a lot of work with fluids; at the von Kármán Institute in Brussels I did some work with instrumentation, temperature measurements, in a solar heat storage experiment," I answered.

Weare smirked. "Ah yes, good old solar energy. Are you an environmentalist?"

I didn't know the right answer. "Well, sort of," I said.

"So am I," he said. "But full professorship is on my list of lifetime personal goals, and I have to do fundable research to achieve that. Then maybe I'll dabble in that soft stuff again."

"What would be the environmental impact of my thesis project?" I asked.

"It actually would be less harmful than many of the other technologies under development. What I'm proposing is to make many underground explosions that will create big pressures on the oil and allow it to be pulled up out of the mountain rather than having to remove the rock and extract it outside the mountain," he said.

"Well, it sounds interesting. Do you think you'd like to hire me?" I asked.

He paused. "I'll look over your résumé and then get back to you. I've got a couple more people to interview. If you don't hear from me within a week, give my secretary a call."

Maybe something else will come up.

That night I stood at the heat transfer solution board and copied down answers to the latest set of problems. It still annoyed me that they didn't just hand these solutions out. But they make the rules and we're engineers and we don't question the rules they make. We just want to solve our clearly definable problems and see an orderly world, even if it's someone else's order.

The solution board is in a locked glass case, under a buzzing fluorescent lamp. There's a little ledge in front of it for your notebook. The lamp illuminates just the board and the hall lights are dimmed, so the solution board becomes its own little world of thought.

Greg Webster, also in the class, was at the other end of the solution board. I'd met him in the dining hall one Sunday morning after the end of the soccer season. He was enrolled in my three classes, plus two others.

"How's your money holding out?" I asked.

"I've got enough saved up in the bank from my two years working on the space shuttle at Rockwell to last the whole year here. But I'd rather not deplete my savings."

How can I hope to compete with somebody who's worked on the space shuttle? I wondered. He'll probably get a Ph.D. here and in five years I'll be watching TV and he'll be smiling and waving as he walks onto *Discovery* as a mission specialist.

"How about you?" he asked.

Should I tell him about Weare? Or about the other department newsletter listings I'll apply to? He's a potential friend, but also a potential competitor.

I finished copying the solution to Advanced Problem 8 and told Greg all my leads.

He replied in kind. "That reminds me," he said. "Frank West

in the Sloan Auto Lab is looking for someone. They just got some big contract with a bunch of engine companies to do some combustion work. I just talked to him today. I would have taken it but it seems like he's really looking for a wrench turner to get the experiment going. I want to hold out for something more theoretical."

"How do you spell his name?"

Wednesday, November 18

West's office was immaculate, with every book perfectly in place in the institute-issue wooden bookshelves with glass-in-wood-frame covers that pulled out and down. A tapestry depicting a hunting scene hung on the white-painted cinderblock wall. The whole place smelled like a truck stop.

"What a beautiful office," I said.

"Thank you," he answered. "I've been trading in tapestries ever since I bought ten of them at a castle foreclosure sale in Holland during my junior year. I brought them back here and sold them for five times what I paid for them."

I handed him my résumé and he looked through it, nodding approvingly. I waited for a question from him about my research projects.

"You seem to have done a lot of bicycling," he said, referring to the entry in my résumé about having cycled in northern Italy for six months. "I was a Texas state cycling champion when I was in high school. You must be pretty good with a wrench."

Milk this for all it's worth, I thought.

"Well, I've taken apart every bearing in my bicycle, cleaned, regreased them, and reassembled them about three times in the past few years."

"Good. How'd you like to work for me?"

"I'd love to," I answered enthusiastically.

"Fantastic," he said. "The funding starts the first week in January. Welcome aboard!"

I shook his hand and walked downstairs a little unsteadily past the corridor to the engine lab. The first thing I saw, lying vertically in the middle of the floor, was a piston as high as my waist. The knot in my stomach tightened some more. But then a clear picture of my $50,000 debt dissolved into the concrete.

I sang to myself:
I got money
I got funding
I got an R.A.
Who could ask for anything more?

CHAPTER

6

Finals

In early December the letter from Stephanie arrived. "I thought you were a nice person. . . . I thought you were innocent. . . . I thought you were not an egotist. Evidemment je m'en suis trompé. I was wrong."

It's good to see she took it so well.

The days became shorter and shorter, Gyftopoulos's problem sets longer and longer. It was cold on the rides to and from Allston. My apartment was cold. The smoke from the power plant on Memorial Drive was thicker, billowier, and at night it was blown more and more to the side by the early winds of winter.

Three weeks left in the term. Two weeks of classes, a weekend, Monday off, and then finals. There is no reading period at MIT. Technology is cumulative; if you can do the last problem set, you're ready to take the exam.

They juggle the schedule to try to prevent conflicts, but there is a finite probability that if you have three classes, one exam will fall on the first morning, one that afternoon, and one the second morning. Mine did: Fluids, Thermo, Heat.

I studied in the fourth floor of the library, downstairs from the main level, where the librarians' offices were. It was windowless and free of distractions.

For Thermo and Heat Transfer, I xeroxed formulas and pictures of problem solutions and stapled them to index cards. They might help me recognize the patterns. Short of full understanding, I could refer to them at exam time.

The first Saturday, Ike Thomas's Gospel singing group sang in Kresge Auditorium. Ike's office was around the corner from Matt's in the heat transfer lab. He'd done his undergrad work at Michigan State, and we sometimes chatted before and after Rohsenow's class. The small audience at the concert was comprised mostly of black students and their families. The singing was joyous, loving, and I felt warm and at home, as if I were back in North Carolina.

Ike played the concert grand piano and sang "Amazing Grace," his rich, sonorous voice resonating with the bass chords, like a voice crying out in the wilderness.

The following week Ike and I were invited to a study session in heat transfer. Four of the guys in the class lived in Ashdown House, the graduate student dorm at the corner of Mass Ave. and Memorial Drive. One of them also had a desk in Matt's office. Actually, I had heard about the study session by accident and sort of invited myself and then asked Ike whether he wanted to come along.

It turned out that these guys had been meeting once a week since the beginning of the term and hadn't invited either of us. It's things like this that let you know who your friends are.

The six of us sat around a table in one of the lounges. The four of them blasted through the week's recommended ungraded assignment quickly, enough to show that they'd all been keeping up with the pace of the class all term. The one at the head of the table leaned forward in his chair, his feet crossed beneath the chair, the upper foot shaking like the Asian semiconductor physics student's in the library two months before.

Ike looked as discouraged as I felt. The session ended after about an hour, and as Ike and I left, we commiserated.

"Those guys will have A's, every one of them," I said. "That'll surely push at least me way back in the standings."

"Yeah, they do seem to know what they're doing," he said. "This place gets me down sometimes. But I just try to keep re-

membering what my grandma from South Carolina used to say
to me when I was little."
   I asked him what she said.
   "God didn't make no junk."

   The Saturday morning before final Tuesday, the senior who
had been building the pedal-powered crew shell for his undergraduate thesis was preparing to launch it with Professor David
Gordon Wilson, his thesis adviser. I was in my office at 9:30 studying heat transfer, but when they asked whether I wanted to help
I said yes. I was reaching the resignation point, when you begin
to think that there's nothing more you can do to study for exams.
It's a combination of saturation, burnout, and a feeling that if you
don't know it by now there's no way you're going to know it by
Tuesday. Besides, I thought, it might help to score some brownie
points with Wilson. Who knows, he might be grading a test of
mine someday.
   "Why don't you fellows bring the boat out, and I'll bring my
car around," Wilson said. He was always so chipper. We loaded
the crew shell onto the roof of his early '70s red VW station wagon.
The boat looked a little funny with the propellor up in the air and
the fiberglass outrigger pontoon strapped to the side, all upside
down.
   With Wilson and his tweed jacket and British accent, I felt
like one of the pioneers of early aviation going out to the testing
ground, walking fast like on the newsreel.
   As we slowly drove around the block to the boathouse, Wilson
said, "The propellor is based on the same design that Paul Mac-
Cready used on the Gossamer Condor. It's very efficient at low
flow rates. We can hope that this test will be successful, and then
the next student can work on making it into a pedal-powered
hydrofoil. My calculations have shown that it should be possible
for one person pedaling a hydrofoil to go faster than the Harvard
varsity eight-oared shell."
   It did make sense when I thought about it. The oarsmen spend
a lot of time just returning their oars to the power stroke. If you
pedal the vessel, you're always in the power stroke.
   There were no crew shells on the Charles that late in the
season, just one woman, who was training for the Olympic team,
standing on the dock at the boathouse after she'd finished her
workout. It was cold and gray and felt like snow.

Wilson and I and the undergrad attached the pontoon to the crew shell on the dock, with the crew shell sitting on two sawhorses and the propellor on its strut attached by the bicycle chain to the sprocket in the middle of the boat. The chain went through a half-dollar-size hole in the bottom of the shell.

We put the shell in the water and let it sit there for a few seconds.

"It appears to be taking on water, sir," the undergrad said as the brown muck flowed through the hole for the chain.

"Yes, well, the water isn't coming in that fast; we'll just have to do our test runs quickly," Wilson said. "We can bail it out between runs if necessary." Stiff upper lip. Pip pip. Cheerio.

The undergrad went first. When he sat in the boat, the water came in a little faster. He pedaled for several revolutions and in half a minute he moved 8 feet along the dock. Then the chain fell off.

"Well, that at least is a proof of concept," Wilson said. "The propellor is designed to give maximum power at about 8 miles an hour boat speed, so we may need to give some thought as to how to get up to that speed."

We picked up the shell to let the water out, and Wilson took his turn, with similar results. Then came my turn.

"Craaack" went the boat as I sat down in it. I saw the two fracture lines move out from either side of the propellor hole and the water came in faster than it had when Wilson was in the boat.

"Maybe you should take the picture now," I said.

I smiled for the camera, pedaled four strokes, moved a couple of feet, and slid back over onto the dock from the boat's seat.

As we lifted the boat out, Wilson said, "Well, that's what design is. You have an idea for how to do something, you build it, you test it, and then you fix the problems that you discover."

That midnight, the last Saturday before Tuesday's exams, the MIT symphony played Mozart's clarinet concerto in Lobby 7. Hundreds of us huddled on the floor—huddled masses, seeking comfort, seeking refuge from the cold and lonely study of science.

Fluids and Thermo were in Du Pont Gym. We were competitors for position on the bell curve, now not playing basketball but rather working problems.

Fluids started at 9:00. I wished Carlos and Matt and Mary

good luck and turned over the typed packet when Shapiro said, "You may begin," over the loudspeaker. His voice echoed through the vaulted aircraft-hangar-shaped room. It was the last kilometer of the bicycle race.

Gemayel and Shapiro handed out the booklets to two twenty five and to two twenty, the undergraduate Fluids class to our right. Gemayel said to Shapiro, "We better not get any of the tests mixed up."

Shapiro answered wryly, "It wouldn't make any difference to the results."

I turned over the typed exam that said again at the top "Open book . . . open notes." They don't bother to make you memorize things here. Instead they let you use anything you can carry and make the problems impossible anyway.

As usual, I looked through the exam for something that looked doable. Surprisingly, Shapiro had put some gift points up front. These were just general information questions, things I could look up in my neatly copied notes, or the general concepts that I had mastered independently of my ability to solve test problems. Within the first hour I had a good third of the points down.

I felt a little high—the bright lights shining down on the white paper as the freshly sharpened number two pencil makes its ordered impressions on the page. Call it test-taker's high, like in a bicycle race when the pack is carrying you along faster than you've ever gone before. There's a focused mental atmosphere in the room, 300 very bright people around you, thinking quietly, quickly, with no random thoughts. You reason, look at the drawings you've made, write the formulas down, and listen for the ideas you need.

At ten after ten, Professor Smith had an announcement for the students taking the undergraduate Thermo final: "There's a typo on Problem 3b." His voice echoed up and down the hangar. "It should be 12 calories per gram, not 120 calories per gram." Evidently a guy who'd walked up to talk to Smith had spotted the error.

Why don't they proofread the tests before they give them out, I thought.

The problem section, worth 60 of the 100 points, involved the same shaft I'd seen on the previous two exams. This time, to add a third degree of difficulty, the rod was spinning:

"(a) Find the maximum speed of rotation at which the oil

flow between the shaft and the sleeve can be considered viscous. (30 points) (b) Find the lifting force on the shaft as the rotation speed reaches 3,600 rpm. (30 points)"

So much for test-taker's high.

I gave it the institute try for the rest of the exam period and figured my total would be around 70. Time to hope that the average was low.

Thermo was a little harder. It did feel like I'd learned something, though. I knew how to do an "ennergy balance and an ennntropy balance," as Gyftopoulos had emphasized. I knew how to draw rectangles and arrows going in and out of them to symbolize the heat or mechanical energy going into or out of the rectangle. The rest was number-crunching detail.

Gyftopoulos walked around the gymnasium as we took the test. He stopped at each table and briefly looked at how each of us was doing. It was his way of showing he cared, but it was unnerving. When he came to my table he gently put one hand on my shoulder, one on the table, and leaned over to look at my number two pencil impressions on the white page.

"Umhmmmm," he said approvingly as he watched me write.

It was better than "Tsk Tsk," but I really wanted to turn to him and say, "Eeeeyesss? May I help you?"

You don't joke around with these guys, though; certainly not before they've made all their judgment calls for the borderline grades.

The next day, from the moment I turned over Rohsenow's final, I knew it was fourth and long yardage. It had been just as well that I'd helped Wilson and his undergraduate thesis student with that stupid boat. Fully half the test dealt with the resistance method of determining amounts of radiation heat flux. Rohsenow had touched on this during the last two lectures.

The idea is that you think of the hot surfaces as if they're batteries. The higher the temperature, the higher the voltage of the battery. Different fractions of the heat are absorbed by different objects, depending on how far away they are, how big they are, and how they face the hot surface. You put all that information into an effective electrical resistance, and then you can solve the set of equations for various hot surface temperatures.

Aha. That's what they mean by modeling. You throw equations at the phenomenon and vary parameters. Generally, you throw equations that you know how to solve from somewhere else, as with the electrical analog model for radiation. Unfortunately, I had never mastered the electrical equations. I knew enough of them to parrot problems in sophomore physics exams, but not enough to transfer that knowledge to another field in the four days before the final when I had two other exams to worry about.

I spent three hours scraping for partial credit points on the other two problems. It was discouraging to watch the other guys in the small classroom working so fast. The radiation questions, if you knew how to set them up, must have had many, many steps.

The day before Christmas Eve I assessed the damage, starting with Beretta. If there was bad news, I didn't want to risk another scene with Gyftopoulos.

"Your final score was really quite low in comparison with the rest of the class," he said deliberately. "Some people did very very well, and some did poorly. We even had to give some D's and F's this time. . . . We talked it over and decided to give you a C."

"How many people finished the class?"

"Forty-five."

I remembered Matt's algorithmic count of 76 at the first lecture. The lower third of the bell curve, the one that would have put me in the middle, had dropped after the first midterm, leaving me grasping at the back of the pack as one grasping for a railing on the back of a receding train car.

I went downstairs to Rohsenow's office. The news would surely be better there. Jamie was the grader, after all, and we were on the same intramural hockey team.

I sat in the seat that was becoming familiar. Rohsenow pulled out the curve sheet from the test. It was a histogram, a graph with the final scores on the horizontal axis and little x's for the number of people in the different ranges extending vertically, like the one he'd drawn on the blackboard after the first quiz. The graph had two humps on it, one centered on 90 percent and another centered on 75. To the left of the two humps were two lone little x's at 60.

Rohsenow explained the graph. "Here are the scores, see. Now Jamie and I sat down and we looked at the graph and we said, well, that hump looks like an A, and that hump looks like a B." He pointed to the 90 hump and the 75 hump. "Then we looked at these two little x's, and we said, well, we could call these a B, but they really look more like a C. You're one of those."

Good for Jamie, I thought. Influence peddling by playing on the same intramural team doesn't do any good at MIT. In a way, the C felt good. It was an honest C. I wondered who was the other one.

"Uh, this could be a problem, sir," I said. "I just talked to Professor Beretta, and he said that I got a C in Thermo, too. I don't know how I did in Fluids, but I doubt it was an A."

"If you have a C in my class and a C in Thermo, the trend would indicate you'll probably have a C in Fluids, too. The subject matter's similar," he said.

Everything's a trend to this guy—points on a graph with a line in between them.

I asked, "What would 3 C's mean for my future at MIT?"

"Well," he answered, "you have to have a 3.5 to get a degree from here. That means you have to have at least as many B's as C's. So if your average ever goes below a 3.5, we put you on probation. If it goes under 3.5 for two terms in a row, we start playing a numbers game. We try to figure out whether it's mathematically possible for you to dig yourself out of the hole by the time you complete all your coursework. If it looks like a long shot, well, we point that out to you and we hope you prevent things from getting ugly by resigning."

It was all so matter-of-fact to him. It's easy to be matter-of-fact when you've been on the right side of every bell curve, even after they've skimmed and skimmed until there's nothing but extra-rich cream left.

"What does this mean in the short term?" I asked.

"First of all, you'll get a letter from the dean," he said. "He'll tell you that you're on probation, and that you should come and talk to me."

Probation. Do I get a probation officer?

Rohsenow continued, "But you're talking to me now, so you can ignore that. Just try to get a couple of B's next term."

The news didn't shake me up as much as it might have. There was, after all, always business school. I walked toward where I'd locked my bike near Building 31 and bumped into Gemayel.

"So, how'd I do in Fluids?" I asked.

"Well, we're really not supposed to tell you until after the holidays," he said.

Right. Don't tell them they're failures until they've opened up their Christmas presents and been well fed at home. The policy must be designed to keep the sidewalks near the tall buildings clean.

"Aw, come on. You can tell me," I persisted. "At least give me a hint."

"Ehh," he hesitated, "you did okay."

I did okay. That meant a B.

CHAPTER

===== 7 =====

The Guild

January 2, 1982

7:30 A.M. Frank West was already on his second cup of coffee when I knocked on his door. It was the first day of my R.A. With an R.A., you take two or three classes per term and work about 30 hours a week in the lab or on a computer. In exchange, you receive free tuition and a stipend of about $600 each month. And the research work ends up in your master's or Ph.D. thesis, so an R.A. kills two birds with one stone.

"Here I am," I said enthusiastically. "What do you want me to do?"

"Your job is to raise the compression ratio of the rapid compression machine, which from now on we'll call the RCM. You'll need to redesign it, conduct experiments over a test matrix of swirl rates and turbulence levels, and investigate parametric influences on ignition delay," he answered briskly.

Gulp. This guy should come with a glossary.

West continued, "You can sit down if you want. I know it's a big job. We want to get results in February, in time for the meeting of the research sponsors. You'll need to design the equipment; Nick Vittoro will be working for you. I want you to keep him busy."

Sure. How can I keep anybody else busy when I don't know what I'm doing. I've never designed anything in my life.

"Uh huh," I said.

"Oh, and about lab rules," he added. "The first rule is 'It's your job and not mine.' The second is 'I don't take any excuses,' and the third is 'Lab hours are 7:30 to 5:30, with half an hour for lunch.' You should be able to get all your lab work done between those hours. Harvard's Physics Department lost a student last year when he fell asleep into his experiment's high-voltage power supply at 2:00 in the morning. He was found dead the next day. We don't want that kind of thing to happen here in the Sloan Lab."

Me neither. "Uh huh."

"You can do computer work at night and read journal articles. And try taking a swim after dinner for half an hour or so. I've found that exercising at that time makes me need less sleep and wakes me up so I can work another four or five hours. Come on downstairs—I'll show you your cell."

It sounded so confining. It was the start of what might not have an ending. Matt had told me that all most graduate students think about is getting their advisers to approve their theses. Real theses. Not a business school forty-page "major paper" that you write over spring break, but a year to two year's effort—if all went well—and West seemed like he'd squeeze as much work out of me as he could before signing.

Past the piston at the door the lab looked like a small factory, with lathes, drill presses, a welding station, and over it all, an overhead crane that ran on tracks to move the really heavy objects. The test cells were small rooms around the perimeter of the main shop. Each housed the equipment for one experiment. It was like a prison workshop scene in a gangster movie, where one gangster tries to drop the engine block on the other one. I even had a cell of my own.

The ordeal would be worth it, though. I'd always been good in math, but when it came to mechanical things I was less than gifted. In high school I tried to rebuild the engine on my minibike after it froze when I let the oil get too low, but that project ended in my taking the minibike to the lawnmower shop. The model rocket I built in sixth grade went up 6 inches, veered to the right, and crashed. And my garage was always a mess, nothing like the ones featured in *Popular Mechanics*, where all the tools are neatly placed on pegboards.

I could keep my bicycle on the road, though, and that was enough for West.

He opened one of the battleship-gray steel double doors to the cell and before he left said, "Here it is. Have fun!"

Thanks. The machine was a mass of gray and brown metal—a tank, bolts, tubes, pipes, wires, switches. I had no idea where to start.

Somebody turned on the radio on the shelf in the center of the machine shop. The song was Glenn Miller's "In the Mood."

I looked at the yellowing, crumbling piece of paper attached with aged masking tape to the gray tank. It read "Rapid compression machine. All systems operational: May 15, 1972." The machine had been rusting while I'd been going through puberty, and now I had two months to bring it back to life.

"We gotta get some eh in hih, Cap'n," the man with gray hair around the edge of his baseball cap said as he opened the second double door to my cell. He wore a blue workshirt buttoned all the way up to the turned-up collar, a blue lab jacket and blue jeans, and work boots that were probably steel-toed. He was a little shorter than I and kind of shuffled into my cell. "I'm Nick Vittoro. What's your name?"

"Pepper White."

"Oh yeah, you're the new apprentice. I remember Professor West mentioning something about you coming along after Christmas. I tell you one thing, Cap'n, we're gonna be suckin' some wind on this job."

I liked the way he said we. "Got any suggestions on where to start?" I asked him.

"Showah. Take it apaht. Get yuh hands on the soul of that old rapid compression machine. Let's bring the A-frame hoist in here and we'll take the front end off it. We gotta let it know who's boss."

Not even an hour into the project and I was already learning one of the most basic concepts in heavy industry: rigging, or moving big heavy objects around without dropping them on your foot or wrecking your back or sometimes doing both. That must be why they call it heavy industry.

"And remembah, Cap'n," Nick said, "you'll get there a lot fastuh and safuh if you keep the Lawd as yah pahtnah."

We took the A-frame hoist from the spare parts area behind the chain-link fence across from my cell. Glenn Miller stopped playing, and the announcer said, "The music of your life." The music added to the lab's archaic feeling. We all know that engines work, so what's left to find out about them? The hot stuff was in the electronics labs around the corner. That's where the technology is high and not mature. But what good is electronics without something real to make or control? Such as a rapid compression machine.

A real four-stroke diesel engine in a real car or truck has a piston that moves up and down two times per engine cycle. Each one-way trip the piston makes up or down the cylinder is called a stroke. Figure the piston is at the top of the cylinder.

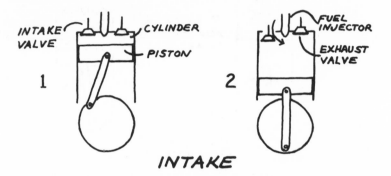

INTAKE

The volume of the cylinder is very small at that point, and a valve (called the intake valve) opens to let air in as the piston moves down. This is called the intake stroke (the cylinder takes in air). When the piston is near the bottom of the intake stroke, the intake valve closes and the piston moves up and compresses the air that's trapped in the cylinder by the closed valve. This is the compression stroke. The "compression ratio" is the volume bounded by the piston and the cylinder at the beginning of the compression stroke, divided by the same volume at the end of the compression stroke.

When the piston is near the end of the compression stroke, the fuel injector squirts diesel fuel into the cylinder. The fuel evaporates and burns, and the heat generated by the burning fuel raises the pressure even more and pushes the piston down. This is the power stroke.

Once the piston bottoms out, the exhaust valve opens and

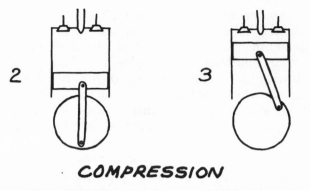

COMPRESSION

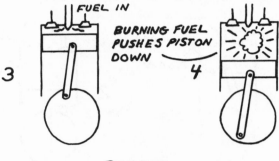

POWER

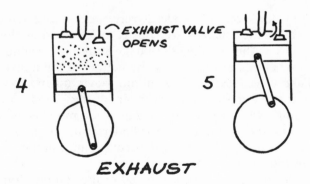

EXHAUST

the piston pushes the burned fuel out of the cylinder to the tailpipe. This is the exhaust stroke.

Then the intake valve opens and the cycle repeats itself. That much I remembered from the science report I paraphrased from the encyclopaedia in ninth grade.

The rapid compression machine would simulate the compression and combustion parts of the cycle.

Before using the A-frame, I made a sketch in my brand-new lab notebook to record how we rigged it. If anything went wrong, we could refer to the sketch to analyze what happened. If our work was successful, the sketch might be helpful for future generations of RCM students.

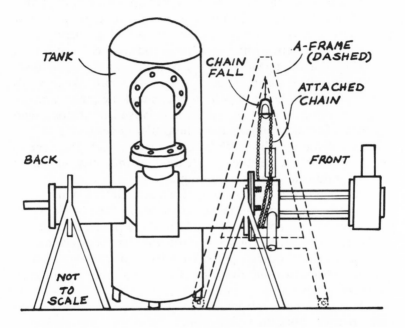

Nick agreed with my setup and we went to work. The A-frame in place and the chain fall wrapped around the cylinder, he said, "OK, Cap'n. Go get a wrench outa my tool box and undo the bolts. I'll hold the chain fall steady."

The bolts loosened with hard tugs and some body weight. Nick tightened the chain just before the last one loosened.

"There's a piston in the front cylinder that we gotta pull the cylinder offa," Nick said. "Here, use this screwdriver to get the cylinder started."

I wedged the screwdriver between the two flanges and eased them apart. As the cylinder moved forward a chrome shaft appeared about a quarter of an inch at a time. Nick and I slowly worked the cylinder away from the rest of the machine.

Two feet out, Nick said, "Easy now, Cap'n, we got just a couple more inches. We don't wanna bend that shaft now. It'd slow things up for me to have to make a new one."

Gently, slowly we freed the cylinder from the piston, leaving the shaft unscathed. "Let's bring this thing onto the workbench," he said, and we walked the A-frame and the cylinder opposite the bench.

"You hold it, Cap'n, while I hoist her up," Nick said, pulling the free end of the chain up a foot or two at a time. Within a few minutes, he had lifted the cylinder to the level of the bench; then we straddled the bench with the A-frame and lowered the cylinder.

"How's that thing work?" I asked Nick, pointing to the hoist.

"It's just the pulley principle," he said. "It's sorta like theyah's a lot of pulleys in theyah. I pull on one end of the pulley and the thing I'm trying to lift goes half as fah. Wasn't it Aristotle who said that if he had enough pulleys he could move the world?"

I wondered whether Nick had his facts straight. The general idea sounded plausible, though. "I thought that stuff all started with the industrial revolution, though."

"No, Cap'n, this kind of thing's been around for a while. How do you think they built all those cathedrals in the Middle Ages? They sure didn't carry all those rocks to the top," he answered.

He had a point. The pulley and the lever had been around for four, maybe five thousand years. They were the first steps, along with the wheel, in using the laws of nature to magnify force by shrinking distance.

"Well, that's enough for now, Cap'n. Time for my roll. You want anything from the coffee shop?"

"No thanks, Nick. I think I'll stay here and try to figure out what these pieces do."

"Okeedokay," he said. "Say, Peppah, I used to teach a machining class. It might help you get your feet on the ground if we spend some time each day going over the basics."

"Thanks. I might take you up on that." The Lone Ranger had Tonto; I had Nick.

Nick went outside and the noise from the Wright Brothers' wind tunnel next door sounded like a squadron of B-17's on their way to bomb Düsseldorf. The radio played "Don't Sit under the Apple Tree with Anyone Else but Me." I half expected to hear an ad for war bonds.

————

If you don't know what you're doing, the first thing to do is to try to look like you know what you're doing. That buys you time. And so I started cleaning up the cell. I removed the yellowed sheet of paper from the tank and scraped the old masking tape away with Nick's screwdriver. I cleared all the old pieces of junk off the available bench space. Then I made a list of the items in the lab as one by one I put them neatly on one of the two workbenches. Some of the devices would never have another use before they either were reborn as a Toyota or went back to iron ore in a landfill somewhere. Others might be adaptable to the new experiment; salvageable, they might save days, weeks of time.

I found an old blue lab jacket with "Don" on the name patch. I put it on. Under one of the benches I found an old pile of notes from West's thesis. They were disorganized and it made me feel a little better to know that for all his surface order there had been at least some chaos in his life at one time.

All the metal was mounted on a 6-inch-thick steel pad with slots running from one end to the other. The slots furnished a place to bolt down all the heavy stuff. I started to clean the little bits of metal out of the slots, but that was too hard and probably a waste of time so I just dusted off the top of the pad. My high school's "shop" teacher, an iron worker, might have had some tips for me if he were still alive.

Five-thirty came quickly. Nick and I washed our hands with Boraxo and he took off the baseball cap, showing a completely bald head except for the gray around the edges.

"See you tomorrow, Cap'n," he said. "Be fresh and ready to learn how to machine."

"Will do, Nick. Have a good one."

7:45 P.M. After my swim—it did wake me up—I saw Frederick Weare, the rock crusher who didn't fund me, in the locker room.

"Have you found funding yet?" he asked.

"Yes, as a matter of fact. I'm working on the Rapid Compression Machine in the Sloan Auto Lab."

"Good for you," he said. "What exactly is the scope of your investigation?"

To get the thing to work and to get out of here. "I'll be looking at the effect of swirl rates on ignition delay in diesel combustion," I said.

"Um hmmm," he nodded again. He didn't ask any more about

diesel combustion because that was outside his realm of expertise. "What kind of instrumentation will you be using?"

"I don't know exactly yet—see, this was my first day and I'm just trying to get oriented," I answered.

"Well, it sounds like a lot of fun. Good luck with it."

Thanks, Fred. Maybe we'll co-author a paper some day.

8:15 P.M. He who fails to learn from history is doomed to repeat it. The theses of experiments past are on the eighth floor of the Barton Engineering Library. Chemical, electrical, civil, nuclear, mechanical engineering. Rows upon rows of black-bound type-written pages, each with three signatures on the front—author, adviser, graduate department chairman. The name of the author is written on the side in skinny white capital letters, together with the year of completion, as far back as the 1940s. Any further back than that and you have to go to microfiche.

I started with West, Sc.D. '71. There were some color pictures of glowing yellow flames. An Sc.D. is a doctor of science, which makes more sense than a Ph.D. since auto mechanics is a lot closer to science than it is to philosophy. Only MIT, Stanford, Cal Tech, and a few other choice schools offer the option of Sc.D. instead of Ph.D. on the diploma. It enables the hyperelite to recognize each other without stooping to ask where they earned their credentials.

I looked in the list of references in the back of West's thesis. He referred to Pyra, '68, whose B.S. was from the University of Prague. Pyra didn't have any pictures, just graphs. I put them both in my stack. Pyra referred to Nayak, '63—B.S., University of Cairo. Nayak had lots of graphs, too, and he referred to Rathle, '59. Rathle had received his B.S. from the University of Alexandria, Egypt, in 1957. Rathle had built the RCM. My apparatus and I were both twenty-five years old.

Rathle's diagrams made the scales drop from my eyes. The machine had three chambers. The front cylinder, where combustion took place, was what Nick and I had removed earlier in the day. The back part of the front part had "nonreturn pawls," which caught the shaft as it went to the end of the stroke and kept it from bouncing backward or being pushed backward by the pressure of the exploding diesel fuel. The middle cylinder had compressed air and a piston four times the size of the front piston. The bigger area enabled the whole shaft to move forward, even when the combustion chamber's pressure was much higher than the pressure in the tank.

The back cylinder had various-size rings in it and was filled with transmission fluid. A piston on the shaft in the back cylinder would slow down the whole shaft to make the compression stroke similar to that in a real engine, where the piston is attached to a rotating crankshaft.

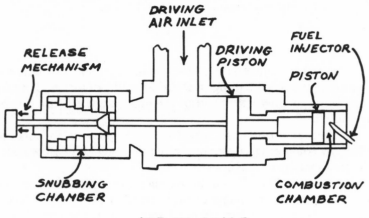

From Rathle back the references were in journals—Taylor, 1948; Selden, 1937; Rothrock, 1932; Moore, 1922; Falk, 1906.

Falk's machine was a vertical tube filled with hydrogen. His shaft had a lead weight on top, and the piston had rope piston rings to seal the gap between the piston and cylinder. He dropped the weight and measured the temperature at which the gas combusted. That first version was simple, almost trivial, but essentially the same as my large gray mass of metal.

Falk referred to LeChatelier, as in Le Chatelier's Principle (1888): "When an external force is applied to a system at equilibrium, the system adjusts so as to minimize the effect of the applied force." Go with the flow.

I looked up Diesel in *Encyclopaedia Britannica*. Rudolph Diesel (born 1858, died 1913), German thermal engineer, was also a distinguished connoisseur of the arts, a linguist, and a social theorist. While at the technical school in Augsburg, he saw a demonstration of the ancient Chinese fire stick. The fire stick, dating to 1000 B.C. or earlier, is like the bicycle pumps that fit on the frame of the bicycle. You put a dry leaf or a dry tindery piece of wood in one end, close it off, give the pump one good rapid compression, and pow, fire. From that demonstration came the idea for his engine.

I felt I was in good company, carrying on a tradition, a legacy.

Diesel developed his engine, amassed great wealth, invested poorly, and for reasons unknown "apparently fell" from the deck of the mail steamer *Dresden* en route to London.

Wednesday

"This heeyuh's a micrometer," Nick said. "You take this and you measure how big something is, in thousandths of inches. The real fancy ones go down to ten-thousandths, but we'll just do the thousandths."

A thousandth of an inch seemed incomprehensibly small to me—how could anything be measured that precisely? How could anything matter on that scale?

Nick continued, "You hold the micrometer like this, see, and you put the two pins just apart from each other on the workpiece." The workpiece was a bar of metal mounted in the lathe. "You want to make the two ends of the micrometer just slip off the workpiece and then you read it. That'll tell you how many thousandths you still need to take off. There's a little rust on this bar, and we can take that off by either pouring Coke over it or turning it down."

I wondered whether there were any connection between the machinists' expression for scraping the skin off a piece of metal and being turned down as a person.

"First we gotta put the tool in the tool holder," Nick continued. "This here's the cutting edge," he said, holding the inch-long piece of metal and pointing out the sharp side. "We're going to bolt it into the machine and then bring it just up to the workpiece by turning the cross-feed handwheel here."

The handwheel had gradations in it so that one revolution of the handwheel made the block of metal to which the cutting tool was attached move a tenth of an inch toward the workpiece. The dial on the knob had 100 hash marks around the outside. The hundred hash marks dividing up a tenth of an inch allow you to move the cutting tool a thousandth of an inch. Like the micrometer, the device magnifies space.

Nick advanced the tool to the workpiece and then moved it forward five thousandths. The tool cut a little sliver through the rust, showing the pure, clean steel underneath. "Now, Cap'n, turn this crank nice and slow and you'll take five thousandths off the whole rod. Let's put a little cutting oil on there first, though."

He put a few drops from the oil can that looked like the kind engineers use to lubricate their trains. The oil smoked when the tool made contact, and I turned the crank slowly and the sliver made a continuous thread of steel as I removed the thousandths from the length of the shaft.

"Very good, Cap'n. Now bring the tool back and you can take some more thousandths off for practice." I took ten more thousandths off and the rod was noticeably smaller on the length where I removed the fifteen thousandths.

"That oughta be enough school for today, Cap'n. I brought in this book for you to take a look at," Nick said, handing me the grease-marked manual that he'd used in his first machine shop class—*Practical Machining*.

The cover illustration showed workers in the sixteenth century operating a foot-powered lathe. First the brick, then the pulley, the fire stick, now the lathe—simple ideas have been around for a very long time.

I walked back to my cell and met Mary on her way into the shop. She wore a lab jacket with her name written on it, and above her name was written "Dynatech."

"Hi, Don," she said, referring to my lab jacket.

"Hi, Mary. What brings you to these parts? I thought you were still a teaching assistant."

"I got an R.A. with West, just like you," she said. "I'm working with Paul Kahn on the Caterpillar engine at the other end of the lab." She looked at the book Nick lent me and said, "Taking up a trade?"

"Let's just say it'll be my recession insurance."

"If you want recession insurance you ought to become a plumber. Machinists will be the first to get laid off."

"Yeah, well, the more versatile I can be the better. Do you want to take a look at my cell?"

"Sure," she said.

I opened the doors. She was impressed by the brown paper

on the workbenches and the neatly laid out equipment and tools. "It looks very professional," she said. "What's that crack up at the top of the wall there?" she asked.

"The machine has taken part of the building with it every time they've done a test in the past. The forces released are like those from a small cannon," I answered.

"Whoa. Be careful. I hope nothing blows up while you're in here."

The danger hadn't yet occurred to me. Then I remembered West's story about the physicist and the laser. And Matt Armstrong had told me that formal occupational safety at MIT is fairly lax because graduate students are supposed to be professionals, and professionals take care of themselves.

"I'll be careful. Can we take a look at your cell?"

"Sure," she answered, as we walked to the north end of the lab.

I read the signs on the doors of the other test cells: "Constant Volume Combustion Bomb: Sponsor: Department of Energy"; "Square Piston Clear Engine: Sponsor: Industrial Consortium"; "Clear Cylinder for Study of Piston Ring Motion: Sponsor: General Motors." I asked Mary whether she knew how these projects got funded.

"There're several avenues. Some of these companies have research budgets that they spend on universities. Half the people in the automotive industry's research departments have degrees from here, and they remember their buddies when they give out the grants. Some of the sponsors expect real results, things that will directly apply to engines, but mostly they're after advances in concepts and understanding of the processes. They get that in the papers the professors and students write that are based on the research. Plus, they get well-trained researchers who can hit the ground running developing products for GM, Chrysler, or Ford. Here we are."

She opened the door to her cell, where there was a blue, newly painted engine with about twenty wires connecting it to a computery looking thing in the corner.

"What's that?" I asked.

"It's the lab data acquisition system. The sensors mounted on the engine send their data to the little computer here. Then it downloads the data files to the mainframe computer upstairs for analysis."

Simple enough. "So how's it going so far?" I asked.

"Pretty good," she said quietly. "The only problem is that my partner on the project is a real dork from Georgia Tech. I don't know how he got accepted."

Maybe he talked bicycles with West.

"Well, I hope everything works out all right," I said. "I've got to go back to work. Every minute of progress now means I'll finish that much sooner and be able to get on with my life."

I looked at the chrome-plated shaft on the front of the machine, the shaft Nick and I'd unveiled when we removed the cylinder the day before. It had a crack about one-third of the way around it, right near the shoulder where the nonreturn pawls caught it. The force of the compressions had taken their toll. I unscrewed the chrome section from the rest of the shaft and carried the baseball-bat-size shaft to where Nick was drilling a hole in a piece of metal.

"Problem, Nick. The shaft's got a crack in it. Is there any way we can fix it? I don't want the thing to break off a year from now when I'm almost ready to finish my experiments," I said.

"We could leave it alone—it'll probably stay straight until it breaks—or I can weld a bead around the whole shaft. That'll make it stronger, but it'll probably bend the shaft a little. It's up to you."

"If the shaft bends, can we bend it back?"

"We can try," he said.

"OK. Let's go for the weld."

We went to the welding area and Nick put on his little welding cap and the leathers that made him look like a torturer in the Spanish Inquisition. He handed me a set of leather gloves, a cap, and a fiberglass welding helmet with a treated glass slit through which to look at the weld. The glass treatment allows you to see the weld but not much else.

"OK, Cap'n. You hold it and turn it slowly, and I'll weld it. If you hold the end you'll be fah enough away an none of that metal will hit, so you won't need leathers."

I put on my helmet, as did Nick. The bright flash of the weld contacted the metal at the shoulder and I slowly turned the shaft. It took about two minutes for Nick to weld all the way around it, layering the temporarily molten metal like cake frosting.

"There. That should do it," he said. "Now before you do anything else with it, put it in that bucket of water over there."

I put the welded end in the bucket, and it flashed the water like a hot frying pan in a sink.

"Keep it in there for a while. That guy's hot all right," Nick said.

After the steaming died down we put the shaft in the lathe. Nick set up a dial indicator, a little round gauge with a pin coming out of one side and a needle on the gauge. If you push the pin in, the needle moves around and tells you how far the pin is pushed in. Nick put the pin against the welded end of the shaft just as he'd put the cutting tool against the piece of steel.

"Time to assess the damage, Cap'n," he said, as he turned the shaft around. The needle went way up, to fifteen thousandths on the dial, then back to zero, and then up to fifteen thousandths and back to zero as he turned the shaft around. "Not too bad," he said. "Now for the hammah."

"What are you going to do?" I asked.

"Give it a tap to make it straight again."

He turned the shaft so the high spot was at the dial indicator pin, moved the dial indicator away, and gave the end of the shaft a quick, sharp tap with the plastic-headed mallet. He set up the indicator again and the high spot was down to four and a half thousandths.

"I think we bettah quit while we're ahead, Cap'n," he said. "This guy's straight enough and he'll last another twenty years."

"OK, Nick. Thanks."

That night the temperature outside was below zero and the key wouldn't go into my Kryptonite bicycle lock. The metal in the lock had shrunk—not much, maybe a thousandth of an inch or two, but enough to prevent the big, warm key from fitting.

At the coffee shop I asked for a cup of hot water, a plastic bag, and a rubber band.

I wrapped the plastic bag around the lock, secured it with the rubber band, and slowly poured the hot water over the plastic. Then I quickly removed the plastic, put the key into the lock, unlocked the bike, and rode home to bed.

The MIT motto is "Mens et Manus"—"Mind and Hand."

C H A P T E R
8

The Taskmasters

And Pharoah commanded the taskmasters, saying ye shall no more give the people straw to make brick. . . . Let there more work be laid upon the men, that they may labor therein; and let them not regard vain words. . . .

EXODUS 5:6–9

Schedule:
Spring '82: 2.651 The Internal Combustion Engine (Heywood)
2.999 Independent Study (Greene)
2.996 Thesis

February 15, 1982

The Energy Laboratory conference room is inside the fourth floor on Amherst Street across from the Sloan School. The rheostat-controlled lights were at full brightness while the Sponsors of the Research ate their choice of the best pastries MIT's catering service could muster. Even the coffee was good.

It was sponsor-stroking time. *Philip Hughes*, an Australian, was director of engine research for Caterpillar. *Sharma*, originally from India, had published a path-finding paper on the theory of diesel combustion in the early 1960s and headed up engine research at John Deere. *Albert Lee* was working his way up the ladder at Cummins Engine Company—he was the last person to work on the RCM before me. And one of my office mates for the year was *Jean Questois*, a rising star from the Paris office of Renault. They were engineers in the most literal sense of the word.

No pinstripes here; brown and light blue were the clothing colors of choice.

Team Sloan had more members. The captain was Professor John B. Heywood, director of the Sloan Lab, graduate of University of Cambridge, recipient of honorary degrees. West was one lieutenant; the other was Chet Yeung. Chet was a new assistant professor, whose Ph.D. was from the Aeronautical Engineering department at MIT and whose bachelor's degree was from the one institute in the world that is better than MIT—Cal Tech.

I was a blighter, as Snoopy called the World War I trench footsoldiers as he flew over them in his Sopwith Camel. So was Scott Rogers, my new lab partner. Scott would do the bulk of the computer work, I the bulk of the experimental work. The third blighter was Ben Radovsky, who worked on the square piston engine in the cell next door. Our mission—and we had no choice but to accept it—was to convince the men in light blue and brown that their money was well spent.

Professor Heywood brought the meeting to order promptly at 9:00. "I'd like to thank you all for coming here today. Our students have been working very hard during the past month and a half, and I think you'll be pleased with the progress that they've made to date." His British accent made him sound even smarter than he was. I wanted to be like him, to command the situation.

"We'll start the meeting with a presentation by Pepper White, on the progress on the mechanical aspects of the rapid compression machine experimental programme," he said.

My knees were shaking. After I've been through a few meetings like this, I thought, any job interview should be a piece of cake.

Professor Heywood continued smoothly, "Then Scott Rogers and Chet Yeung will discuss some thoughts on the computer model of diesel combustion we'll be developing. After lunch, we'll hear from Ben Radovsky and then take a tour of the lab. Before Pepper starts, though, I'd like to remind you all that we hope to expand the consortium programme to include more sponsors, and if you know of colleagues at other engine companies or oil companies who might be interested in participating in the programme, we'd be most appreciative of your putting us into contact with them."

I put the stack of transparencies with the cardboard frames like the ones Gyftopoulos used next to the overhead projector and turned the projector on while he finished. I stood next to the screen until my cue came.

Ben dimmed the lights. All the faces around the conference table were lit up by the light of the screen; only the faces showed against the darkened background of the room, as in a theater. The eyes were focused, intelligent, good, and decent, since there is no room for lies in engineering. In science you can lie and fudge the data because you don't have to make anything work. In engineering the product is the proof of your honesty.

First slide. "I'd like to talk about our general objectives, our specific short-term objectives, some of the things we've accomplished in the past several weeks, and the schedule for the coming months."

My knees started to shake less as the audience smiled and listened attentively. I was using the right lingo.

"First the general objective: We'd like to get the machine up and running and determine the range over which we can conduct our experiments. That means we need to determine the maximum pressure and temperature we can obtain from the machine, and also how high a swirl rate we can obtain, with and without combustion."

Next slide—diagram of machine. "As you can see, the machine has three chambers. The front is, of course, the combustion chamber; behind it is the driving air chamber, connected to a compressed air storage tank; farther back on the shaft is the snubbing chamber, filled with transmission fluid and rings of varying inner diameters. The piston in the snubbing chamber slows the shaft motion down during the compression stroke. By varying the order of the rings, we can make the motion of the shaft and piston simulate that of an actual diesel. The nonreturn pawls will lock the shaft in place when it has moved fully forward. We thus have the ability to look at combustion occurring at constant volume." The bright faces were still smiling. I'd learned a lot of words in the past six weeks.

I went on to tell them about taking the machine apart and putting it back together, about fixing the shaft with Nick, about measuring and drawing a new piston with new bronze-Teflon one-piece piston rings, about having it machined and feeling it fit into the shaft. About the first unsuccessful test of the whole machine.

At the end there was a warm round of applause, and on the way to the coffee and Danish table, West said, "First class." Maybe I'm not such a dummy after all, I thought. Maybe I just didn't know the system during the first term, the system that encourages dropping any course in which you're below average.

Before the lunch break, Sharma asked for monthly progress reports from us. Oh no, more work, I thought. Evidently so did Professor Heywood.

"They're bright young people, but there are many demands on their time and it might impede their progress on the research," he said.

"Do you mean to tell us that the people you're producing for us won't be able to write a brief paragraph once a month saying what they've accomplished and where they're headed?" Sharma retorted.

Professor Heywood hedged without flinching. He was still in control, the quintessential grantsman. "Perhaps the reports could be prepared every two months," he said. He knew that he would have to review them, that his secretary would have to type them, that he might have to meet with the whole group just to discuss that one subject. It could easily kill a morning that would be better spent writing his book.

"Every two months would be fine with me," Sharma said, and the others agreed.

February 17

Professor Allen Greene's office was in Building 7, on the second floor overlooking Mass. Ave. and the student center across the street. Following up on our conversation after his Energy Engineering lecture in early October, he'd agreed to take me on as an independent study student in January. I remembered the incident in *The Paper Chase* when Hart was honored to be asked by Kingfield to help him prepare a scholarly article; I thought this might be close to equivalent.

Greene ran the Institute for Applied Systems Engineering (IASE), a midcareer retraining ground for the engineering profession founded to do what Harvard Business School and the Kennedy School of Government do for their respective trades.

IASE is one of the mechanisms by which MIT maintains its close links to industry. Mid- to upper-level engineers or research and development managers come to MIT, take a few classes, maybe do a small project, meet a lot of professors, and later hire the professors they meet as consultants to figure out how to solve their problems.

Like me, Greene was an outsider. The IASE was his fiefdom, apart from the mainstream departments, apart from the traditional tenure track. His Ph.D. was from the University of Illinois, and his positions at Union Carbide, the World Bank (director of technology development), and Ohio State (dean of engineering) did not quite measure up to the MIT professor goal—getting tenure and starting a multimillion-dollar company. He was good enough for me, though.

When I entered the antechamber of his office, his secretary was typing little blue index cards with his appointments and things-to-do on it. To hyperachieve you have to be hyperorganized.

His phone was busy when she first tried to buzz him, but after a few minutes of her telling me how hypnosis was helping her quit smoking, he buzzed her to send me in.

At four in the afternoon his office was bright with the western sun, bright enough that he'd turned off the fluorescents above his desk. His office was corporate-looking, like Gyftopoulos's, only bigger, with two couches in an L around a coffee table in addition to the desk, chairs, bookcases, and blackboard.

He shook my hand and said, "Sorry to keep you waiting; that was the president of Ford on the phone and I don't like to cut him off. Here, have a seat." He sat on one couch, I on the other. "How are things going for you here?"

I didn't tell him about being on probation. "Oh, pretty good, I guess. I'm doing experimental work in diesel combustion at the Sloan auto lab. Professor Heywood heads that up, and I'm also taking his engine class this spring, plus the independent study with you."

"John Heywood is very good," he said. "And your experimental work will help you understand what's possible and realistic, even if it's a little on the researchy side. We can try to balance that with some real-world design problems. I'd like you to work up a computer example for my book as your major project, but first we'll take a few weeks to go over some problem-solving techniques I've developed over the years."

He talked to me with respect, as a near-peer or at least a future peer. It was refreshing. I wondered whether he was a nice guy or if I was improving. He opened up the manila folder on the coffee table and said, "Let's go up to the blackboard and . . ."

Oh, no. Not this again.

". . . I'll work an example to show you how to solve steam cycle problems." He drew a grid on the blackboard and a diagram of a steam power plant—a boiler where the water is heated by the flame or by the nuclear reactor; a turbine that is forced to spin by the high-pressure steam generated by the boiler; a condenser to turn the low-pressure steam back to water; and a pump to push the water into the boiler. This is how the world economy is powered—anything that uses electricity is effectively a little fire. He put little hash marks at various points in the diagram and numbered them.

"What you want to do is start at one point in the cycle and work your way around. For each point in the cycle, you put a line in the table. Each column in the table is a variable, like pressure, temperature, energy, entropy. In any design problem you'll be given certain constraints and your job will be to devise a workable solution that satisfies the constraints," he said.

The two of us filled in the table of known quantities for the cycle, leaving blanks for the unknowns. The approach was orderly, methodical, simple.

The session was a tutorial in the Oxbridge sense: at Oxford and Cambridge there are no classes; instead students meet regularly with tutors. I wished MIT encouraged more of this, but it's very time-consuming for the professor, and if he spends his time teaching and explaining things, there won't be time for the real work of bringing in research funds, consulting, publishing and delivering papers, making a name for oneself. Besides, if you can't figure out everything by yourself, you probably don't belong at MIT. And they wonder why students kill themselves.

Greene said, "It'd be a good exercise for you to finish this between now and our next session. First do it by hand and then we'll see about putting it on the computer. I've also got another problem for you, the balloon-filling problem. I want you to figure out how the volume for a balloon will vary as a function of time if you fill it with a large constant-pressure tank of air. And as a third item, try to come up with some examples or analogies for energy that isn't useful because of high entropy. You can make an appointment with my secretary for ten days to two weeks from now for our next session."

I picked two weeks. I might need every day.

February 19

The steam cycle was easy. The balloon was a different story. It was a combination of thermodynamics and fluid mechanics, with that most dreaded of all things, a "deformable control volume." Usually volumes are fixed, and at steady state—i.e., things don't vary with time. A 3-inch-diameter pipe will typically stay 3 inches in diameter, and you can draw an imaginary box around it and account for mass, energy (whatever that is), and entropy (*really* whatever that is) by invoking the appropriate conservation equations. Or as they say at Harvard, all the gazintas gots to gazatta. Everything that goes in has to come out.

Not so in the case of a balloon filling with air from a large tank at constant pressure. There the volume is always changing, until the pressure in the balloon is equal to the pressure in the tank, or until the balloon pops. This is the advanced course. I began my attempt at a solution.

Step 1. Define problem: Draw picture. Think about what the problem involves physically. He just stated it verbally but I need to say it with symbols.

Assume a pressure, say 3 pounds per square inch above atmospheric pressure. Look for key words in his problem statement. *Large* referring to the tank means that it's not affected by what happens to the balloon—i.e., the imaginary tank keeps pumping air out at a constant rate and never empties. Now think about what will happen. The balloon will fill up until the pressure inside it equals the pressure in the large tank. Those are initial and final states. The balloon is going to stretch, and energy will be stored in the balloon both in the air pressure and in the tension of the rubber.

Step 2. Go to Barker Engineering Library and look through every book on thermodynamics to see whether the example has been worked out in print before. Notice that tables of contents are almost identical for all the thermo books. Fail to find worked-out solution of balloon-filling problem. Quit working on the problem for the time being.

One week later

7:00 A.M. Shave. Brush teeth. Rinse. Spit. Step 3. Flash of inspiration. Redraw picture on paper towel . . .

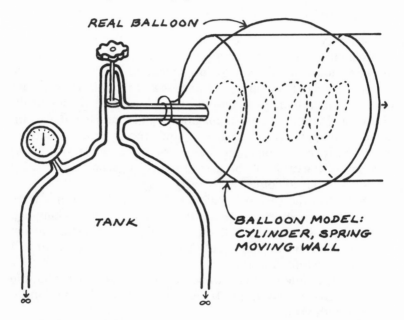

The old picture is intractably complex because the geometry of the balloon's expanding is three-dimensional and I'm not a mathematician, I'm an engineer. If I convert to the new picture, I can clearly see the stretchiness of the balloon lumped into a spring that can expand and contract, and I can see the expanded volume aspect as a movable balloon skin wall with very little mass, moving in only one direction. If the equations for the simplified approach are similar to the equations for the real balloon, I can predict the behavior of the real balloon with my simplified, one-dimensional equations. *This* is what they mean by a model.

Step 4. Redraw new picture, showing the motion of the balloon skin.

As air enters the balloon from the tank, the balloon skin moves (A_2) and the spring stretches. Now to remember the problem. Find

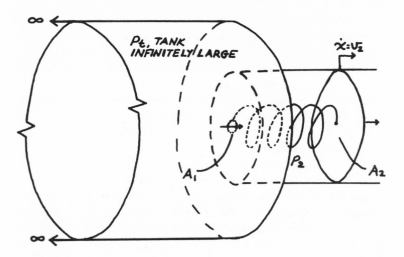

how the balloon volume varies with time. The volume of the imaginary, one-dimensional cylindrical balloon is just its length times the constant area of its circular movable skin. The problem reduces to finding how the balloon length varies with time. I'm making progress.

February 27

Professor Heywood's Internal Combustion Engine class was on the third floor of Building 38, in another interior room with dimmers.

Heywood favored the handouts and slides approach to lecturing. He distributed copies of what would be on the screen and pointed to the diagram and made notes on the transparencies with different colored pens. This was efficient both for him and for us. We would not waste time trying to redraw what would be easier for him to photocopy, and Professor Heywood would not get chalk dust on his beige corduroy jacket.

Heywood was trim and looked younger than his forty-five years. Maybe the bicycle ride to and from his house in Newton every day helped. He was one of the many mechanical engineering professors who cycled to work even though funded by oil and car companies—he valued efficiency.

He'd received tenure young, and although smarter than most

of the faculty, he hadn't started a company. He preferred to write his book, to consult when asked to, to be a distinguished scholar. One day I saw him eating his lunch and looking out onto the trees of Killian Court, perhaps thinking about how MIT wasn't quite as pleasant an environment as Cambridge or London's Imperial College, but the pay and the taxes were better here, and America's auto industry wasn't dead yet. Perhaps one day the Sloan Lab would be the Heywood Laboratory, and *labbratory* would be pronounced the British way.

The day's lecture concerned volumetric efficiency, or how much air you can push into a can. If the bottom of the can moves up and down, you have something like the heart of an internal combustion engine, a.k.a. the cylinder. If you can figure out how to push more air into the can, you can put more fuel in and then use the more air to burn the more fuel. It's sort of like blowing up a balloon.

Toward the end of the lecture, Professor Heywood mentioned that the volumetric efficiency of an engine decreases markedly as elevation above sea level increases and air becomes thinner.

The fellow sitting next to me in the front row just right of center raised his hand and was recognized by Professor Heywood. "Yes, Ari."

"You are absolutely right, Professor. Thees phenomenon was a great problem for my tank batallion on the Golan Heights. Fortunately, it was also a problem for the Russian-made Syrian tanks."

"Thank you for mentioning that," Professor Heywood said. "That's a good example of how important an issue volumetric efficiency is."

Professor Heywood finished his lecture and I introduced myself to Ari. He looked as if he was in his late thirties or early forties and his hair, parted on the side, was graying and thinning a lot. He wore glasses, a plaid shirt, and jeans and had a bit of a paunch.

"How do you do, Meestair Pepper White," he said. "Would you like to join me for a cup of coffee at the student center?"

"Sure," I said. As we walked and talked he told me a bit about his background. Presently a major in the Israeli army, he'd been born to Romanian Holocaust survivors just after World War II and then raised in Israel from the birth of the nation. He had graduated from the Technion in Haifa with degrees in both mechanical engineering and industrial management and was on the second of three years of leave from the army to get a Ph.D. at MIT. A general had done precisely that, and the degree to end all degrees had helped that general advance from major and colonel. Ari hoped the same would happen for him.

After coffee, Ari said, "Come, my friend. I want to show you something in the room next door here." We entered the video game room, in general occupied by the geekiest of the geeks, the ugliest acne-ridden prototypes of what people expect of MIT nerds. Instead of thinking about how to have a life, how to maybe go out on a date, they while away their leisure minutes looking at a cathode ray tube and make rapid gestures with the buttons below the screen. If I ever felt ugly or fat or like I had a bad complexion, I'd go to the video game room and come out feeling ready for a modeling career.

(Some of the video geeks had a major advantage on the games; they knew where the hacks were. A hack is a trick encoded by the programmer who designs the machine so that he can play the game forever at whatever bar he happens to be in. Since half the people who program the video games are from MIT, and many of the programmers from MIT worked for video game developers during high school or during their summer jobs, there is a fair amount of insider video hack trading. It's a constant source of annoyance to the people who control the video game industry.

It's only fair that there should be some mastery of these machines by MIT students. The first video game, PONG, the little black and white bars that I moved back and forth with a joystick when I was a freshman at Hopkins, was invented as a semester project by two students in course six one eleven, MIT's Digital Electronics lab.)

Ari put a quarter on the ledge below the Tank Commander screen to establish our place in line. When our time came, he said, "You go first. I will pay."

"Thanks. Could you give me a little briefing on how to work this thing?"

"Certainly. You need to put one hand on each joystick. If you want to go forward, you push both joysticks forward, and you pull both back if you want to go backward. Each joystick controls one of the treads of the tank, just like in a real tank. If you want to turn right, push the right one forward and pull the left one back, and you do it the other way to go left. When you've lined up on the target, press both buttons on top of the joysticks."

He put the quarter in and I gave it a shot. It was fun to see

the barrel of the tank move up and down with the simulated noise
of the tank corresponding to whichever way I was turning to avoid
the enemy fire and shoot on the pillboxes. Ari's coaching helped—
"Right . . . back . . . forward . . . left . . . now fire!"—and in my
thirty seconds I knocked out three of the pillboxes. I could get
good at this after a few hundred quarters.

Then it was Ari's turn. He stood farther from the machine
than I did and bent over so his torso was almost horizontal. "I get
a better feeling for the machine this way," he said.

Boom, pow, left-right-forward-back—Ari was a master. He
jerked the joysticks quickly, decisively, grunting as if all his nervous
energy were channeled into reflexes and fast response. Three minutes and 97 pillboxes later one finally got him.

"You must play this a lot," I said.

"Not this one, actually," he answered. "I developed my abil-
ities with the real thing during the Six Day War and the October
War. And this one is much easier because I am not afraid for my
life when I play it. I find it very relaxing."

February 28

Back to the balloon. Step 5. Refer to picture from Step 4. Think
about problem again. Remember fluid mechanics study session
with Mary et al. and Bernoulli looking over the bridge on the Arno
at the two rocks. If the pressure in the tank is not a whole lot
higher than atmospheric pressure, and the air is therefore not
compressible, I can call it incompressible flow and use Bernoulli's
equation. That will tell me how fast the air will flow from the tank
into the balloon, depending on how much pressure there is in the
tank compared to how much is in the balloon.

I can also say that everything that goes into the balloon results
in enlargement of the balloon. That's another equation, called the
continuity of mass equation.

And finally, I can balance the forces on the skin of the balloon—the stretchiness of the balloon has to be balanced by the air
pressure inside and outside the balloon. That gives me three equations and five unknowns.

Now all I have to do is show how x varies with time, so I can
graph the position of the balloon and Greene will think I'm a hero.

Step 6. Dust off differential equations book from sophomore
year at Hopkins. A differential equation deals with things that move

in time, like the piston of an engine, the earth, and the moon—or the skin of a balloon being blown up.

Everything in the differential equations book deals with "linear" differential equations. That means that the second term, the x-dot-squared term, means I can't solve this using any methods in that book. I'm multiplying the velocity by the velocity, and that makes it "nonlinear."

Step 7: Punt. This is what you do at MIT when the institute or the problem set has painted you into a corner.

March 2

Greene looked quickly through my steam system solution, checking off the steps with his Cross pen. Then he asked me to go to the blackboard to present my solution to the balloon problem.

"Now *that* is a good idea," he said of my making the balloon expand in only one direction. "You know, in my years as a manager, I've found that there are people who are creative and can invent things and then there are people who can analyze things that the creative people have invented. Not many people can do both, but this solution shows me you might be one of them."

Kvel city. This guy's bound to give me an A. They won't be able to kick me out, after all.

I went through the steps for him and showed him my insoluble set of equations. "This is my answer," I said. "Unfortunately, I don't know how to solve it, to be able to graph the position of the skin of the balloon as a function of time. I thought you might have some suggestions."

"Well, if you brought that problem to me at Union Carbide, I'd get the head of the applied mathematics department in here and one of his people would solve it on the computer," he said. "But you want to know at least enough to talk knowledgeably with the applied math types and prevent them from billing too many hours to the project. Let's go down the hall to the Apple and I'll show you how to boot it up."

The computer room was a corner office the size of a large closet, with windows on both walls and a desk and the Apple. The windows looked out onto a seven-story courtyard; since the room was on the second floor it never received direct sunlight, but the soft diffuse light and the tree just outside the window made me feel I was in a cloister's cloister.

Greene put a diskette into the machine and turned on the on switch. I presumed that's what he meant by "booting it up."

"I'll just write a three-line program that will add two numbers for you to show you how to get started," he said.

His fingers blurred around the keyboard, like a concert pianist's. Unlike speech or writing by hand, which have natural speed limits on how fast information can be transfered, the computer could receive information almost as quickly as he thought. He must have done well in touch typing class in high school.

When he was done, the screen said "Input A," and I typed 3. "Input B," it said, and I typed 5. "A + B = 8," it said.

"You've programmed before, haven't you?" he said.

"Well, just a little in college, but that was always on a teletype terminal with the yellow paper that was connected to a big computer in an air-conditioned room down the hall. This looks a little different."

"It's the same in principle," he said. "There's a programming manual in the drawer here, so you can refer to that if you need help. What I want you to do for our next meeting is to set up the equations you showed me in such a way that you can step through little increments of time and see what happens to the skin of the balloon as the spring in your model stretches and the pressure in your balloon rises. Try to organize the equations so the information will flow from one equation to the next, so that at each step in the program, the computer has all the data it needs to go on to the next step. Oh, and read up on 'subroutines' in the programming guide. You can use them to break up a big, complex problem into several smaller, simple problems. It'll make debugging much easier. For now, let's go back to my office and go over the examples of entropy you've come up with."

Landfills, overeating, smoking, drug addiction—all the ills of modern life had come to mind during the past two weeks, but I knew he'd want something more specific.

"Well, the other day I was at the crosswalk at Mass. Ave. and I saw somebody trying to parallel park in a space that was about 6 inches too short for the car. For the length of the block there were 2 or 3 feet between the other cars, sometimes as much as 4 feet. So if you added up the little pieces of space you'd probably be able to fit three or four more cars into the block comfortably. But the little pieces of space by themselves were useless. That's the best I could come up with."

"That's a good one," he said. "You could make the analogy that space is the equivalent of energy, and the shortness of the space is the equivalent of entropy. The longer the space is, the more ordered a system it represents and the more useful it is. That's good. I like that. I think you're making progress."

C H A P T E R

9

Spring

March 15

The Ides of March. The first day above freezing, and time to blast the mental cobwebs out. Time to go on a bicycle ride. My escape route was out Trapelo Road through Belmont.

The pressure was still constant, but with only two exams scheduled for the term, there was more relaxing time. Up the first major hill, Belmont Hill, I remembered my old cycling coach's telling me to sit back in the saddle and pull on the upstroke. He said that would allow the muscles in the front of my legs to relax and let the used blood flow out and the new blood flow in. If I always pushed on the front of my legs the tension would build up and my legs would feel tired and I'd be dropped from the pack.

It was sort of like Heywood's description of an internal combustion engine. Fuel goes into the cylinder, gets burned, then pushed out and exhausted. If you kept the exhaust in the cylinder, there wouldn't be room for the fresh, unburned fuel and air, and your car would stall.

At the Route 128 overpass, I looked both ways up and down the eight-lane highway. On both sides were continuous lines of two-story buildings. The sign on the side said, "Route 128: America's Technology Highway." I rode on, past Honeywell's Electro-Optic Division, past Raytheon's Bedford Missile Systems Division, past Digital, past E.G.& G.

All these places were either founded by or heavily populated by MIT grads. The Harveys have most of their power in New York, but the most powerful Techies live and work within twenty miles of Building 7. I wondered what it would be like to work in a low-rise building with cubicles and very few windows.

On through Concord Center and past Ken Olsen's house. Ken Olsen graduated from MIT in '50, went on to work with Professor Jay Forrester on computer memory technology in Project Whirl-wind, and from there spun off a company—Digital Equipment Corporation. Ken is worth a billion or two and still lives in a modest home.

Farther on, I saw the fruit of Gyftopoulos's industry. Well, not the whole fruit, because you can't see the whole house from the street because the driveway's so long. Next door was the house of the other Thermo Electron founder, George Hatsopoulos. George showed that you don't have to be a professor at MIT to make a million bucks. In his case, a Ph.D. in mechanical engineering and a good idea for how to measure the concentration of nitrogen oxide in automobile exhaust were sufficient.

Back toward town Thermo Electron was less than a five-minute drive from their houses. Maybe, if I worked hard, I could emulate all of them.

The ride felt good, and after my shower, it was Apple time. Greene had given me a key to the computer room and a floppy disk.

It was two o'clock, and sunny, and if I'd had my druthers I would have happily continued cycling on to Concord or Carlisle or Acton or Harvard, but that's not why I was in Cambridge.

The cloister, facing inward, shielded from the street, with the tree just outside the window and the diffuse sunlight brightening the upper part of the pink limestone walls, was a peaceful sanc-tuary. Here it was just my thoughts, and the wit of the manual written by two guys who hadn't gone to college, Wozniak and Jobs.

Okay Apple. I'm a user. Be friendly.

Apple taught by example. The language was BASIC, the lan-guage in which most people learn to program. In BASIC, it's fairly easy to follow the logic of the sample programs. I typed in the sample programs, and they worked. This began to establish a cause-and-effect relationship for me; if you type in the right thing and don't misplace parentheses and don't misspell anything and do it absolutely, perfectly, uniformly right, it works.

By six o'clock I'd finished the manual. It was sort of like listening to a Paul Desmond record and trying to pick out the improvisational riffs and play them by ear on my clarinet. I'd pick it up a phrase at a time, and once I knew what Paul Desmond was doing, what chords he was working from, what scales he was embellishing, I could experiment on my own, maybe change the order a little bit, try different permutations of the notes. Before I knew it I was a programmer. You imitate the patterns, and by accident you discover new combinations and develop your own style. The time disappeared and I became lost in it and it became almost fun, not work.

After sunset the office light made the window a mirror, and I saw myself beside the computer and imagined the *Newsweek* picture of "MIT's White," the brilliant young engineering professor whose research is solving the world's energy and environmental problems. I'd wear a V-necked pullover, lean back in the desk chair, and have my hands clasped behind my head and elbows out. The bookcases in the background would be full.

Back to the balloon. Time to refer to the equations and the drawing. Greene had said I need to think of the flow of information in any algorithm (solution method) I write. That means I need to take my three equations and arrange them in an order so that the result of one calculation will feed into the unknown side of the next calculation, that answer will feed into the unknown side of the next calculation, and so on. This is how I will march through time and blow up my balloon.

Mr. Apple's logo is an apple with a rainbow on it and a bite out of it. The apple is the fruit from the tree of knowledge. The rainbow is the promise that one flood was enough. A bite sounds like a byte is 8 bits. What does it all mean?

March 21

The office is home base for graduate students. Mine was upstairs from the lab, near those of Chet Yeung and West. There were five offices at the end of the hall. Ari's was on one side of mine. One of Ari's office mates was a Russian who'd left the Soviet Union in '58 with his family. Scott Rogers was on the other side of me. Ben Radovsky was across the hall.

Steve Geiger shared the office with Ben and Mary. Mary had set up a fish tank, and they also had a coffeepot and a big drafting table in the center of the room. Often those of us from neighboring offices would walk in, make a cup of tea or coffee, pull a chair up to the drafting table, and talk camshafts. Mr. and Mrs. Tung from Beijing were next door. They often boiled seaweedlike materials that gave off strange smells in their adapted electric coffeepot.

The office becomes the core of your sense of community. Every department is divided into subspecialties. Anyone you meet in a class may be in a different group, so you have no reason to see him or her outside or after the class. There may be an occasional chance encounter on the infinite corridor or in the student center coffee shop, but other than that, you lose contact. It's part of why the institute is such a lonely place—the knowledge and the students are segmented.

I chatted with Mary while drinking tea at the drafting table, and West interrupted.

"Mary, we need to talk about the fuel system. Paul's not pulling his weight in the experiment and—"

The phone rang.

West picked it up, answered, "Mary's in a meeting now. Call back later," and hung up.

Mary's face turned red with rage. She stood up and said to West, "Don't you ever do that again. I don't care who you are or what kind of power you have. You have no right to intercept a call like that."

"Well, I think I do," West said. "What do you think, Pepper?"

It was a scummy thing to do. You have power, and, because I'm on probation I need all the powerful friends I can get. "No comment," I answered.

West continued. "Well anyway, Mary, I want you to cover for Paul. We've got to keep the project moving."

After West was out of earshot Mary said, "Why didn't you stick up for me? I thought you were my friend."

"You did pretty well for yourself. I didn't want to get involved. Besides, he's keeping me out of debt," I said.

"Well, I guess we know where your priorities are. Thanks. Thanks a lot."

"Hey, look. I'm sorry. I'll try to make it up to you someday."

March 25

La chasse aux fuites. The search for leaks. I'd fired the RCM at a compression ratio higher than ever before attempted. That was the good news. The bad news was that the pressure at the top of the stroke was about half as high as needed. That meant there were leaks.

Machinery leaks when two pieces of metal are next to each other and the pressure inside the machine pushes out whatever liquid or gas you're trying to compress. I asked Chet Yeung, the new assistant professor, who was gradually becoming my adviser as West was preparing for the start-up of his company on Route 128, for help.

Chet knew everything. Born in Hong Kong, at age five he had built Heathkit radios. One summer during high school he worked as a machinist; another summer he worked as a draftsman in a machine tool plant. Yet another summer he worked as a computer programmer. This was all before he graduated from Cal Tech with an applied mathematics degree. Chet wanted to be a mathematician, wasn't quite good enough to be a great one, but was well on his way to becoming a great engineering professor.

"So you have to put some O-rings in," he said. "And you have to look at every surface to see where the leakage paths might be and put them there." Chet pulled one of the ten notebooks off the bookshelf behind him and turned to a page in it that described O-ring design. An O-ring is a skinny rubber donut that fits in a groove and prevents the air or water from leaking.

Chet made a quick sketch of the groove dimensions, made a list of the O-ring sizes, then sent me down to Nick to have him machine the grooves.

Nick was milling a part, and "Begin the Beguine" was playing on the radio.

"You hear the news, Cap'n?" Nick asked. "A plane just took off from Miami and had to turn around. The mechanic who rebuilt the engine forgot to put some O-rings in and the bearing oil almost all leaked out. Imagine that. 'S lucky no one got killed."

O-rings are important.

March 29

All O-rings in place, it was time for another firing. The shaft was in its backmost position, held in place by a little piece of metal in a slot in the back of the shaft. There was a pendulum, basically a pipe with a hinge on one end, at the back of the shaft. The idea was to raise the pressure in the tank and then let the pendulum swing into the back of the shaft. The little piece of metal was strong enough to avoid breaking with the pull of the shaft from the air pressure, but not strong enough to hold when the pendulum hit it. The pendulum was the pipe that broke the shaft's back.

Chet, Scott, Nick, and I were in the test cell when we tried the first firing with the new O-rings in place. The shaft was set up and I opened the valve to let the driving pressure on the tank build up.

The air made a hissing, ringing sound as it filled the tank and the gauge climbed up through 10, 20, 30 pounds per square inch (psi). The first thunk noise came at 52 psi. I closed the valve. My pulse was up to 90.

"What was that?" I asked.

Nick answered from the back where he was holding the pendulum. "I remember that one, Cap'n; that's the first one. Nothing to be afraid of. The metal's just adjusting itself."

"Keep raising the pressure," Chet said from across the cell where he was adjusting the brightness of the oscilloscope. The oscilloscope was just like the ones I'd seen before in Weare's lab, basically a TV set with only one channel, or trace. Its beam of electrons went from left to right on the screen. As the pressure rose in the RCM's cylinder, the electron beam would be deflected upward and make a glowing graph of measured cylinder pressure versus time. The oscilloscope was our eye on the world of the very fast, the things that happen in small fractions of a second.

At 90 psi there was another thunk and the tank started to creak.

"That's as high as it was ever run, Cap'n. Any more pressure is unexplored territory," Nick said as he crossed himself with his free hand.

"Let's raise it to 110," Chet said. "There's still plenty of safety factor at that level. We'll need at least that much pressure to push through the pressure the cylinder will develop with the higher compression ratio."

The loudest thunk yet came at 105 but nothing blew up, so I kept going to 110 psi. My pulse still rose with the pressure. I closed the valve.

"Ready, Nick?"

"And waiting, Cap'n."

Nick let go of the pendulum.

It was over in an instant like a gunshot. The trace on the oscilloscope bobbed up and down.

"Looks like good news and bad news," Chet said.

"What do you mean?" I asked him.

"I think there are no more leaks, but we need more pressure. The piston went forward, bounced back, went forward, bounced back, and as the compressed gas cooled, the piston finally made it all the way forward."

All in half a second.

Chet added, "We're going to need a stronger tank, maybe a new starting mechanism, maybe a new shaft. Let's take a look at the shaft. Nick, do you have your micrometer handy?"

"Yes, sir, Professor," Nick said.

After we pulled the shaft back into prefiring position, Chet tightened the micrometer on the pendulum end of the shaft and then moved it down the shaft to the back of the machine.

"That's what I was afraid of," he said as the micrometer became looser and looser along the length of the shaft. "We'll need a new shaft, too. This one has been stretching with the higher force, so it becomes longer and skinnier. Before it was like it was supporting a Toyota; now it's supporting a Cadillac."

New tank, new shaft, new starting mechanism. How many months will that add to my term in the cell?

April 20

Spring was fully with us, consistently warm at last. The daffodils were out, the sky was blue with some big breezy clouds, and the sailboats were on the Charles again. I felt newborn when I met Mary in front of the Green Building.

"Did you hear about Gyftopoulos?" she asked.

"No. What about him?" I said.

"He had a heart attack."

So he's a human being after all. I wondered whether he'd had a near-death experience, whether he'd floated up above his body for a few moments in the valley of the shadow of death and said it's not time yet—there are too many more students to teach—or whether he'd just blacked out and there was nothing but the pain in his chest.

"Is he OK?" I asked.

"Yes. I heard he just got out of intensive care. He'll be in the hospital for a couple of weeks, but they think it's a mild one. He'll probably have to take off some weight and quit smoking," she answered.

"I sure hope he pulls through. He's a good man. By the way, what ever happened to your dorky lab partner? I haven't seen him around the lab for a while."

"He was booted out. They just sat him down and said to him that he couldn't do research and now he's gone. I think he's doing some kind of computer consulting or something," she said.

These guys play for keeps. If you can't produce, you're history.

April 22

I bumped into Jim Stuart going down the infinite corridor. The Ivy League knowing look had faded, had been beaten out of his eyes by all the 50 percents he'd scored on problem sets and exams. His calculator was on his belt.

"What's the deal with the calculator, Jim?" I asked.

"What about it?"

"It's on your belt. Don't you remember? I bet you would have thrown spitballs at anyone in your high school who did that," I said.

"Oh," he paused. "Yeah. Well, it's actually a really convenient way to carry it. The case protects the calculator, and it frees up my arms to carry books and other things without worrying about dropping it."

Function is greater than form.

May 12

"You made a good start, and I would have expected more progress by now," Greene said.

"I need some more time, sir. Things should ease up in the lab during the summer, so I should be able to finish off the balloon problem. Besides, this whole business of computer modeling is kind of new to me. I'm just totally stumped on how to make the equations flow."

He said, "It's important that you figure this out for yourself. I could teach you, but there's a big difference between learning and being taught. You know, it's sort of like trying to learn the language in a foreign country. Say you go out to the market and you want to buy something that's not on display—apples, for example. If you know 100 words in the language, you'll use all of them trying to communicate that 101st word that you need. In the process you may learn a few more words from the shopkeeper. When you finally hit on that 101st word, and you're taking a bite out of the apple, you've internalized the knowledge, and you'll never forget it. Capisce?"

"So what do I have to do to get a B?" I asked.

He answered, "If you can make your balloon model work as you've now set it up and produce meaningful results with realistic pressures and elasticities, I'll give you a B. I'll give you till the end of the summer to do that. If there's any time left after that, you can make the model a little more realistic and I'll give you an A. This isn't related much to energy engineering but it's a good problem and that's why we call it independent study. By the way, have you come up with any more examples of entropy?"

"Uh, yeah. I've thought of a couple more," I said. "I used to race bicycles, and the key to doing well in races was always to be in a 15-man breakaway from the 100-man field. Once the breakaway is a minute or two ahead of the pack it'll never be caught. The guys in the break work together smoothly, and you only have to fight the wind one-fifteenth as much as you would if you sprinted off the front of the pack by yourself. The pack generally can't organize itself to bridge the gap, so the breakaway's lead just gets bigger and bigger."

"Umhmmm," he answered. "So the flow of information as to how to share the wind load more efficiently is more efficient in the breakaway than in the pack. Better information flow means better organization and lower entropy. I like it. What's the other example?"

"I read in the *Globe* that Boston is windier than Kansas, but Boston isn't as good a place for windmills because the wind direction is always changing. So a windmill in Boston would spend a lot of time turning to face the wind, and by the time it faces the wind, the wind direction may have changed again," I said, and drew a picture on his blackboard.

"So in the limiting case," Greene added, "the windmill will turn back and forth and never face the wind long enough to produce any power. The windmill turns, but that turning results in no power delivered to the propellor. You're beginning to internalize entropy."

May 15.

Heywood's exam was in Room 1-134. I made a point of arriving early, finding the janitor to open the locked door, arranging my books and notebooks, finding a wall outlet, plugging my borrowed calculator into the wall outlet, sharpening my twelve number two pencils, flossing my teeth. Everything was in order at 1:15, fifteen minutes before the exam would start.

My scores on the four problem sets and the term project were above average. I was definitely in B territory, unless, of course, I choked on the final. A well-below-average score would put me into C-land and onto the street.

I went outside to sit on the Henry Moore sculpture in Killian Court. I tried to clear my thoughts, to be receptive to the inspiration I'd need to pass. The fresh-cut lawn smelled sweet when I closed my eyes.

At five minutes to launch I went back to the classroom. Ben Radovsky and two other guys were standing next to my desk and laughing. A little closer, I saw my calculator broken on the floor, and the twelve number two pencils at rest randomly underneath the neighboring desks.

"What happened?" I asked, panic-stricken.

Ben said, "I didn't see your calculator cord and I tripped over it."

There was no tone of apology in his voice. Obviously, my calculator setup was a faulty design and had presented a hazard to the public. Never mind there was less than a foot between my desk and the wall outlet; never mind that any thinking human being would have walked around the other way.

"Yeah, and what's so funny about that?" I asked him.

"Well, you've got to admit it's kind of funny that you set things up so carefully and tried to plan it all in advance and then this happens. It's the kind of thing that would happen to Woody Allen," Ben smirked.

"Well, I'm screwed without a calculator," I said. "Do you have an extra one?"

"No, I only brought one, and I need it."

Ari tapped me on the shoulder.

"Here, my friend," he said. "I brought two extras. Don't worry; it's fully charged."

"Oh great, thanks a lot. You've saved my life," I answered, wanting to give him a hug. "But why'd you bring three?"

He answered, "It's just one of the principles of good engineering—redundant systems."

CHAPTER
10

In Control

Schedule:
Summer '82: 2.023 System Dynamics and Control (Miller)
2.999 Independent Study (Greene)
2.996 Thesis

In early June Gyftopoulos walked out of the Walker dining hall. He looked a good twenty pounds thinner, and he walked slowly, more tentatively than before the heart attack. He'd wakened up to the fact that he wasn't going to be at MIT forever; you could see it in his eyes. For the first time I felt I had something he didn't— fifty or sixty years ahead of me. When he said hello, his voice was a little tentative, like his walk.

"Yes, I'm recuperating fine, Pepper. Thank you for asking. I'm starting by coming in to work two days a week, and gradually I will work back up to five."

"It's good to see you back, sir."

"It's good to be back."

I squeaked out the B in Heywood's class. It wasn't that my performance on the final was stellar, but that over half the class's performance was at least as murky as mine. So murky that Professor Heywood, in the critique he handed back with the exams,

wrote, "While some of you showed complete mastery of the concepts presented, many of you did not show the organization and
clarity I would have expected. Each of you might ask yourself,
'Would I want to send this exam to my parents to show them the
great work I'm doing at MIT?' "

He knew how to put the needle where we would feel it. But
a B is a B and I'm here for another three months minimum.

The institute is laid back in the summertime. Because the
undergrads are away, the nervous energy level is reduced by several orders of magnitude. You generally take only one course, and
professors go on vacation. The MIT day camp is in session, and
fresh young counselors lead large groups of little kids to the swimming pool and the gym.

Several friends were gone, though, and I missed them. Matt
Armstrong had finished his master's degree in record time—
1 year—and was off to a job for $35K as senior research scientist
for Owens Corning. Michael Picardi had stayed in TPP, had earned
A's in all his classes, but had never found funding; he transferred
to Princeton, where they gave him full financial support. Ike
Thomas received two C's the second term, and, like Mary's lab
partner, was given the boot. And Amrit, the squash player who
thought that energy was easy, had landed a job modeling world
oil demand for OPEC in Vienna.

MIT is unlike law, business, or medical school. People come
and go on their own schedules, so there is not, for example, a
"Class of 1984 Mechanical Engineering Master's Degree Students." There's no cohesion; there's nothing but your own ability,
or lack thereof, to meet people and make friends.

My only summer class was Two-oh-two-three—System Dynamics and Control. It's an undergraduate class, but the summer
version was populated mainly by what Rohsenow affectionately
referred to as "the Navy Guys." Like the ones I'd met in Rohsenow's heat transfer class, they were generally older than the other
graduate students and were working toward master's degrees.

The smart navy guys had been to the academy at Annapolis,
or Purdue, or maybe Georgia Tech. There was a good percentage
of dumb ones, too, and I thought they would help the curve on
the tests. However, the navy teaches teamwork, organization, and
discipline: the navy guys help one another on the problem sets, their

files of previous exams are impeccable, they work hard, and they concentrate well. They're also used to sleep deprivation. These qualities can make up for stupidity, so I would have to work for my grade in this class, too.

"Feedback control systems are what makes anything that works work," David Miller said to the class in Building 13. "Everything is inherently unstable, and the feedback loop takes an unstable system and changes the system equation to make it into a stable system. For example, walking is unstable; just look at a baby trying to figure it out. He or she hasn't yet figured out or programmed himself to know the right gains to apply to his servo-motors—his muscles. So he hits the stops a lot, or rather the carpet. But gradually we do get our gains tuned, and we can walk."

David paused a second, then continued, "But before you can control a system, you need to be able to model the performance of a system. We've worked out a number of techniques for doing this. That's the first part of the course. Then we'll go on to figure out how to find the gains we need to apply to the open loop systems we've put together in the first part of the course. That's basically what controls are—modeling open-loop systems and finding closed-loop gains, where by *gain* I mean how hard and fast you push the system to do what you want."

Model model model. Eventually I'll be able to use that word without blushing. David certainly did. He looked as if he were pushing thirty, and had a curly mop of hair that he said his son's little league teammates pulled on, saying "Is this real?" He was exuberantly bright, talented, enthusiastic. He hadn't yet finished his Ph.D., so he was close enough to our level to have some compassion for our slowness. Plus, he really seemed to love to teach.

His Ph.D. would put him among the MIT-cubed ranks that Mary had told me about. These are the talented few whose undergraduate grades are good enough to get them into MIT grad school, who then pass the doctoral qualifying exams, and successfully defend their doctoral theses. Good enough undergraduate grades means almost straight A's, because if it meant any less there wouldn't be room for graduate students from anywhere else—like me.

David's Ph.D. thesis was to make a little underwater robot work. Once he was done, it would be able to crawl around deeply buried shipwrecks, the *Titanic*, for example; pick up debris; and send video camera messages back up to the control room of the ship on the surface.

He continued his lecture. "So basically once you know how to model things, you can model anything. It doesn't matter whether it's a mechanical, fluid, thermal, chemical, electrical, or biological system. The concepts of modeling are the same. Do any of you have any examples from what you're doing you'd like me to go over?"

Holy kill two birds with one stone, Batman. I raised my hand. "I've been working on this one problem, how to model a balloon being filled up with air." The word *model* rolled off my tongue naturally.

Without missing a beat, David drew the picture that had taken me ten days to intuit in March. He quickly set up the equations I'd been trying to program on the Apple and expressed the problem in the parlance of two-oh-two-three. The only difference from my model was that he gave mass to the skin of the balloon and added something he called a dashpot.

"And so your balloon problem will be a matter of accounting for the energy flow from the pressure of the fluid to the mass of the skin of the balloon, the elasticity of the skin of the balloon (the spring), and the internal friction of the balloon (the dashpot). The dashpot always slows down the motion of the mass, whether the balloon is expanding or contracting," he summarized. "If you put a feedback loop on the system, to, say, maintain a constant pressure in the balloon as the pressure in the tank varies, you'd have the same problem designers of airplane pressurization systems face."

So there's a reason to learn to blow up a balloon.

June 22

Time for another dog and pony show—a research sponsors' meeting. The men in brown and blue had flown in from Peoria, Davenport, and Columbus to see whether we'd made any progress. Actually, it was a good idea for them to come every four months because in the last three weeks of the four months we made a lot of progress.

"We gotta get some results for the meeting," Chet had said just after Professor Heywood's final. It was always something. So we'd cranked to replace what we could of the components of the RCM. The new driving air pressure tank was in, and we had mounted it in place. The new shaft was on order, and we knew there was no hope of further trials of the whole machine until after the meeting. The target then became a matter of completing as much other hardware in the test cell as possible.

Scott and I had split up the machine into the front half and the back half; he would design the pieces of the new starting mechanism on the back, and I would design the fuel delivery system on the front of the machine.

And then there was the electronics to sequence the whole thing. This involved assembling black plastic boxes and electronic components. I put them together on the basis of Chet's designs— I drilled holes into metal plates, spray-painted the plates battleship gray, screwed the electronic components onto the plates, and connected them with wires and solder. The process made me understand how uneducated people can work on assembly lines and produce very complex equipment without having any idea what they are doing.

On the front end of the machine, one immediate goal was to construct a support to fix the cylinder to the metal slots on the test bed. It was a two-day job; Nick and I cut pipes and plates, set up one of the plates on the machine, and welded the four angle-cut pipes between that plate and the plate on the test bed. Then we spray-painted the whole thing silver. It amazed me how good it looked when we were done—like something in *Popular Mechanics*.

My talk was just after the coffee and cream cheese Danish break. I summarized the leaks we'd detected and the hardware we'd assembled.

The guy from Caterpillar said, "So what you're telling us is the thing doesn't work yet. When *is* it going to work? I have to go back and report to my vice-president, and he's getting a little antsy. You know, what with the strike and everything, money's been getting a little scarce and we might have to cut the—"

Professor Heywood stepped in to the rescue. "Well, as you know, these things do take time. We expect to see a lot of progress during the summer when the pressure of classwork is less for all of us, and I'm sure that by the next meeting we will have all the components operational and have a test firing or two."

Thank you, Professor.

During the lab tour that afternoon the guy from Caterpillar

said he liked the front support Nick and I had built. It could be interesting to work for him; if only they weren't located in Peoria.

That night after midnight, Ari and I were the only ones left in our offices.

"How's it going?" I asked him.

"Oh, not too bad," he said. "They could be better, though. My doctor said I have to stop how do you say 'burning the candle from both ends,' but I don't have much choice. Every day it's stay here till 1:00 A.M., then go home to my wife and children, then up at 7:00 to get the children ready for school and back here at the lab by 8:00. Seven days a week I am here for two years so far."

"Well, after you work your way up to general and on to defense minister and on to premier, you'll know it was all worth-while," I said.

"Maybe if I'm lucky I'll be a general. But the rest is politics, and you know, my friend, we are engineers, we do not lie, and politics is best suited for people who lie. Look what you people did to Carter. He was a good man, maybe even a good engineer, an intelligent man, an honest man, and your country spat on him," he answered.

He offered me half of his bologna sandwich and I sat down in the old green Naugahyde office armchair across from his steel-gray desk.

"How can you get by on so little sleep?" I asked him.

He answered, "Typically when I am on duty in Israel we live on four hours sleep. It's all a matter of what you're used to. There we had four hours so it would not be much of a decrease to zero hours. You know your Thomas Edison never slept; he just took fifteen-minute catnaps every four or six hours. But even in the army with the few hours of sleep, even during the wars, *nothing* there is as hard as this place. The Six Day War was hard, but at least it was only six days. Sometimes I wonder whether I'm going to make it out of here alive."

"Hang in there," I said. "I'm sure you'll do fine. At least you've got the talent and the ability to work. I often wonder whether I have either."

"Talent is a gift, my friend. And the ability to work, if you can stay here long enough, that is something you acquire. You become like Nehemiah, with a sword in one hand and a shovel in the other hand, and nothing is able to bring you down from your work."

July 10

Chet, West, and I drove to United Technologies Research and Development Center in Hartford to pick up the fuel injector. In diesel engines, the piston compresses the air in the cylinder, and it heats up the air, just as a bicycle pump does. At the end of the compression, the fuel injector squirts fuel into the cylinder; the fuel then vaporizes and spontaneously ignites.

At the R & D center, the guys with Ph.D.'s had their own little offices with cinderblock walls and steel-gray desks like the one I had at the institute. Unlike my office, though, they had windows, which were a nice touch even if you couldn't open them. Their offices encircled the pigpens, where all the underlings—the newcomers or guys with just master's degrees—worked at computer terminals and drafting tables arranged in neat rows. If American industry wants better engineers, it occurred to me, why don't they give them better working conditions? Then the brightest ones might decide against going to business school or law school to get a private office and a decent salary.

West was nearly totally out of the picture now; his company was rolling along with a grant from the Department of Energy for a report that would sit on somebody's shelf. But he had a buddy at UTC who had a spare EFIS fuel injector. That was what we would use for our experiments.

EFIS stands for *electronic fuel injection system*, which was developed by UTC to improve tank performance. The only problem was that, like many other things developed for the army, it worked great in the research lab but was too complicated to work well in the field when the low-tech-but-reliable Russian tanks stormed toward Brittany.

It would suit our purposes well, though, because in the RCM, the fuel injector only had to fire once per experiment. And the EFIS could do this better than any standard fuel injector.

Chet, West, and I went to the workshop in the back of the building. It reminded me of the Sloan Lab. We went to the quiet, glass-enclosed office on the side and met the foreman. He picked up the telephone and said over the PA system, "George Brent to the office. George Brent to the office." The foreman gave no further information, and for all George Brent knew from the tone of voice on the PA, it was pink slip time.

"George, these gentlemen here are from MIT, and we need to set them up with an EFIS injector for some research they're doing. I'd like you to help them out," the foreman said.

"I'd be happy to, sir," George said. George was a friendly, middle-aged mechanic, with graying hair greased back, black shoes, and white socks; he reminded me of Riley in the "Life of Riley" TV show. He was like Nick, but younger.

George took us to the EFIS injector he'd set up on the lab bench. "See, it's got a solenoid here; that's just a valve that operates with an electromagnet. So what you do is cut the power to the magnet and then the valve opens and the fuel goes out of the tiny holes in the tip of the injector."

He flipped a switch and a small white cloud that smelled like diesel fuel burst out from the tip of the injector.

George continued his explanation, "You know, it's interesting how we build these things. We make all the pieces, mostly rods and cylinders that the rods fit in, and then we give some of the ladies in the plant a box of rods and a box of cylinders. They take the rods and test them in the cylinders; they can tell by the feel in their fingers whether or not the dimensions are correct. It's a lot cheaper than machining the parts to a ten-thousandth of an inch tolerance."

High technology.

Anybody can have a good idea, even a stupid person. My good idea was to ask George whether he had any spare pieces of the EFIS, together with the complete unit that we'd come to pick up. I didn't have any real reason to ask for the junk pieces; it just seemed that I might be able to figure out how the thing worked if I had them handy. I could play show-and-tell. By myself.

On the drive back from western Mass., I sat in the backseat and slept some while Chet and West talked in the front.

"Do you consult?" West asked Chet bluntly.

"Yeah, a little bit. I do some work on the side for the people who funded my thesis," Chet answered. Chet didn't seem to care about money. He was more into the science and the theory of it; he would follow in Heywood's footsteps.

"What's your billing rate?"

"Fifty dollars an hour."

"They must be laughing at you, pal," West chuckled. "If I were you I'd go for at least a hundred. They'll pay it; they've got the bucks."

At the tollbooth at Route 128 a flatbed truck pulled up beside us. Its cargo was wrecked cars with the exterior sheet metal stripped off; the joints and marrow were bare. There was a spring on an axle, and a dashpot—the shock absorber. The chassis looked like a mass, just like in David Miller's class.

July 15

At the laundromat I pondered how much the spin cycle should run its motor to wring the moisture from my clothes, and how the spin cycle energy compares with the dryer's heat energy. What combination of spin time and dryer time would result in the least total energy use?

I picked up the aquamarine paperback that somebody'd left on the next dryer. The back cover was a picture of a man and a boy standing next to a motorcycle.

Two sentences stood out. The first said, "The steps in the scientific method are: (1) statement of the problem; (2) hypotheses as to the cause of the problem; (3) experiments designed to test each hypothesis; (4) predicted results of the experiments; (5) observed results of the experiments; and (6) conclusions from the result of the experiments." The second was like unto it: "An experiment is never a failure solely because it fails to achieve predicted results. An experiment is a failure only when it also fails adequately to test the hypothesis in question, when the data it produces don't prove anything one way or another."

The statements explicitly summed up what Chet, West, and Professor Heywood had implicitly tried to tell me. We had tested the machine to see whether it could take the higher pressure. The answer was no, and the conclusion was to rebuild parts of the machine. Scott and his computer modeling would predict results of the experiments. We would do the experiments, I would analyze the data, and he would conclude what changes were required in his computer model.

The book was *Zen and the Art of Motorcycle Maintenance*.

August 12

I got an A. David gave me an A.

I wondered whether he gave everybody A's, because, who knows, one of the navy guys might review a grant application of his some day.

There were three weeks left before my Incomplete with Greene would become an F and I would be driving a cab.

The fact that August was cool and not its typical humid self, which makes it pleasant to be in an air-conditioned room with a computer terminal, didn't make things any easier. If it hadn't been for the demands of the lab and David's class I probably could have knocked the project off in a week or two at the beginning of the summer.

I remembered Greene's assignment: program the incompressible balloon-filling problem with realistic parameters; for example, a typical balloon volume might be 100 cubic inches, pressure on the inside of the balloon might be 2 or 3 psi, and a typical stretchiness (elasticity) might be close to that of a skinny rubber band. I looked at my set-up of the equations—my model.

The killer is the square term. If it were an ordinary differential equation, marching through time with the solution would be a piece of cake. How to deal with the square term?

Solution. Go to the library again. Somebody somewhere sometime must have bashed his head up against this. Maybe even Bernoulli himself tried to solve this type of equation as a follow-on grant from the Medici or Sforza Foundation.

I could ask Chet to give me a hint, but that would be cheating. But going to the library is not cheating. If by chance someone has already done this I'll be a free man. I went via a hall on the fourth floor of Building 4 with photographs of bats and gymnasts and a bullet going through a jack of diamonds, and on up to Barker Engineering Library. Before going to the card catalog I read the funnies and the sports, took a nap in one of the soft, cushy, leather chairs, and checked the price of the stock I'd been following since seventh grade. I didn't own any of the stock but it had done very well.

The card catalog was compact; it all fit within the space of several washing machines. It was smaller than the card catalog in the humanities library.

Okay. Let's start with "balloon." Maybe someone's done a thesis or written a book about it. Let's see. Ballistic missiles; ballistics, exterior; here we go: balloon.

"A 2-Dimensional Model for the Inflation of a Limp Intra-aortic Balloon." "The Occlusive Filling Problem—see Heart." "Balloon Behavior in Restrictive Fluid Environments." All these reports are talking about hearts. I don't care about hearts; I need to know about real balloons.

Next step. Maybe it's in a thermo book. Look under T. "Thermal Pollution." "Thermonuclear Devices." "Thermodynamics." Here's an interesting one: "Reflections on the Motive Power of Heat and on Machines Fitted to Develop This Power," by Carnot. Carnot was the nineteenth-century Frenchman Gyftopoulos always talked about. Even though Electrical Engineering, Course Six, double E, is the hot topic at the institute now, the double E's would be nowhere if it weren't for the mech E's like Carnot and Diesel, who made the shafts turn the generators. Most of the thermo books had the same call letters so I'd camp out in that section of the stacks.

The balloon problem involves "Differential Equations, Nonlinear," so I also wrote down the call letters for that section. And just for good measure, I looked up "Fluid Mechanics." On to the seventh floor.

Barker is shaped like a big doughnut. The doughnut hole is the domed space in the center where you read the funnies and sleep in the leather chairs. The fried dough is the large-radius circular hallway on the inner edge of the stacks. You can walk the loop, almost not perceiving that you're turning, and end up where you started. But if you're alert you're different at the end of every lap.

Differential equations and numerical analysis techniques books were useless. They all were a bunch of lifeless Greek letters like sigma and subscripts like i. I remembered Professor Kollman in Belgium telling me that a "mathematician writes out an extremely long and complicated solution to a problem, with, say, one or two hundred logical or algebraic steps. Then he or she condenses it into the shorthand of mathematics with all its Greek letters and subscripts and superscripts, and publishes it in a form that no one else can understand." That was why I was neither a mathematician nor a physicist.

In the doughnut I felt I was in the same mental marathon

with Bernoulli and Newton. OK, their mile times are under five minutes and mine are over ten minutes, but it's still the same race. The crowd is the same and the pain is the same and maybe all of us will make it to the finish line. I had the advantage of a library and packed ground before me.

Next stop. Fluids texts. Useless again. Many looked as obscure as the mathematics texts—lots of subscripts.

Last stop. Thermo. Ditto except for one text: "Practical Thermodynamics," published in England. It didn't solve the problem, but it had one that was close. One example stated, "A common problem in industry is filling a small tank from another vessel in which the pressure of the larger vessel is assumed not to vary as a result of the process. Tapping fluid off a pipeline of liquid or gas is a real-world example of such a process." So Greene knew what he was doing when he gave me this problem.

Other than that the library was a dead end, but I still learned. Each field's textbooks had nearly identical entries in their index sections. The presentation order varied, but within a given field each book said more or less the same thing. The set of knowledge is finite, manageable. That's why the Barker card catalog is so small.

My bicycle tire was flat that evening so I took the bus home to Allston. I jotted notes, thoughts that had come to me while I looked through the library.

I reviewed the equations:

The force balance on the balloon shell;
Bernoulli's equation for the flow into the balloon;
Flow continuity from the tank to the balloon.

I checked off the problem's constants, as Greene had suggested. These will go along for the ride in the analysis, and later on they can vary. The trick now is to make the equations flow.

Think. If I can solve my equation for the speed ("dx by dt, or $x$dot") of the skin of the balloon, I can multiply that d by dt by a little dt and find a new position of the skin. In my equation that balances the air pressure force with the balloon elasticity, a new skin position will give me a new balloon pressure, which will in turn give me a new skin speed, which will in turn give me a new skin position, which will in turn give me a new balloon pressure, et cetera, et cetera, et cetera, until the balloon breaks or the pressure in the balloon equals the pressure in the tank.

In freshman calculus the trick was to take long, curvy lines and make them into short, straight lines. I want to graph x, the balloon position, versus t, time, using little slices of time.

I redrew the picture I remembered from calculus.

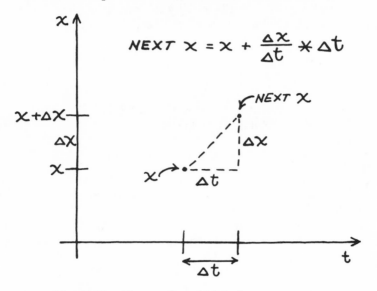

I could call NextX = x plus *dx/dt* * *dt*.

Time to write the software.

The Apple handbook explained a "for" and "next" loop. This is the heart of how a computer solves things "repeatedly."

I'll create an index, call it I, that's a substitute for t, time. Time is just a place holder, a reference mark, a hash mark on a graph. If only there were more of it.

I'll say "for I = 1 to 100," as if I want to track the balloon for 100 1-second intervals. At the beginning of each second, I'll calculate the speed of the shell of the balloon. I'll multiply that speed by 1 second to find how far the balloon goes in that second. That will give me the next position. I can taste the solution now.

One last problem. How do I tell the computer that I want the time increment always to be 1. If I'm at second number 43, how do I know to multiply by 1 and not 43? There's got to be a trick.

There is a trick. At each step, define a last step. For example, if I'm at step 43, the last step will be 42. The step size will always be one. In the program I'll call the last step "last$I$" (computerese for "last I"), and the program will start with last$I$ equal to zero. I'll calculate the balloon pressure, the speed of expansion, and the new size of the balloon (x) by programming

$x = x$dot $* (I - $last$I)$.

Then I'll make the present I (1) equal to the last I, so when I go on to the next I (2), I'll get 1 by subtracting the last I (1) from the present I (2). The program for the Apple will be:

```
10 LastI = 0
20 For I = 1 to 100
30 Pb = Pa + (k * X)/ A2
40 Xdot = (A1/A2) * SQAROOT (2 * (Pt - Pb)/ Ro)
50 X = X + Xdot * (I - LastI)
60 LastI = I
70 Next I
```

It's so simple. How did it take so long for me to arrive at the solution?

I looked out the window of the bus. I'd stayed on it for three miles past my stop, and it was turning around at Watertown Square. Space and time had collapsed in thought.

August 25

I showed my solution to Greene and he said, "That's fine. I'll give you a B if you stop now. If you want an A, though, I'll give you another week, and you can change the model to accommodate the case where the skin of the balloon has mass."

No problemo. I made a slight change to the program and left the solution on his desk four days later.

September 2

I wore my, or rather Don's, lab jacket around the institute. It made me feel a part of the place. The scared faces of the newcomers further fed my confidence. I bolted up the stairs to Greene's office to receive my A.

Greene's secretary had put on thirty, maybe forty pounds, and she bobbed a stopwatch on a string back and forth to prevent herself from running down to the machine in Building 6 to get a pack of Camels.

She pulled out my file. "You got a B," she said.

That snake. I did the extra work and he gave me a B anyway. If he'd given me an A, the A would have canceled out one of the C's from the first term on my grade point average (GPA). I don't care how many high-level contacts he has. We made a deal and he was backing out of it.

"Is he in now?" I asked.

"Yes, would you like to see him?"

"Yes. Right away."

I went in. He was sitting at his desk, glasses on, reading proceedings from a meeting of the National Academy of Engineering. He stood up to greet me.

"Why'd you give me a B? I thought we had an agreement."

We both stood still, on opposite sides of his desk.

"Yes, we did, but in the end, even though you made a good effort at solving the additional piece of the problem, the write-up you submitted, well, it just didn't have the polish of what I could in good conscience call 'A' work. I could let you look at copies of some term projects I've given A's on, and I think you'd agree."

"But why didn't you tell me, give me a chance to do more work, to fix it?"

"Well, there comes a time when you just have to close the books on a project. You've done good work, just not A work. I'm sure just one B won't bring your grade point average down that much," he said. He must have thought I had mostly A's. In a convoluted way he'd just given me a vote of confidence.

"Yeah, well, it won't help that much either. Maybe you're right. It's time to cut my losses and press on."

I'm off probation.
I belong here.

CHAPTER

11

Sigma Delta

Schedule:
Fall '82: 2.70 Introduction to Design (Wilson)
2.14 Feedback Control Systems (Brooks)
2.996 Thesis

September 3

"Is this Pepper White?" the voice at the other end of the phone said. "I'm calling from the Dean of Student Affairs' office. An opening for a tutor has just come up, at Senior House. Would you be interested in interviewing with the housemaster?"

"Sure. What do I have to do?"

"Just call Professor Dorsey at Senior House; his number's in the directory. You can set up an appointment with him."

Yeah baby. Maybe there's a chance for a tutor position after all. A tutor at MIT is what state schools call an R.A., short for resident assistant, and what Harvard calls a house fellow, because Harvard likes to give important sounding names to people.

In the springtime between bicycle rides I'd applied for tutor positions at several undergraduate dormitories: at MacGregor, where the tutor suites have million-dollar views of Boston; at

McCormick, the all-women dorm where the fundamentalist families send their daughters ("Hey, maybe their boyfriends need counseling," I said to the housemaster); and at Bexley, the acid rock dorm across Mass. Ave. from Building 7. At Bexley, rumor had it, the chem majors synthesized their own LSD, and the FBI was just aching to make a bust. At Bexley, I made it to the first round of tutor elimination.

April 1

The interview consisted of the twelve tutor candidates sitting around the living room of the housemasters, Professor and Mrs. Jacob Levy. None of the candidates, if they thought like me, would be very disappointed if the other eleven were run over by a dump-truck at the Mass Ave. crosswalk. About thirty of the one hundred Bexleyites asked general questions. Our job as candidates was smoothly, deftly, to answer a question at an appropriate time of our own choosing.

The kid wearing the Led Zeppelin T-shirt posed the question, "So, like, if I were on a bad acid trip, like, and if you found me, like, what would you do?"

It seemed as good a time as any for me to speak up. "Well, your business is your business; I mean if you want to fry your highly gifted brain out, go ahead. I'll call an ambulance and get you to a hospital where they can take care of you, maybe pump your stomach out, and keep you from hurting yourself. As for myself, I haven't taken so much as an aspirin for about eight years, and I've been fairly healthy and happy."

Buzzer sound. Wrong answer.

The biochem major sitting next to me, with longish hair, beard, and mustache, hit the mark a little closer.

"Well, I've done about every kind of recreational pharmaceutical there is, and I've got a notebook full of recipes, which might come in handy for you guys, heh heh. As far as the acid trip scene, I'd like talk you down like I once did for a friend of mine. I'd say something like, 'It's OK, you're coming to the runway, you're not going to crash and burn, man, just go easy with the stick, nice and smooth, we'll get you down, that's it here we go it's all right.' I'd say something like that until you came down off it."

Buzzer sound. Right answer.

September 3 again

My appointment with Professor Dorsey was at seven and I took the scenic route to Senior House—down the Charles from Mass. Ave. The sailboats in the late evening sun and the real world of Boston's skyline in the background made me think back to the year before, when I was a technological infant. I'd gotten better; I knew it. Now if I could just talk my way into being a tutor I'd be able to pay my debts.

There was a little chill in the air, and it made me remember the fall in Brussels, and Stephanie. I hadn't called or written since December, and neither had she. Water under the bridge in Bruges. I wondered whether she'd found someone else.

Into Senior House's cornerstone was chiseled "1917." In 1917 my mother's father marched across Flanders to Paris. Past the glass entryway to the courtyard enveloped by the L-shaped dormitory and the wall of President Gray's backyard, Jimi Hendrix played "Purple Haze" loudly on speakers pointed out of a fourth-floor window.

The fast-falling dusk was made darker from the shade of the trees in President Gray's garden, lighter by the light of the bonfire ahead in the courtyard under the tall tree. A kid with long hair and lots of zits and a black T-shirt with "Visit Hell" written underneath a flaming design of Building 7 walked past toward Ames Street. I said hello.

He returned no response, no nod, no noise, no acknowledgment of my existence.

Two women walking arm in arm also ignored my greeting.

A tall guy wearing a ponytail, an earring, and a garment that is worn by some Indian men but we in America call a skirt said hello. I didn't say hello.

Near the fourth-floor window, where the speakers played Hendrix, the larger-than-life version of Mary's "Sport Death" T-shirt hung from the balcony. The skull, the stars and stripes, the "Only life can kill you" in the skull's teeth, waved gently in the bonfire's breeze. This place is even worse than Bexley, I thought.

Another guy with a ponytail spun around the tree from the tire swing. He arched his back horizontally outward from the tire, and the centrifugal force thrust his ponytail outward as he missed the bonfire by a hair's breadth and his head never came near the tree; he was a tetherball with an on-board microprocessor. He'd probably calculated his trajectory on his computer and knew precisely what his margin for error was.

"Yeah, Sport Death!" one of the bonfire bystanders said. Sport was a command—to defy, to taunt. The bystander wore a yellow T-shirt that said, "Dare to be friendly," and I asked him for directions to the Dorseys' apartment.

"Sure, it's right down there on the left toward the river, on the second floor of Crafts," he said with a happy tone to his voice.

I sat down with Professor Dorsey and he explained the situation. "Well, you see, the Atkinson tutor was off doing some genetic engineering research in the Australian outback for his thesis work at the Whitehead Institute, and he contracted some strange disease out there and is under observation in a hospital in Sydney."

"Gee, that's terrible; I hope he recovers." But not real soon.

Professor Dorsey continued, "Freshman rush week is coming right up, and the students aren't back yet except for a few. Typically, it's a pretty wild time, and to keep the whole place from blowing up, I think we really need our full complement of tutors."

"I thought it was all seniors; isn't that why they call it Senior House?" I asked.

"No, it's the senior house, the oldest dorm in the institute. There are all classes here, and also some graduate students. Part of the issue for rush week is that this place is usually the freshmen's last choice—it's generally a tie between here and Bexley. Nobody wants to live here; they'd rather live at the more middle-of-the road dorms like Macgregor and New House up the river, or at the frats; there's even been talk about shutting down Senior House as a dorm. So we'd really like to have as many tutors on hand as possible, just to keep an eye on things and to be a friendly face for the lost freshmen."

"I think I could handle that," I said. "Are you interviewing anyone else?"

"Well, you're the first person who's called, and the dean's office wasn't able to reach anyone else today. You seem like a nice enough person; I think you'd be fine. I'd just like to ask one question of you, though. Where'd you go to high school?"

Kind of an odd question, I thought. "Winston Churchill High School, in the Washington, D.C., area," I answered.

"Good. That's a relief. What with the blue and white striped shirt you're wearing, and the khaki pants, and the topsiders, I was afraid you might be a preppy. I don't think a preppy would get along well here. When can you move in?"

"Tomorrow," I said, happy at the prospect of leaving my sloping tenement in Allston.

"That's great," he said. "Now let me briefly summarize your duties as a tutor. First of all, the term is pretty much a misnomer because, well, frankly the undergrads are generally smarter than the graduate students, except for the ones who went here as undergrads and the ones who came here from Cal Tech. Besides, the students who have friends tend to tutor one another, or they get help from someone who took whatever class it is the previous semester. Your main purpose as a tutor is to make the environment in the dorm a little more human, and to be on the front line of knowing whether anyone is having emotional problems," he said.

"Uh huh."

"You see, we're in a sticky position here; on the one hand the undergraduates are allegedly adults and are accorded all the freedoms of normal society. On the other hand, many of the undergraduates spent their spare time in the computer room at their high schools so they didn't really have a chance to develop socially. And Lord knows there's no time for them to develop socially here. So if one of them goes over the railing and through the ice in the dead of winter, there's a good chance that his parents will sue the institute for all it's worth. Part of your job is to help us prevent that from happening. Oh, and by the way, we'd like you to host a study break every two weeks, and once each term you'll be required to host a whole-house study break."

That makes, call it seven study breaks per term, at, say, one hour to get the milk and cookies, one hour for the study break itself, and one hour to clean up. That's twenty-one hours. Now figure five hours per term of suicide prevention duty, plus two or three hours of actual tutoring, an occasional tutor's meeting, and I'm up to about thirty hours per term of actual work, times two terms equals sixty hours. The rent's probably worth about $250 a month, or $3K a year, plus another thousand for food, that comes to $4K, divided by sixty is roughly $65 bucks an hour, tax-free, so before taxes that would be about a hundred an hour. That's almost as much as some of the profs make consulting—what a deal.

"Would you like me to give you a tour of the dorm?" he asked.

"Sure, that sounds great."

We walked past the bonfire again and started with the Runkle entry. An entry is a subset of Senior House, with a separate entrance and stairway and hallways. John Runkle was an early president of MIT, whose major contribution to education was high school "shop" class. I asked Professor Dorsey whether he had any clues as to where "Sport Death" came from.

"I don't know; it's just sort of a battle cry around here. One story has it that a Senior House student was taking skydiving lessons and his chute didn't open. That was supposed to be the ultimate in 'sporting death.' I tried to check that out and couldn't find any documentation on the story, though. Another, maybe more plausible explanation is that the first painting, here on Runkle fourth, was done by a kid whose roommate was the first MIT student killed in Vietnam."

It's odd how traditions take on a life of their own and when you get right down to it nobody knows what they mean.

We walked down the length of Runkle fourth, with the Hendrix music at its loudest through the open door to the speakers. Hey Joe, where you goin' with that gun in your hand . . .

"Here's the original," Professor Dorsey said, pointing to the skull mural. "Let me show you the Munch reproduction down the hall. They call it Captain Nemo."

It was equally larger than life—*The Scream*, the face of anguish. I was glad Runkle fourth was not in my entry. Professor Dorsey led me to Atkinson, and on the second floor landing, a tall athletic-looking student dictated a letter: "And my computing staff will be able to complete the task within two man-months. Yours sincerely, DLM."

"Dianne, this is Pepper White," Professor Dorsey said. "He'll be replacing Nabil as the Atkinson tutor."

Dianne sneered a little, as if she thought, "What are you guys trying to pull? Why are you bypassing the democratic process?" I hoped that her sneer wasn't an indicator of sneers to come from the people in Atkinson. Best to nip this in the bud by trying to be friendly.

I asked her, "Who's the letter to? Are you starting a company?"

"I've been in computer consulting since ninth grade," she said impatiently. "I've got a staff of about eight subcontractors here in Senior House, and I provide the marketing and client servicing."

"Golly. That's pretty impressive," I said. As Professor Dorsey and I left, she whistled between her teeth, "There's a place in France where the alligators dance." I didn't get it immediately, but in a minute I knew it was a subtle slam of my preppy appearance.

Even so, Atkinson felt a little more friendly than Runkle; somebody had mellow jazz by Bob James playing on a stereo. Whereas Runkle reeked of pot and incense, Atkinson just smelled of one part dirty clothes, one part twenty different kinds of shampoo, and twenty parts air.

The apartment was perfect. It had a refrigerator, sink, bedroom, living room—all the comforts of home. In its location, the rent would probably have been $300 a month, thus raising my effective hourly rate.

Back at the office, Ari gave me some advice. "You are in a very touchy position, my friend," he said. "The students might organize to get you thrown out. You would not only lose your free room and board; I think that might hurt your performance as a student here as well. So what I think you should do is have each floor over for dessert. There are maybe eight or ten of them on each floor; am I correct? That is a small enough group that you will be less nervous, and if you make a fool of yourself, the information will travel secondhand, not firsthand. This is what I did with my troops in Israel; it is the old principle of 'divide and conquer.' Oh yes, and one more thing. Encourage them to settle their own disputes as much as possible. Otherwise they will drive you crazy if they want to make you the referee all the time."

"That sounds like good advice," I said.

"Oh, and there's one more thing I forgot to mention," Ari said. "The food you serve them for the first time has to be very good and served elegantly. That's what we do in Israel when terrorists holding hostages demand food. It weakens their resistance." Mind bending 101.

September 7

Rush week is just the first dehumanizing experience for poor little MIT first-year students. I remembered orientation week at Hopkins. I knew who my roommate would be and where my room would be. Driving up to Baltimore from Potomac, with the '68 Mercury Park Lane stuffed full of my stereo equipment and bicycle and clothes, I was still terrified. There wasn't room for my parents, so they took the train and I met them there. I think I would have been more terrified if I were a dormless person from the beginning, as they are at MIT.

At Hopkins—OK, it's a much smaller undergraduate school so they can manage these things more easily, and some alumni have warm enough feelings in their hearts to give it an endowment so they don't always have to be grubbing for money and cutting budgets—at Hopkins my happiest memory of orientation was sitting on the sun-drenched grass with my freshman orientation group and my adviser, Jerry Cohon (B.S., Penn; Ph.D., MIT) and talking about environmental engineering and how to save the world. Orientation week was a nurturing week, an opportunity to meet people, make friends, invite them over to my dorm room for tea.

Not so at MIT. Boom, you sniveling little nerd, who probably never went out on a date in your life, welcome to getting your last choice in living arrangements. Welcome to fraternity brothers patting you on the back and putting a sticker there that says, "This guy's a loser" in the underground code. Welcome to being abandoned by acquaintances who promise they'll wait when you go to the bathroom. Welcome to hell.

Howard Gelman was the first to arrive for vanilla ice cream and fresh blueberries served on glass plates with silver plated spoons from the Dorseys' flatware set. Howard was a short, fat freshman from New York. He had a whiny voice and wanted to major in Course Six. High tech. Double E. Electrical Engineering and Computer Science; pronounced "EEKS" in short form.

It was time to start earning my free room and board.

"So," I said. "How are things going for you?"

"Ummmm. Ummmm. They could be better. I'm here, aren't I?"

How do you talk to somebody like this? "So," I said. Pause. "Where'd you go to high school?"

"Science," he said, referring to the Bronx School of Science. If he were a talented musician or actor this would be Juilliard and his answer would have been the School for Performing Arts. But he was good in math, better than the best in Manhattan, and this was MIT.

"What room are you staying in?" I asked.

"303. It's just a temporary assignment. I really wanted to be in MacGregor but they were full. I'm going to see whether I can transfer there next term."

Good luck. Once they see their views there's only one way a room is going to open up, and I doubt you'd want to get it that way.

When is someone else going to show up, I wondered. This is too awkward. "Well, the rest of the people should be here any minute," I said.

"It's a Poisson distribution, how people arrive at any queue," he said. "If eight people will arrive between now and 7:10, that will make nine total in fifteen minutes, or once per every fifteen over nine minutes. The probability that two more people will arrive here by 7:05 is e to the minus six times six cubed over three factorial. Do you have a calculator?"

This kid's good. Let's get him trained and out of here, doing something productive like figuring out how to deploy troops in Europe or decoding Soviet cable transmissions.

"No, I prefer to do the easy ones in my head," I said.

A woman who wore a black shirt with the red letters sigma delta walked in. "Hi," she said. "I'm Cindy Brooks. I live next door."

Brooks. That name sounds familiar. Oh yeah, Professor Brooks is teaching my advanced controls class this semester.

"Are you any relation to the professor?"

"I'm his daughter."

Professor Kingfield at the law school had a daughter, too. But that story's already been written.

"Say, I like your shirt," I said, referring to the black football jersey with red letters on it. "What does sigma delta stand for?"

"Sport Death. Sigma Delta is the Senior House sorority. Actually we're looking for guys who want to be little brothers for some of the pledges."

"What does that involve?"

"Well, everyone is born with 100 purity points, or things they haven't done," she said. "Our pledges have to fill out the form, and that's how they get their preinitiation score. To get admitted, they have to reduce their score by 10 percent. The postinitiation score is the number on the back of the shirt. As a little brother you would help them accomplish that. The list is on the computer system in Building 35."

Everything can be quantified.

"Well, I don't think my friends at church would approve. Maybe you ought to talk to Howard here."

Two others came in and took their ice cream out of the freezer. One was from Ghana; the other was a sophomore math major from Poland. Dianne, the woman dictating the letter to her client the day before, walked in.

"So what's the deal here?" she asked. "Are you trying to butter us up floor by floor so we won't organize to get you kicked out and then select a tutor democratically? Are you playing some 'divide and conquer' game?" She was smiling, as if she didn't mean it, but was just testing me, seeing whether she could put a verbal service ace past me.

"Say, who do you think is going to win the World Series this year?" I asked. That works in most circles; in most circles no one even notices it's an evasive maneuver.

"No no no no no. You're not getting off that easy," she volleyed back.

"Well, what would you do in my situation?"

"No answering a question with a question. I asked first," she said.

The other six students ate their ice cream, half-listening to the Polish mathematics student say that everything is mathematics and all engineering is just glorified technician work, half-listening to the verbal exchange near the door.

"OK, yes," I said.

"Yes what?"

"Yes, like everyone else on the winning side of this con game, I'm a money-grubbing sleazeball who greased my way into this position. What do you want to do about it?"

"Oh, nothing. I was just curious. Say, is that an Italian racing bike you've got there? Maybe we can go riding sometime."

September 15

The phone rang; it was my mother.

"Pepper, your father's in the hospital again. They don't know whether it's a heart attack or cancer or what. He's got a fever and he's on all kinds of medication. They don't know whether he's going to make it this time, and maybe you should come down to—"

"I'll be on the next plane."

Alone with him in the hospital room, I looked at my father. He was asleep, with electrodes taped to his bare chest underneath the hospital gown; the fever hadn't left him. Next to the bed there was an oscilloscope with a blue screen, monitoring his vital signs. It was like the oscilloscope in my cell at MIT.

I wondered whether the nurses and doctors looked at him the same way I looked at the rapid compression machine, as a device with inputs and outputs, generating points on a graph, points to be analyzed, discussed, reasoned through, argued about. Maybe they did think that way so they could distance themselves from the ones that didn't make it.

Please don't let him die now. Please. Let us have him for a few more years, maybe long enough to see his grandchildren.

The nurse came in to take his temperature.

"That's odd," she said. "It went down a degree in the last half hour. Maybe he's turning the corner and getting better."

It was probably just a coincidence.

Or was it?

CHAPTER

——— 12 ———

Two Seventy

Enough of the Calorics were still at the institute to field a C-league soccer team again, although many had moved outward and upward to professorships at good schools or high-paying jobs in industry. Carlos was still here, though, and Dave Orlowski, too.

The score in the game with TEP was 0–0 late in the second half. I was at left wing as usual, Carlos at right, Dave at center.

Robin, the left halfback, passed up to me; I one-touched it to Carlos. He shot toward the goalie but Dave deflected it and we won in textbook style.

October 19

"We define *suboptimization*," Professor Wilson lectured the design class, "as elegantly solving the wrong problem. Rearranging the deck chairs on the sinking *Titanic* is an example." Speaking of sinking ships, I wondered how Wilson had progressed with the pedal-powered crew shell we'd launched almost a year before.

Course Two Seventy, Introduction to Design, was on my list of required undergraduate courses. It was the scariest, biggest hurdle between me and my master's degree because two seventy had The Contest. Engineers and designers compete every working day of their lives to make the best product at the lowest cost. What

better way to round out your engineering education than to compete directly, in a contest to build the best device to perform a
stated task?

Wilson continued, "Now I'd like to change the subject a bit
and talk about The Contest. This year The Contest will be a little
different from those of years past. Instead of giving you all the
same bag of materials, as Professor Flowers has done, this year
you'll have to buy things from a 'store,' and we'll give you a
'budget' of $12,500. Also, you'll have to put in some microelec-
tronics. One of the teaching assistants, Nigel Adams, thinks that
no mechanical engineer should leave MIT without having wired
up at least one integrated circuit. The point of this year's contest
is to lift the most weight up a hill, and you'll receive a 500-gram
bonus weight if your electronics works. Furthermore, this year
we'll have preliminary elimination rounds during the third week
in November, in which you'll be able to test your device several
times. The Contest itself will be on Monday night before Thanksgiving."

I really should read some of those handouts, I thought. All I
knew was that some weight had to go to the top of a ramp in
twenty seconds, and with just a little tiny electric motor and two
little tiny springs, together with whatever else was available in the
"store." All the components had to fit within a geometric space
about as big as a breadbox, and within a financial space of 12,500
funny dollars.

October 26

"I better get moving on this stupid thing" was going through my
head with nagging regularity, so I finally went down to the shop
of the 400-pound technician named "Tiny" and looked at the
course. It had two halves; The Contest would be run one-on-one,
and the halves were mirror images of each other. Scales were on
either side of the center line, and it looked as if there were several
ways to go up successfully. There was a plywood winding road
on one side of the terrain. Bounded by the road was an astroturf-
covered obstacle course, including a "cactus" (a metal green U on
a stick), designed to prevent us from all going up the middle.

I looked at the course and couldn't decide what to do, so I
checked out the sample "store" items: a 2-watt motor for $1,000;
wood strips, $250 each; screw, $50; copper welding rod, $75 per

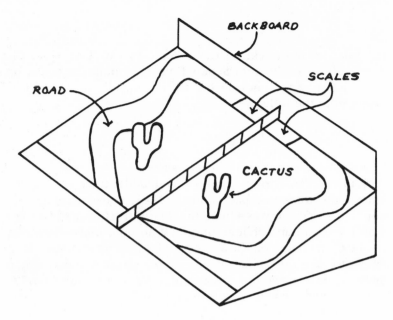

meter; tongue depressor, $25; rubber band, $100; and a four-gate microcomputer chip for $500. When I'd finished handling all the items, I looked at the course again. A couple of ideas had come to me during the inventory. I met two juniors at the course.

"I think the road is definitely the way to go," one of them said.

I agreed. "All you have to do is build a little truck that goes up the road; it would be pretty easy to make something that carries a Coke bottle full of gravel and steers itself up the road," I said, "or you could go underneath the 'cactus' here, or build a wide off-road vehicle that goes around the cactus, or how about a counterweight system that lifts the weight up like the elevator in the Eiffel Tower?"

We talked a while longer, and they, too, had many ideas. I went back to my office. The stew had begun to simmer.

"Why don't you build something that extends an arm out there like a crane?" Ari suggested. Not only had he driven tanks, he'd also designed them, and I valued his opinion. Extending an arm out would add another dimension to the problem. How could I fit something 4½ feet long into a 2-foot-long bread box?

October 28

9:47 P.M. "A fire truck!" It came to me as I walked out of the Sloan Lab on my way to Senior House. I'd build an extension ladder just like the ones on fire trucks, and it would push the weight onto the scale.

October 29

At noon I went to the fire department to see how these things work in real life. There was a hook and ladder truck at Lafayette Square; the truck had been built in 1941, and the ladder was mounted in 1960. It was a huge aluminum structure, and I looked at all the cables and pulleys for almost an hour and couldn't for the life of me figure out how it worked. Lieutenant Shaughnessy offered to take the ladder out for me on Saturday morning and demonstrate its extension, but Saturday was to be a study day, so I just sketched a few mechanisms and left.

November 5

The class of 160 students was divided into 10 "recitation sections." These met for an hour once a week for more interactive instruction than was available in the larger lecture format. Tom Bligh, the professor who'd known more about Lindbergh than I did the previous fall, and with whom I'd proposed to heat Kansas farmhouses with windmills and heat pumps, was my recitation instructor. He gave personal consultations to about 20 of the 160 students in the class. Tom would determine my grade.

One advantage of having a meeting with your recitation instructor every week is that it forces you to do something. The meeting was sort of like the progress reports we prepared for the research sponsors in the Sloan Lab. So I was up past midnight the night before, trying to figure out how to build my fire engine ladder.

"I'll cut the wood into three strips of equal width, and then glue two of the three into an L-shaped beam. That should be fairly strong, it's easy to make and cheap," I said. My classmates and I had started calling materials cheap or expensive, as if the assigned "costs" had real meaning.

Already little design details started popping up. How many cross braces/rungs should I put in my ladder? How wide should it be? How will I extend it? It was time to be arbitrary. Start with five cross braces and see whether that's enough. If not, put more in. I began to write more and more notes to myself. "Just build the thing, get it working and tested," I kept telling myself. So I spent Friday night with epoxy and wood, and a piece of stainless steel 1 inch thick to hold the wood together while the epoxy hardened.

November 6

My L-beams came out really well. The epoxy hardened; I would never have believed wood could be that stiff. Expecting a mob at eight, I arrived at Tiny's shop, but most people slept in and I found an available drill press on which to drill the holes for my copper rods. I put five rungs in two feet, and again I was amazed at the stiff, light results.

It took all morning to drill the twenty holes, and by the time I finished the place was hopping. Everyone had backpacks filled with wood strips and welding rod; for most of them it was the first day of construction. Some built frames, some built drive systems for their 2-watt motors, others machined wheels from masonite on the lathes.

By 1:00 my beams and welding rod began to look like a ladder and somebody said, "That's the best track I've seen yet."

I said, "Thanks, but it's not a track, it's a ladder."

He said, "Oh. Well, it's nicely built, whatever it is."

2:00 P.M., and I had my string interlaced among the rungs of my ladder so that it extended fully when I pulled on one end. It worked! But when I put a weight on it it hardly extended at all.

"Resolve weight support problem," I wrote in my lab notebook—and what a problem it was. If I aimed the ladder at the scale, there would be a constant angle between the end of the ladder and the terrain below, but the height of the ladder end would vary as it would climb the hill. I was sure I didn't want to design a wheel assembly that would contract as it climbed the hill. Time for a bike ride.

November 7

9:20 P.M. In the middle of my mechanical drawing assignment, I couldn't keep my eyes off the ladder. I kept thinking, How am I going to support that weight? The ladder looks great, but it will never work as is. There's got to be a way to support the weight.

And then it came. The light bulb appeared over my head and I took some rubber bands out of my desk drawer. Why not shoot the ladder out with rubber bands, then winch a weight up the "track"?

12:40 A.M., and I was still tossing and turning in bed with the ideas of different ways to shoot the ladder out and haul up the weight: obsession was beginning. The word obtained new meaning. The letters dripped as at the beginning of a Bette Davis movie and I realized that two seventy had me.

November 8

"Now this is a good piece of engineering," Tom Bligh said as he examined my ladder. "You know I don't see how some of the people who take this course can do the slipshod work they do and live with themselves. For an engineer, there should be no other way to do things than with high quality."

"Well, I've got the advantage of having effectively worked as a lab technician for almost two years, and I've seen how to set things up and build them right," I said. I tried to be modest, but I realized that all I had to do was to keep up the good work and I'd have my second A.

"Yes, well you've still got a lot to do and not a lot of time to do it," he said and I agreed. "Let's try shooting this out with the constant force spring."

He wound up the ladder and put one stage on top of the other with the spring fully stretched. "You stand over there across from me," he said. "Watch your eyes." I was about five feet from him when he let go. The upper stage flew right into my arms. "I think it's got enough pop to go up the hill; what do you think?" he asked.

"I think I'm in business but have a lot of business to attend to," I said.

"Just get it working as quickly as you can," he said.

November 9

Tasks: legs, nonreturn mechanism, cart to pull weight up track, pulley, drive system for motor, frame. Details, details, details, enough to drive you crazy. Forget electronics for now: it's only worth 500 grams. But I have to work on other problem sets, too, and I have to maintain some semblance of progress with my thesis work on the rapid compression machine. *Aargh.* So this is why MIT is the best engineering school in the United States, which means in the world.

9:00 P.M. "Ari, it's becoming an obsession to me. I can't do anything else or think of anything else. There's so much to do, and I have to keep things rolling, and I'm running out of time."

"Yes, it's like co ca heen," he answered.

"Like what?"

"Co ca heen, you know, you breathe it in," and he took a big breath through his nose, "and the more you breathe in the more you want."

"That's it exactly," I said as I went back to look at my machine.

November 10

Time to review the budget: constant force spring, $500; wood strips, $1,750; masonite sheet, $1,000; motor, $1,000; welding rod, $350 . . . $4,600 total. Almost $8,000 left. Time to plan for the next day. Organized procrastination is useful because deciding what you're going to do in a machine shop usually takes longer than doing it.

I've got to design that frame. It's easy, but I can't overcome the inertia keeping me from that subproblem. If I can build the frame by tomorrow night, though, I'll be in good shape.

November 11

Veteran's Day and did I go to the teach-in on nuclear war? Nooooooo . . . as John Belushi would have said. I worked on my two seventy project.

4:00 P.M. I waited for my falafel in front of the Great Dome. A bearded man, thirty-seven, walked down the steps toward Boston. He wore blue jeans and leather and wood from his knee down. A Vietnam veteran, he made time for peace.

9:00 P.M. "Do you realize what destruction there would be?" Ari said vehemently. "It would set you back at least 100 years. Essentially you are living on the work of all the generations before you. There must not be a nuclear war."

I was a little surprised because I thought Ari, the staunchest anti-Soviet hawk I knew, would assure me that the weapons were necessary to keep the bear in its cage. "And what's more," he said, "there was nobody there, no students, nobody. Don't you people care at all about this? It could be the end of the world and there'd be no one there."

"But I have my two seventy project to worry about," I said. "I'll be there next year."

"Next year it will be something else."

November 12

Contestants arrived at the machine shop with machinelike-looking devices. Fewer and fewer carried backpacks with wood strips in them, and more and more carried boxes with partially completed devices. I was still at the backpack stage.

3:00 P.M. Professor Bligh was out, so I spoke with Professor Griffith. He parked his bicycle next to Heywood's, Weare's, and Wilson's. Like them, he consulted to the energy industry. Like them, he bicycled to work because he valued efficiency. He said, "The point is, you could spend two hours on this project, make a catapult, and put a weight up on the scale, or you could spend two years on it, and put the effort of the space program into it. We're trying to teach you to make decisions based on limited time and resources. That's what the real world is like all the time."

7:00 P.M. Freak-out time. I wondered how many nervous breakdowns this course had produced. I was slipping on my personal schedule and goals. I had to build that frame, but it involved so many details I didn't know where to start.

I talked to Ari. "Calm down," he said. "You've done good work so far. Just keep it up and don't let the pressure overwhelm you."

"You're right. But tonight I'm so wound up I can't think. I've got to go skating." So I went to the rink. There were about a hundred skaters there and the ice was really chopped up—only fifteen minutes after the Zamboni had cleaned it off. The Zamboni looked more comprehensible to me. I wanted to take it apart and see how every little piece of it worked.

There were many skaters there, starting and stopping abruptly. Skating is like grinding one's molars together for MIT students, and ice hockey is the most popular intramural sport. After fifty hard laps, I went to Senior House for my good night's sleep of the week.

November 13

Raining. Thank goodness for that, or I'd have probably blown the whole day cycling to avoid working on my project. I went upstairs in Building 3 to where the practice track had been set up. There was one other guy in the room. He had a machine with big masonite wheels and wooden hubs and was trying to make his grappling hook catch the backboard and winch his truck up to the scale.

I *had* to build the frame. That meant: figure out heights of wooden pieces to cut and cut them. Then make a list of tasks. 1. Cut two 3-⅝-inch pieces. 2. Cut two 5-½-inch pieces. 3. Cut two pieces 7³⁄₁₆ inches long. 4. Epoxy pieces together. 5. Cut welding rods. 6. Cut notches for clearance. The only way to keep your sanity in this kind of thing is to make lists and then check things off.

The student machine shop was open all day and there was no unemployment in the basement of Building 3. Every lathe, every bandsaw, every milling machine, every drill was in constant use. Wartime. Innovations researched, developed, manufactured in minutes, hours. Only 120 hours left. No time to procrastinate. Two seventy is the organic chemistry lab of engineering. Organic lab gives premeds operating room pressure; two-seventy gives engineers production line pressure. People began to ask one another, "Does it work?" Each time I heard the question my commitment to make it work was heightened.

9:30 P.M. I sat in the men's room (3-126) and felt the whole building vibrate from the whirr of the machines in the basement. On each trip up and down the stairs from the workshop in the basement to the testing ground on the fourth floor, the display of the best machines from the year before caught my eye. They were in the case across from Mikic's office; the best machines from my year would be there in January. I became less tired.

11:00 P.M. A moment when all machines were off. I missed the noise. Someone turned on the bandsaw.

November 14

To do: Read Sunday comics in library after lunch. Drill holes in extension to catch it as it flies apart. Glue base together. So much to do. So many piddly details to attend to.

8:50 P.M. I needed familial support so I called home.

"I have some sad news for you, Pepper," my mother said. "Your dog just died."

Why does it have to happen all at once? Why didn't I wait until after the contest to call so I wouldn't have to worry about this? After I hung up, I kicked a plastic cookie tray and it shattered.

Ari ran over to my office and found me sobbing. "You have to get back in control. The professors here don't care what happened to you; they just care about what you produce. Now go and wash yourself and go back to work. You must finish the job you've started." He said it as if I were one of his soldiers who was shell-shocked. He was firm, and I appreciated it.

12:30 A.M. The frame was complete. I was one day behind schedule, but at least I could sleep.

November 15

A.M. go to class; P.M., work on electronics.

"How do I use this wire-wrap tool?" I asked Cindy.

"It's easy," she said as she used the tool to fix two wires around pins on my chip. "There. You try now."

It was easy. Another mystery of technology had vaporized for me. Cindy finished wiring her circuit, and another undergraduate woman asked me for help.

"It's easy," I said, and I showed her how to attach the wire. She was beautiful, and I reminded myself that when I was a freshman she was in sixth grade—don't even *think* of asking her out on a date.

6:30 P.M. After rewiring it three times, my circuit finally worked. If nothing else, I would win the 500-gram bonus weight.

November 16

My mechanical drawing test was intuitive and short, but unfortunately I didn't receive page two and would have to finish the test later in Bligh's office. Just when I was beginning to think I was smart. I'd completed the frame, the electronics, the ladder. All that remained was to build the drive system. So what if that would be the hardest part? I was running out of money. I couldn't afford the "cost" of the ready-made rods that the store sold, so I'd have to turn down a cheaper square bar on the lathe. That would take only three hours. Not only was I inventor, researcher, production line worker, and cost accountant; I was a micromicroeconomist trading time—i.e., labor (i.e., my sleep)—for capital, i.e., ready-made goods.

Four hours later I finished machining the shaft.

November 17

7:00 A.M. Thirty-six hours left until the first trials. I went to the Sloan Lab early so I could recruit Nick to help me set up the lab's lathe to machine the masonite for my drive wheel.

9:55 A.M. Go to pick up calculator and books for rest of mechanical drawing test. I said to myself, "Just pretend you're at West Point and you always have a test every day."

10:45 A.M. Back to get more help from Nick.

12:10 P.M. Nick went to lunch.

1:20 P.M. Thirty hours left. I can't blow everything because of a nonfunctioning drive system. The machine looks too good to miss the finals. I've got to finish it. To do: 1. Solder wires to motor leads. 2. Turn down motor shaft. 3. Build drive system. 4. Make bearings for drive system. 5. Build drive system. I wrote it twice for emphasis.

I knew I'd need every hour. I was so nervous I couldn't solder the wires, so I cheated a little bit and Mary calmly, quickly soldered them for me.

8:00 P.M. I jokingly asked Nigel Adams, the teaching assistant, "Are you going to keep the two-seventy machine shop open all night?" I half-wanted him to say no so I could get some sleep, half-wanted him to say yes so I could fight to the wire.

"Yes."

11:00 P.M. Fifteen people in the machine shop, not to mention ten in Tiny's shop and ten upstairs testing at the track; somebody brought in a boom box to keep us going through the gang-all-nighter. People sang along at the top of their lungs. You could just hear them over the whirr of the machines.

2:00 A.M. Both shafts done. Time to turn down the drive wheel to make it fit in the bearing.

3:30 A.M. Press fit drive wheel onto shaft. Make quick decision on drill sizes.

4:00 A.M. The wheel was on the shaft. If you make it to 4:00 A.M., the back of the night is broken. I met Eddy, the janitor who'd kept me from hurting myself the year before. "No time to talk, Eddy, I'll catch up with you later," I said.

6:30 A.M. My wheel's axle moved easily in the bearing I'd made by drilling a hole in a piece of black Teflon. There was hope. Time to clean up so nobody would know the thirty-five of us were there all night. What would the institute's insurance company say?

8:00 A.M. Doughnut and yogurt for breakfast.

8:15 A.M. Nap time.

November 18

My digital alarm clock said 12:50 and my test was at noon. *Aieeee!* Get into clothes in a second and run across campus. At my lab I couldn't read the clock. It looked like 11:30, but sort of like 12:30 and I couldn't tell the difference on three hours' sleep. "Calm down," I said to myself. "Call the time."

"At the tone the time will be 11:32 and 20 seconds."

1:30 P.M. Chet could be rough around the edges at times, but deep down inside he was a good guy. I asked Chet for help with the drive system.

This was one of the times his helpfulness showed through. "Just put it together like this and glue it with 5-minute epoxy," he said, and the two of us finished construction before 2:00.

3:00 P.M. I met Cindy Brooks at Lobdell. She had a tray with five sandwiches and she sat at my table.

"I was hoping you'd sit here," I said.

"Uh. Oh, gee, I just sit wherever." She was embarrassed. Next time don't come on so strong, I thought.

"Why so many sandwiches?" I asked.

"This is my food for the next thirty hours," she answered. "My preliminary round is tomorrow."

"Well, good luck. See you later," I said.

4:00 P.M. Drive system operational!

5:00 P.M. Testing on the track. The ladders didn't deploy the way they should. Go downstairs and put stops in. I kept threading the string wrong, and the sections jammed against each other. But it had potential. The string wound around the winch shaft just like on a real winch.

7:00 P.M. Trials, round one. Professor Blanco, another recitation instructor, said, "We just want to see something that has a good chance of working on Monday." More hope.

My first round. The ladder went out but as it extended it fell under its own weight. I went downstairs to make supports to catch it.

8:00 P.M. Make supports. How do I do it? I don't have time. I'm sick of making all these stupid decisions. Where are the drill bits? How long do I make the rods? *Aieee! Aargh!* I had to leave the shop, hit the wall, and stand against it and try not to burst into tears. The stupid thing almost works. If I don't make it to the finals all the time I've spent is wasted. Then . . . Calm down. All you have to do is drill a couple of holes and put some welding rod in. That'll do for tonight.

I did and it did. The ladder didn't make it to the scale but it went far enough to keep me in the arena of hope.

11:00 P.M. I walked down the stairs and encountered a youngish looking sophomore.

"Sniff, sniff."

"How's it going?" I asked, putting on my "tutor" hat.

"It doesn't work," and the sniffs became sobs.

"When's your trial?"

"Tomorrow. I've been up all night for the past three nights and it still doesn't work."

How I know how you feel, I thought. "I know what you're going through. If it's not possible to make the whole thing work, why don't you set some personal goals for the next few hours; say, try to get one or two subsystems to work."

"I've already gotten all I want to out of this stupid course."

Wimp.

Cindy was downstairs, outside the store, working next to a guy from the Aeronautical Engineering department.

"I can't believe how friendly people are in this department," she said.

"Maybe it's because we have wider career options than you aero guys," I said.

"Yeah, like making toasters instead of killer satellites," Cindy added. "Or toys. Wouldn't it be fun to work for Mattel Toys?"

For the first time in my life I thought I could work for Mattel Toys if I wanted to.

Friday, November 19

Rest day, and time to catch up on neglected details, e.g., paying bills.

11:00 P.M. Finished skating. The plaque in the athletic center rang true: "Not the quarry but the chase; not the laurel but the race" (Burgess, 1885).

'Round midnight. I spray-painted the ladder rungs silver. It would look good if nothing else.

November 20

This was supposed to be my day for cycling because my device was supposed to work, but Bligh suggested I change the design to a ladder with a hinge at the back and a wheelbarrow wheel on the front. That might solve the falling-under-its-own-weight problem.

So that means: 1. Break epoxy bonds on the beautiful base I built last weekend. 2. Build a wheel assembly for the ladder's front. It was a lot of work but my only chance. Professor Blanco once said that he spent seven years developing a product only to have it stolen by a German company. "You have to be able to change," he said. "You put in so much work and you think as you whine, 'But it will take so long to change . . . I did so much already . . . I don't want to change it.' But you have to be flexible, willing to forget about all the time you spent going one way, and then turn around and go another way. Otherwise, you will not survive."

4:00 P.M. Cindy's machine was a grappling hook launcher with a quality of construction second to none, even mine. "Are you going to make it?" I asked her.

"I hope so, but I'll be here almost all night tonight and tomorrow night," she said.

"It's a beautiful machine. You should really sprint to make it work. You've got forty-eight hours and then you can sleep," I said.

9:00 P.M. I had to figure out how to make the stupid wheel for the front of the stupid ladder, so I had to go upstairs. The guy who'd pulled up eight pounds the Sunday before was there with his grappling hook. He was talking to a Course Six geek.

"I think design is one of my strong points," he said.

Shut up, you nerd.

"Yours didn't work Thursday, did it? It looks good but it didn't work," he said as he watched me experiment with the heights of my ladder supports.

"It'll work," I said, and his chiding made it more imperative. This kind of thing is a good way to tell whether you're a Type A.

He continued his conversation with his friend. "My dad went to Harvard. I got in there but I didn't want to go there. I figured I'd be more of an engineer if I went to MIT. He was disappointed."

"My dad's MIT cubed," the other one said. "He works at Draper now. And you'll never guess where my mom went."

"Simmons?" the eight-pound guy said.

"You got it."

"Are you dating a Simmons woman now?" Mr. Grappling Hook asked.

"No, but I go to a lot of parties there."

"Not to change the subject, but this class makes you become like family with all the people you stay up all night with. It's kind of fun," G.H. said as I left the room.

1:00 A.M. Sunday morning. I've got to glue this wheel but I don't know how to make it. It's taking forever just to decide just how to just cut just one piece of wood. Besides, all the drills are unmarked and all the rulers and micrometers have been swiped so I'll have to eyeball everything. Besides, I want to go to sleep.

Fight it. Stay with it. Just make the thing work. Don't worry about how well. Just make it work. Just cut the pieces of wood and glue them together. Make the wheel on the belt sander. So what if it looks like something from "The Flintstones"; it's still better than nothing.

4:00 A.M. The epoxy was setting and the wheel looked good. The design had become me, and I had become the design.

November 21

2:00 P.M. Twenty-nine hours left before the contest in 26-100. Cindy said, "Did you hear about what happened at Harvard yesterday? At the football game, right after one of the touchdowns, a small pipe sprang out of the field. Then a balloon started inflating. It was black, and it had MIT written all over it. Finally it blew up and yellow smoke came out of it. It was on the front page of every newspaper in the country. It's got to be the hack of the century. Some of the people in two-seventy were in on it."

Score one for MIT.

7:00 P.M. Cindy looked at her grappling hook launcher. "I'm so depressed," she said. "It's not going to work. This thing keeps splitting and the bearings fall out."

"Why don't you try turning the wood 90 degrees so the bearing won't be trying to break it apart?" I suggested.

"That's a good idea. But I also need a rubber band for my drive system and there aren't any left like the one I had and I have to go work at the Pritchett snack bar and I'm exhausted."

"Look, you can't give up now. You'll never forgive yourself if you do," I said.

"I'll think about it."

10:30 P.M. I chatted with Ari about pay policy at MIT. I opened my desk drawer and found ten rubber bands of all sizes and shapes. I went to Pritchett to give them to Cindy but she was already off work. She was in her dorm room.

"I found these and thought they might help," I said. She looked through them and found one that was perfect.

"Oh wow. These are great. Thanks a lot."

1:10 A.M. Eighteen hours to launch. Don't quit! I wrote it in my lab book to keep me going. Two students wore Walkmen while they worked. I wondered how they could concentrate.

3:00 A.M. Started testing. Ten other people were testing their machines. Mine almost sprang up; the Flintstone wheel worked nicely, but there was too much friction in the rope and the motor stalled.

4:30 A.M. Cindy was at the test track.

5:00 A.M. Try different combinations of springs and string; I screwed up the threading of the string for the winch twice. Mr. eight-pound G.H. walked in.

"I thought there'd be nobody here," he said.

"Admit it; you just came here to gloat," I sneered.

6:30 A.M. Trials proceeded but the machine still didn't work. On the last trial I misloaded the springs. I had to hit something after that trial failed, and a box of computer cards was the closest thing. I tried to put them back in the box in order, and told myself to leave a note on the box some time after the contest. I left eight people in the testing room at 7:00 and gave the machine a coat of red spray paint.

November 22

Nineteen years ago John Fitzgerald Kennedy was assassinated. 10:30 A.M. The phone rang. It was Tom Bligh. "Is your machine working?" he asked. "I have to make the list for tonight, and if it doesn't work by 2:00 you won't be in the finals."

"If you hadn't called, it surely wouldn't have worked because I would have slept all day. I think I can make it work by 2:00." I went back to the track and forty people were there, making last-minute adjustments, testing, and making more last-minute adjustments. "Oh s–," "Oh f–," emanated at a frequency of about twenty times per minute.

I reran the aborted trial of the night before. It almost, almost reached the scale and Professor Blanco was impressed. Tom Bligh walked in, and another light bulb lit over my head. "How about I be one of the placebos?" I asked. "Let me have one more spring and my machine will work perfectly."

Since the contest was a one-on-one elimination like in a tennis tournament, some rounds would have an odd number of contestants, or some no-shows. Instead of letting anyone luck into the next round by a "bye," two-seventy tradition was to have a "placebo," an entry that would oppose the opponentless player. Like a sugar pill, the placebo was not an official contestant, but it could be effective.

"That's a good idea," Tom said. "Let's go for it."

4:00 P.M. "I talked with a lieutenant with an Irish last name about borrowing a fireman's helmet and raincoat for a contest at MIT. Can you think of who that would be?" I asked the fire chief.

"We're all Irishmen," he answered. "But come on up to the firehouse and we'll see what we can do for you."

6:45 P.M. Room 26-100 was already full to capacity, but I found one of the last aisle seats. I held my machine like a mother holds her baby. There were a lot of paper airplanes being thrown.

7:00 P.M. Professor Wilson quieted the crowd. "Before we start, I would like to squash an ugly rumor that has been circulating. There will not, I repeat, there will not be a large crimson balloon inflating on our stage tonight." A chill-breaking roar went about the crowd of six hundred. "We'll go one-on-one for as many rounds as it takes to get a winner. The first round will have forty contests, the second will have twenty, etc."

The first contest was between a miniature football player that kicked the weight onto the scale and a miniature truck that went under the cactus.

"Punt, punt, punt, punt," the audience shouted, and boom! the little football player kicked a film canister football for a field goal through the arms of the cactus and beat his opponent.

Eight contests later the opponent of the grappling hook guy didn't show. "We need the placebo," Professor Wilson said. I walked to the stage with my red and silver "fire truck" and my fireman's helmet and raincoat.

"Pla-cee-boh, pla-cee-boh, pla-cee-boh," the crowd chanted.

I walked to the starting ramp. I put my device down. I hooked up the power wire. Professor Wilson flipped on the power.

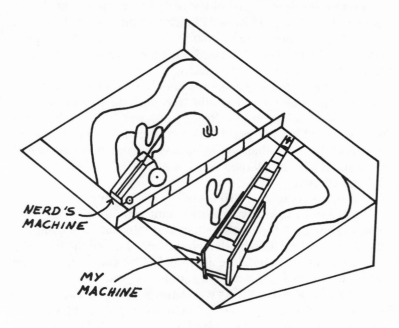

"Thawockkk!" My spring-loaded-Flintstone-wheel-fire-engine-ladder put a 1-ounce deflection on the scale in a tenth of a second. The grappling hook shot off to the side, missed the backboard, and Mr. G.H.'s truck was dead in the water.

I looked at Professor Wilson. Professor Wilson looked at me. "That was great, Pepper."

C H A P T E R

13

Is Suicide Painless?

November 21

I helped Griffith and Bligh and Wilson lift the pieces of the contest out of 26-100 after it was over and went back to my tutor apartment at 11:00. Boy, am I glad that's over, I thought. Now I can coast for a bit, maybe until Christmas. Ah, now I can sleep. Yes, a nice restful sleep for the next four weeks.

I walked past the Monopoly game on the third floor landing and they said, "Great ladder, Pepper. Wicked awesome."

Aw shucks, it was nothing.

"The engineering director of Campagnolo cycling components was in the audience. He's a buddy of Wilson," Dianne said. "Maybe you can hit him up for a job."

"Yeah, that'd be great. Maybe I'll try that."

Kvel, kvel, kvel.

I congratulated Cindy on her performance; her grappling hook made it to the semifinals.

"Oh, by the way," she said, "John Dorsey left a note under your door. He said it was important."

It's always something, isn't it. If it's not one thing it's another thing. Just like Gilda Radner's grandmother Nanna Rosanne Rosanna Danna always used to say.

"Please see me. Come by my apartment if you're in by 11:30."
Oh, no. Maybe they want me out and I'll have to start buying
groceries and paying rent again. I walked over to the Dorseys'
apartment in Crafts.

"Hi, John. What's up?"

"It's Steve Watson," John said. "He's having serious emotional troubles. He's depressed and lonely and already worried
about finals. The psychiatrist's office and one of the religious counselors have both talked to him, and they think he's close to round-
ing the bend. He's almost finished his undergraduate work in three
and a half years and he's not even nineteen yet. I think he's in
the process of realizing he doesn't have a life."

At nineteen, he was born some time between the Cuban missile crisis and Kennedy's assassination.

"Gee, that's terrible," I said. "Who's Steve Watson?"

"He's one of the students on your entry. Haven't you gotten
to know every one of them? That's part of your tutor job, you
know. Anyway, we'd like you to keep an eye on him, maybe
recruit some of the students in the entry on his hall to do the same,
have them be friendly to him, you be friendly to him, try to make
him feel that his last three and a half years were not a total emotional vacuum."

"I'll do what I can, John. And hey, I've done my best to get
to know everyone. Well, maybe not by name, but by face anyway.
I mean before every study break, I put the signs up and then go
and knock on every door. Can I help it if this kid is always at his
lab?"

"No, you can't, and I'm sure you're doing your best. The main
thing to do is to take care of Steve. I've been housemaster here
for three years and there hasn't been a suicide yet, and if I can
help it there won't be any for as long as I'm here."

"Ditto for me, John. Do you have any suggestions for how I
should talk to him?"

"Just try to be natural; don't let on that you're keeping an
eye on him. Try taking an interest in things that are interesting to
him. I heard he likes to play chess. Maybe you can have a game
with him or encourage the other students to do the same."

It's really too bad that I, a paid staffer, have to be paid to be
nice to this kid, I thought. Nobody else has the time or the incli-
nation. There are loners at every school but MIT is a magnet for

them. And what do you get when you put eight loners on a dormitory floor? Eight very lonely people.

December 11

After a restful Thanksgiving, and after several attempts at finding him during the week and a half following the vacation, I met Steve. There was a noteboard on his door that said, "Should I kill myself?" and beneath it there was a Yes column and a No column. There were seven hash marks under No and two under Yes. Somebody'd written, "Jump, jump" to the side of one of the Yes marks. On the bottom someone else's hand had written, "Life's a bitch, and then you die." It must have made Steve happy to know that people cared.

Steve had pale skin, a receding case of acne, a little brown beard on his chin, and a mustache. He was slim, tall, and quiet. Of course he was quiet; that's why he didn't know anyone.

"Hi," I said when he opened the door. "I'm Pepper White, the tutor. I haven't had a chance to meet everyone yet, but I'm trying to make sure I meet everyone and let you all know that there will be a study break every night during exam week. And if you ever want to come by and chat, feel free to knock on my door."

"They put you up to this, didn't they?" he said.

"Up to what? Say, is that a chess set there? I like to play chess, too. Maybe we can have a match sometime."

The depression must have weakened his resistance, the cynicism that he'd absorbed from the environment. "Sure, that would be nice," he said. He cracked a smile, apparently thankful for any offer of friendship.

"How about tomorrow at 1:30 in the afternoon?" I asked.

"OK."

Dianne started bowling with a real bowling ball and empty two-liter ginger ale bottles as the pins. Thunk! The ball hit the heavy oak door next to Steve's. Three of the ten pins went down.

"Hey, can you keep it down there?" I said.

Dianne retorted, "How am I going to get any better at this if I don't practice?"

"Say, Dianne, do you know Steve? He's a math and physics major. You've taken some physics classes, haven't you?"

"Oh, yeah, sure, OK," Dianne said, quickly figuring out what I was hinting. "Aren't you in my relativity class, Steve? That Professor French, he can really lecture, can't he? I'm having a little trouble with the material on the Schwarzschild radius for black holes. Could you help me conceptualize it?"

"It's a pretty easy concept," Steve said, his confidence growing at the chance to explain something to someone. "The mathematics is a little hairy—I mean, it's a singular point solution for a differential equation—but the idea is that as you approach a black hole, and you come within a certain distance of it in the space-time continuum, there's no turning back."

"You mean you sort of get sucked into it, like in a sci-fi movie?" Dianne asked.

"Yeah, that's it," Steve said. "Did you understand the problem about the twins, one of whom leaves earth and travels at close to the speed of light and he comes back sixty years later, and his brother has aged sixty years but he hasn't?"

"Sure," Dianne said, "that's special relativity, and I think I've got a handle on that."

Dianne started to explain the problem, and I figured she had Steve covered for the time being so I excused myself and said, "I'll see you at 1:30 tomorrow for that chess game, OK, Steve?"

December 12

Sunday. Steve was still asleep at 1:30 in the afternoon. When you're depressed, all you want to do is sleep, and when you're at MIT, you have very little time to sleep, and therefore all you want to do is sleep and your body feels the same as when you're depressed and it's hard to tell whether you're depressed or just tired from all the work. I knocked repeatedly and waited outside. Come on, Steve, answer the door.

He finally answered after about five minutes. He was groggy-eyed, and said, "Oh, yeah, I forgot about our chess game. Can we do it some other time? I'm going to play a guy in Runkle at 2:00. Thanks for waking me up, though. I might have missed my match otherwise."

"Sure, there's no hurry for our match. Have a good match with your partner," I answered, glad that he had a friend.

December 13

Monday evening at Lobdell's cafeteria Steve sat down by himself at the table next to me, then saw me, and picked up his tray and brought it over to my table. "How's the studying going?" I asked.

"Oh, pretty good. Thursday and Friday are going to be rough, though. I have a final on Thursday morning, a final on Thursday afternoon, and a final on Friday morning."

"Whoa. Three in a row. I know how hard that is. The same thing happened to me a year ago. How'd your chess game go yesterday?" I asked.

"Oh, pretty good, but it didn't last all that long. I checkmated him in twenty-three moves, a little over half an hour."

So much for camaraderie. Steve ate fast, faster than I, like he was nervous thinking about his exams. So fast that little pieces of bread got caught in his beard. He cleaned his plate before I finished my salad. He seemed tense, and I didn't want to keep him from his work, so I said, "Hey, don't let me keep you. If you need to get back to studying, feel free to head back to the library or wherever."

He looked hurt, like I was trying to get rid of him, when in fact he probably wanted to sit and chat about anything but exams until the cafeteria closed. But he didn't know how to communicate that verbally, and I was a little too slow to pick up on it from his body language.

He picked up his tray and said meekly, "Uh, yeah, maybe I better get back to my studying." By then it was too awkward to ask him to sit back down, so I let him go.

December 14

Tuesday evening, after Day 1 of exams. Two seventy had a token final exam, a piece of cake after the contest, and Bligh gave me an A. That, plus the A in David Miller's System Dynamics and Controls for the summer, canceled my two C's from the first term, making my overall average a respectable B. If I could keep up the improving trend, maybe by the time the doctoral qualifying exams (a.k.a. qualifiers) rolled around they'd write off my first term to being my first term, and I'd have a shot at M-I-T, P-H-D, M-O-N-E-Y.

I relaxed in my tutor apartment living room, read through the Mechanical Engineering department newsletter in a leisurely fashion, and saw an intriguing item.

"EE, ME, Physics students wanted to participate in Perpetual Motion Machine Debunking Contest for national television show. Three individuals will be selected to compete against a three-person team from Berkeley. Contest will be held in Berkeley in January; round trip air fare and accommodations will be provided. Apply in no more than 1,000 words to Chedd Angier Production Company, Watertown."

Berkeley is a lot more pleasant than Boston in January. It's worth a shot. It would be a really nice entry in the old résumé if I'm selected. There's no minimum application length specified, and I'm pretty sure I won't get it anyway, so I'll crank something out in five minutes.

Why I Want to Be a TV Star

1. I want to be rich.
2. I want to be famous.
3. I want to be a professor at MIT and this might help.
4. Ever since I was a child I've had a fascination with perpetual motion machines and this would be a dream come true for me.
5. I already know the answer. It's impossible to prove something's a perpetual motion machine because however long it runs there's always going to be some more perpetuity during which you can't know whether it will still run because you aren't there yet.

December 19

Well, the job is done; we made it. Steve's made it through exam week. He'll be home in no time and I can really relax. 6:10 P.M. The phone rang.

"Hello, this is Mr. Watson; I'm Steve's father. He was supposed to be home this evening and he wasn't on the plane. Professor Dorsey is out but he gave me your number. Can you try to find my son?" His voice was shaky, as if he feared the worst.

"I'm sure he's fine, sir. I saw him yesterday and he seemed fine. I'll go and check his room; then I'll put my laundry in and then I'll check his room again. I'll try to find him and have him give you a call."

The tally mark was up to three yeses and eight nos. I knocked on the door. "Hey, Steve, are you in there?" I knocked on the door harder. "Hey, Steve, come on man; open up the door. Your father called and he's worried about you."

No answer. I went to put my laundry in the washer.

I saw that Steve's light was on when I walked back from the East Campus laundry. Every time I'd checked on him before and he wasn't there, the light was off. If the light was on he had to be in there.

Knock knock knock. "Come on, Steve. Quit playing games, man." My heart began to beat fast, like when the pressure built in the tank for my experiments. Knock knock knock. No answer. The Dorseys were gone for the weekend so I went to the lab to call one of the deans.

I caught Dean Robbins just before he left for a Christmas party. "Yes," he said, "it sounds like it could be an emergency. Maybe you better call Bill Thompson and have him come over. He's the on-campus dean on call. Here's his number."

Dean Thompson was also on his way out to a Christmas party. "I'll be right over. Why don't you go ahead and call the campus police? They've got the master keys and can open up his room."

I met the campus policemen, two of them, in front of Steve's room. One of them pulled out a ring with about a hundred keys on it and said, "It should be one of these."

My heart continued to pump like it pumped in the cell. The campus policeman tried one key. It didn't work. Another. Another. Ten keys. Fifteen. Number 16 was the right one. God, I hope this kid's alive.

The light was still on. Steve was lying on his bed. An empty half-gallon of Jack Daniels was on the floor next to the bed, on top of a stack of *Penthouse* magazines. The campus policeman felt for Steve's pulse.

Steve woke up. He was glassy-eyed, semicoherent, in the depths of the depths. "What . . . the . . . hell . . . is . . . going on?" he asked. The campus policeman suggested that I talk to Steve alone for a while.

"Look, Steve, your father's worried sick about you. You didn't answer your door, so I didn't have any choice but to call the campus police. We just wanted to make sure you were all right."

"I'm all right, all right," he said a little more coherently. "Who the hell do you think you are busting into my room like that?"

Dean Thompson arrived before I had a chance to answer. "What's going on, Steve?" he said firmly, like the rock of Gibraltar, yet with some compassion. "And what do you want to do about it?"

"These people just broke into my room. I want to see their search warrant," Steve said.

Dean Thompson asked to see me in the hall. "Listen," he said, "I'm going to go call the psychiatrist that he's been talking to, and I want you to go get Steve's home phone number and we'll have a talk with his father."

Dean Thompson went back into Steve's room. "Mr. White and I are going to be away for a few minutes. For your own safety, I'm requesting that the campus policeman stay nearby while we're gone."

Steve slammed the door. It was locked when we returned. The campus policeman opened it again. Steve was on the phone with his father.

"Steve, I'd like to talk with your father," Dean Thompson said. "Will you hand me the phone?"

Steve hung up. "No."

"Give me the phone, Steve," Dean Thompson said.

"No," more defiantly.

Dean Thompson put two hands on the phone and pulled it away from Steve's body but Steve held on to it and fell toward Dean Thompson. Steve regained his balance, tried to pull the phone back, but his hands slipped and the screw under the case cut his thumb and he screamed.

"You cut me. You cut me. I'll sue you," he said and then put his thumb in his mouth to suck away the drops of blood.

"Do you have that number, Pepper?" Dean Thompson asked, and he called Mr. Watson.

"Yes, Mr. Watson, this is Bill Thompson at MIT. Steve's upset but I don't think he's in any danger of hurting himself." He paused and turned to Steve. "What do you want us to do, Steve?"

"I want you to leave me alone. Twenty-four hours from now I'll be a product of this place, not a problem for it," Steve said, a little mellowed. I gave him a bandage from my tutor's first-aid kit.

"What would you like us to do, Mr. Watson?" Dean Thompson asked. "Yes, we can arrange for a taxi to take him to the airport tomorrow if you'd like. And for now, Mr. White will spend some time with him. Both Mr. White and I have Christmas parties to go to, so we'll be busy for the next two or three hours, but Mr. White will check in with Steve after he returns from his party. Is that all right with you, Steve?"

"Huh? Oh. Yeah, sure," he answered from his bed.

Dean Thompson finished the phone call with Mr. Watson and asked to talk to me in the hall again.

"Just chat with him. Maybe play a game of chess with him. Try to cheer him up a little bit."

"OK, sir, I'll do my best," I answered, and Dean Thompson left.

Pawn to king four. Steve was black; I was white.

"So what's the point of staying here?" he said rhetorically.

"Well, you've invested a lot of time in your studies, and you're almost done, and your parents have invested a lot of money in your studies—I mean they could have bought a vacation home for cash for what they've spent to put you through here—and you're just at the beginning of being able to put your knowledge to use."

"Right. So what's the point of putting the knowledge to use?"

"To do good mathematics research or to write efficient computer programs. To extend the frontiers of knowledge."

"And what's the point of extending the frontiers of knowledge?"

"So that products can be developed to improve the quality of life."

"Oh, you mean like video games and high-definition television, I suppose. Is that what you mean by improving quality of life?"

Maybe I need a swig of that whiskey, too.

"Well, we're getting out of my realm of expertise. Maybe you should talk to a minister or your psychiatrist about it."

"I've been talking to both, and they totally contradict each other and it just makes me more confused and depressed. You want to know something else? You know how some people dream in black and white, and some people dream in color? You know what I dream in?"

"No, what?"

"Equations. It's like there's no room left in my conscious or my subconscious for anything else. There's no relief from it. There's no escape. I Hate This Fucking Place."

"I know how you feel. But you've made it through. I'm sure you did great on your exams. You've got a great career ahead of you. Just hang in there—oh, excuse me, poor choice of words. Just try to relax for another day, go home, and you'll forget this place and feel relaxed and well-educated in just a few days."

"Checkmate," he said. "Twelve moves. You did pretty well."

I returned from the party at 11:20. I brought Steve a pint of chocolate Häagen-Daz and a package of Mint Milanos. That combination had always helped to lift my spirits. I figured we'd watch "Saturday Night Live" together while we split the goodies.

There was a clipping from *Penthouse* on his door. In bold print from a magazine article: "When somebody screws you up, you have ways to make him pay. I'd be more specific but that would take the fun out of it when I do it."

Knock knock knock. "Steve, are you in there?" Knock knock. "Steve, it's me, Pepper; I brought you some ice cream and cookies." Knock knock.

No answer. Oh no. We shouldn't have left him by himself. But he's an adult; he's a college graduate; we had to give him his space, accord him his rights.

"Hello, Dean Thompson, it's Pepper here. There's a strange note on his door and he doesn't answer when I knock."

"Call the CPs again," he said. "I'll be right over."

I called the CPs, put the Häagen-Daz in the freezer, went downstairs, and knocked again. Still no answer. High blood pressure time again. Hurry up, CPs; he may have just a few breaths of air left.

The CPs were quicker this time, and they knew which was the right key. The light was on but the room was empty, as was a second half-gallon of Jack Daniels by Steve's bed. Dean Thompson arrived. "We should never have left him alone," he said. "Sergeant, call the dispatcher and put the force on alert. Cover the tops of all the stairwells, the roofs of the Green Building and Macgregor. Have two cars patrol Mem. Drive and the Harvard and Longfellow bridges. Pepper, you know what Steve looks like— why don't you drive with the sergeant here. I'll walk up and down the sidewalk on this side of the Charles."

There was a plan for this contingency.

I drove with the sergeant. We were both quiet. I remembered failures: giving up physics, not keeping up in bicycle races, leaving Stephanie, two C's in one term at MIT. I had a life, though. That always kept me going.

The sergeant pulled a U-turn by the Hyatt. "You know any prayers, kid?" he asked.

"I learned the Twenty-third Psalm when I was a kid," I said.

"Why don't you try saying it to yourself, not out loud. I'll do the same thing."

"OK."

There was no one beside the still, frozen, snow-covered waters of the Charles, no one on the footpath above the seawall. We drove back and forth slowly, stopped occasionally to look out across the ice. My pulse rate went down, but my chest and my stomach felt weightless, like when a roller coaster plunges. I tried to remember the words to the psalm.

On the seventh drive past the sailing pavilion, the dispatcher said over the radio, "We found him. He's all right. He's been in the TV room at the student center the whole time."

The sergeant and I drove to the student center, where we met Steve, Dean Thompson, and the CPs. "Saturday Night Live" was almost over.

"Steve, we're going to have you sleep in the infirmary tonight, under observation. Then the campus police will help you pack and drive you to the airport tomorrow morning," Dean Thompson said authoritatively.

"You know, Steve," I said to him as tutorly as I could muster, "you've caused a lot of grief for a lot of people tonight."

"This was my last chance to even up the score."

Sunday Morning

Dean Thompson called at ten. "He's on the plane. The CPs had no problem taking him and his things to the airport. They took him all the way to his seat and watched the door of the plane close, so we're sure he's on his way."

Another product of MIT has been shipped. But do you have a receipt?

C H A P T E R

14

Perpetual Motion

January 2, 1983

"Yes, this is he," I said.

"We'd like you to go to California as one of MIT's contestants in the perpetual motion machine contest on January 20," the producer said. "We received thirty applications for the three spots, and everyone here at Chedd Angier Productions agreed to accept you sight unseen. Your application had real chutzpah."

Yippee. A free trip to California. Nationwide television exposure that any struggling young comic would kill for. If I play my cards right, go to aerobics class, pump some iron for the next two weeks, and take charisma lessons, maybe some New York or Hollywood producer will see the show and say, "This kid's great. Let's sign him up for a vapid sitcom." Thirty K per episode sure beats an engineer's $30K per year.

"Thanks a lot. What were the other applications like that made mine stand out so much?"

"Most of the others submitted six-page notarized essays on perpetual motion, with figures and drawings, and reference letters from professors. They all looked the same after a while. But yours stood out. We've also selected two others on the basis of our interviews. One of them came to the interview wearing a tuxedo and a red carnation. He's quite an accomplished trombone player."

"That sounds like a friend of a friend, a guy I chat with in the infinite corridor every month or two. Is it Dan Wagner?"

"Yes, that's him. And the other one is a senior in Mechanical Engineering, Tim Neuberger. He's extremely bright. I picked him because he said the most interesting intellectual experience he'd had was reading the Talmud. I think the three of you will make a good team."

January 3

Literature review. Perpetual Motion. I referred to my notebook from Gyftopoulos's class. Problem set 3, Problem 1: "Prove the Impossibility of a Perpetual Motion Machine of the First Kind (IPMM1)—4 out of 10 points." Problem 2: "Prove the Impossibility of a Perpetual Motion Machine of the Second Kind (IPMM2)—2 out of 10 points." These will be no help. I remembered asking Professor Gyftopoulos whether the toy bird that you put next to a glass of water would qualify as a perpetual motion machine. When its beak goes into the water it's pulled down by the capillary action of the water going into the wick on the beak. Then it rocks back and forth, with seemingly no energy input.

Yes, Professor Gyftopoulos had said, you are right in saying that is not a perpetual motion machine, because you have perpetual motion but no transfer of energy out of the system.

We haven't seen a perpetual motion machine, something that puts out more energy than goes into it. Since we haven't seen a PMM, we'll say that one can't exist, because energy, whatever that is, is conserved. Since energy is conserved, there can be no perpetual motion machines of the first kind.

A perpetual motion machine delivers power perpetually, with no energy input. A PMM of the first kind "purports to deliver more energy from a falling or turning body than is required to restore the device to its original state." An example of this is a closed-loop waterwheel and pump joined together.

If the waterwheel generated more power than the pump needed to push the water back up to the top of the waterwheel, the waterwheel could generate power perpetually without any fuel. But despite many attempts, no one has devised a system that achieves that. If they had, the Persian Gulf would be no more than a pleasant vacation spot.

An article in Encyclopaedia Britannica describes the various attempts at perpetual motion: Edward Somerset, second marquis of Worcester (1601–1667), produced a machine around 1638 or 1639 and operated the device for Charles I and his court. In the same century, the Dutch physicist W. J. Gravesand inspected the machine of the Frenchman Offyreus and was impressed by its construction, although he was not allowed to inspect the interior of the machine. Gravesand wrote about the device in a lengthy and detailed letter to Newton.

The simple drawings in the encyclopaedia looked primitive compared to our high-technology devices today, but they looked just as sophisticated as many of the two-seventy design contest machines, including my own.

January 4

I asked Chet Yeung for permission to take the time off to go to the contest, plus a week of vacation time to bicycle in the Bay Area, to lose some weight for the cameras.

He asked abruptly, "Why'd they pick you?"

"Gee, Chet, I don't know; maybe they wanted somebody on the team to make the other two guys look smart."

"Yeah, well, I guess you can have the time off. I should go along on that, though. If they really wanted to have a team that would solve it, they'd have someone like me along," Chet said.

I wondered whether he'd posed as a graduate student and put his name in the hat for the team selection. I answered, "They only want students on this thing. Okay, I know you *look* young enough to be a student, but you'd have an unfair advantage. You're gifted."

"Yeah, well, just try not to embarrass the institute by what you say on TV," Chet said. "Let the other guys do most of the talking."

Thank you, Chet, for that vote of confidence.

"Oh yeah, but before you go I want you to do some runs of a computer model I've put together to make sure the RCM simulates the stroke of a real diesel engine. I think the guys who worked on the machine before us may have messed up the assembly of the snubbing chamber," Chet said.

I left his office and went to talk to Professor Gyftopoulos, to ask him for reference materials on perpetual motion machines.

"That's very interesting. I wonder why they picked you," he said. "They liked my application."

"Well, look for places where irreversibility may occur in the machine. There will certainly be friction, and there will certainly be an energy supply within the machine. Do what you can to locate these."

Greene was a little more positive. "Congratulations," he said. "That's quite an honor, being picked as a representative from MIT."

I'm glad somebody thinks so.

"You'll have some tough competition from Berkeley, though. But it's a lovely area. I hope you're giving yourself time to take in a few of the sights."

"Yes, I'll cycle there for about a week. Do you have any suggestions as to how to think about the problem?"

"Yes, well, look for where there is degradation in the quality of the energy. Most of the attempts at perpetual motion machines over the ages have included sections where energy is removed from the process and other sections where it's put back into the process. The problem is that wherever you have energy flow, in real life you have entropy increase. You remember that with your cycling example."

"Thanks for your help, sir," I said. "I'll let you know when the show is on."

January 6

More salt mines. Chet showed me his model for the motion of the piston of the RCM and made a copy of the program on the lab's Digital (Ken Olsen, '50) VAX computer. Chet redrew the machine for me on a piece of green and white computer paper.

"So you see, the idea in modeling the motion of the shaft is to write Newton's first law for the moving shaft; at every point in its motion, the sum of the forces on the shaft will equal the mass of the shaft assembly times its acceleration at that moment," he said. "We got the driving air pressure from the tank, and then we got the pressure of the gas in the cylinder pushing back on the combustion chamber's piston, and then we got the back piston dragging along and slowing the whole thing down, depending on how much space there is."

I remembered Greene's balloon problem, how I'd made the balloon expand in just one direction.

Then I looked at the RCM diagram again and translated it into the language of the model.

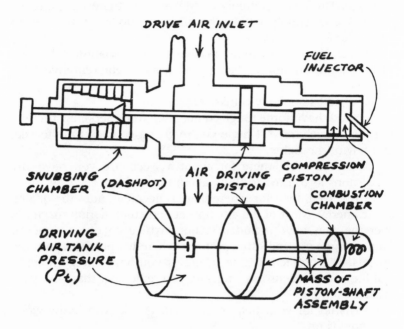

Chet continued, "So what I want you to do is take the machine apart in the back and determine the ring geometries available and the snubbing piston diameter. Then I want you to change the order of the rings in the computer until the forward motion of the shaft matches the motion of the shaft in a real engine."

I wondered why or whether it made much difference how the compression profile took place or whether Chet's point was, This is something we can control to make the experiment match real life better and therefore more useful, less questionable when we present a paper in Detroit, so we have to do it. It can be done; therefore, we do it. But there was another lesson to be learned here.

My task was to take the machine apart, take the dimensions of the centerless disks, input the dimensions in the computer, and play with the order of the centerless disks until the piston moved through them as required, all on the computer. The alternative was trial and error—i.e., take the machine apart and put it together again and test it until we achieved the same result.

Chet had set up the program so I only had to input a list of the ring diameters and see what happened. I took the RCM apart and put it back together ten times in an hour, just by changing the order of the ring diameters in the computer's input statement. In the real world, engineers do this kind of thing all the time because it is much cheaper to pay an engineer to set up a computer model and hack away at it than to pay a machinist to hack away at blocks of metal.

I hacked for a few more hours that Friday but I made no progress. On Monday morning Chet said, "Don't worry about that problem; I finished it over the weekend."

"Why, Chet?" I asked. "I thought that was my job. You let me start it; why didn't you let me finish it?"

"I didn't want you to waste any more time on it. We gotta put the machine back together and do some firings before the consortium meeting in March. What with your week off and the next semester coming up we gotta make a lotta progress in January," he answered.

This was Chet's style. The micromanager. Chet was stuck between a rock and a hard place in having me as a student. On the one hand, the point of my working on the experiment was for me to be trained as an engineer. On the other, perhaps more significant, hand, the point of my working on the experiment was to obtain results, publish papers, promote Chet to full professorship, and retain the sponsors' income stream.

So when in my lumbering way I took too long to do things because I hadn't done them before and my thought processing wasn't as lean and mean as Chet's, he'd step in and help me. Or sometimes, like over the weekend, he'd jump in and do the task himself.

That afternoon, Nick and I reassembled the ring assembly according to Chet's specifications. I felt the way Nick must have always felt, carrying out someone else's design, not knowing why it was that way, not being mentioned in the paper but knowing it was still better than working on an assembly line.

Nick lowered the chain fall into place and I put the twenty bolts through the holes and into the threaded holes in the machine.

I said to him, "I wonder whether anyone likes this kind of work."
"Whadaya mean by that, Cap'n?"
"Well, do you like this kind of work?"
"Of course not. I gotta do it. It's a living," Nick answered.
"That's what I mean. I wonder whether communists like this kind of work."
"Don't talk that way, Cap'n. Communists are bad; they don't believe in God."

January 14

The guy in the seat next to me on the night flight to San Francisco International was an astrophysicist. He had a storybook life: he spent half his time doing research and teaching at Harvard; the other half he spent working on laser-induced fusion at Lawrence Livermore Laboratory.

"Look at those stars," he said. "Just look at them. You could almost touch them from up here, they look so close."

I switched places with him and couldn't see much of anything, what with the glare from the cabin lights.

"You know," he said, "it's really a strange thing we're doing right now. We're inside an aluminum tube, traveling in the air, six miles above the ground. It's such an odd thing. I wonder what future generations will think about it."

January 18

I bicycled from Berkeley to Livermore to meet my friend from Belgium who'd been working for U.S. Windpower for the year and a half that I'd been at MIT.

"What makes them work well," he said, "is that the wind blows steadily through the pass here for about eight months of the year. Unfortunately, January isn't one of the months, so none of them is turning for you."

"Why does the wind blow one way only?" I asked him.

"The Sacramento Valley is like a giant solar panel. During the day, it heats up, and the air rises. As the hot air rises, it has to be replaced by air from somewhere. The air from somewhere is cool air from the ocean. It funnels its way through the pass here."

I remembered Greene's balloon problem. The ocean was like

the higher-pressure tank. The valley was the balloon; the Alta Mira Pass was the pipe between the tank and the balloon.

January 20

Contest day. Dan and Tim and I received our syllabus for the day. Dan wore his tuxedo and red carnation, Tim wore his normal plaid shirt and slightly short (i.e., high-water) corduroys. I wore the MITAA (MIT Athletic Association) sweatshirt that Cindy lent me, blue jeans, and Don's lab jacket. The red of the sweatshirt would show up well on the video camera, according to an article in *The Globe*.

Berkeley's team had one MIT physics undergrad, who was doing his Ph.D. in astrophysics, plus two Berkeley undergrad computer jocks. From the moment he opened his mouth, it was evident that it was Berkeley's MIT guy who would pose the biggest problem for us.

The contest would consist of first an introduction and toss of a coin by Dr. Glenn Seaborg, Nobel chemistry laureate, who is best known for his work on isolating and identifying elements that are heavier than uranium (plutonium, for example). Then Dr. David Jones, the machine's British inventor and acclaimed self-promoter, would present the machine briefly. We would have a chance to ask him questions, and then we would break into our respective hotel rooms for discussions. At that point, we could request any test equipment and would have private access to the machine twice. At the end of the day we would present our results, and Dr. Jones would decide the winner.

Before the camera started rolling, we sat in the room with the motionless machine. Dr. Jones gave it a good hard push, at what looked like its full speed. It stopped in about half a minute. "Umm. Excuse me, ladies and gentlemen, but I think I'll need a few minutes alone with the machine."

Everyone left the room except Dr. Jones. Twenty minutes later we went back in. The machine was a spinning bicycle wheel mounted in a rectangular steel frame. At the top of the frame were two cigarette-box-size boxes with what looked like potential solar cells, and at the bottom of the frame was a larger box with two 3-inch metal disks on top. On either side of the wheel's hub, a rod extended down to a separate disk that moved up and down opposite the disk on the lower box. Copper tubes also aimed at

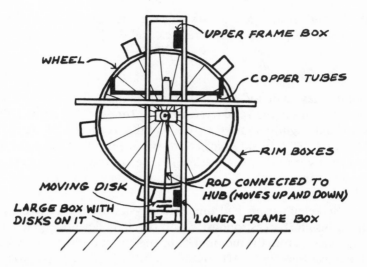

the rim, set at such an angle that perhaps they could be blowing the wheel around.

Before the toss, the sound guy said, "I'm getting some static on the mike near the machine." This was a hint.

Team MIT won the toss, so we asked the first question. Tim asked, or rather told, Dr. Jones, "If I go into outer space, and I throw a rock from a space capsule, it will keep going at its initial speed more or less forever. But that's not a perpetual motion machine, because the rock doesn't deliver power outside itself. Your machine doesn't deliver power outside its own motion, so in the thermodynamic definition of perpetual motion machines of the first and second kind, your device fails."

Dr. Jones was taken aback. Dr. Seaborg nodded his head up and down slightly. The camera caught it all.

Dr. Jones answered, "The fact remains that this machine moves continually. I challenge you to define why."

"How much did it cost?" I asked. If we had an upper bound on the materials cost, we could eliminate propulsive methods such as a micronuclear reactor in the lower box or a microwave receiver from a transmitter elsewhere in the room.

"A few hundred dollars in equipment and hundreds of hours of labor and aggravation on my part," Dr. Jones answered to laughter from the studio audience.

The MIT physics guy from Berkeley's team asked, "How long have you run it continually?"

"It's been on display in a number of museums over the past several months, for periods as long as three weeks," he answered.

My bicycling eye came in handy. "Is the wheel out of true for a reason?" I asked.

"No. It's just the stress of shipping," Dr. Jones said.

One of the non-MIT Berkeley guys asked, "How much does the whole thing weigh?" What a stupid question, I thought.

"About 100 pounds."

We broke for our respective hotel rooms.

Tim started our discussion. "I think he was kind of ticked off at my first question to him. We're going to have to come up with an explanation that's really right if we're going to win this thing. That microphone interference from the sound guy was a golden hint, though. There must be some electromagnetic field interaction in some of those boxes. Let's ask for a transistor radio. When I was a kid I used to take my transistor radio, tune it between channels, turn up the volume, and put it next to things like my father's stereo, the back of the refrigerator, my mother's hair dryer. It drove my mother crazy, but I could sort of track what was happening in the air by the noise the radio made."

"OK," Dan said. "I'll write that as one of the items of test equipment we want. What about the tubes?"

"They could be blowing on the rim and providing enough force to overcome the friction in the wheel's bearings," I said. "A friend of mine in Belgium smoked a lot and we used his cigarettes to see what air flow was doing, so maybe we should put cigarettes and matches down on the list, too."

"Check," Dan said. "Let's first do a power analysis on the wheel. We know that before Jones made the machine work continuously, it took about half a minute for it to come to a stop. That means that when the power isn't being tranferred from wherever to the wheel, the energy of the wheel will be dissipated in about 30 seconds. We can calculate the energy stored in the flywheel effect of the movement of the wheel, and divide by 30 seconds, to find the order of magnitude of the power required to overcome the air resistance and the friction of the bearings."

Good idea, I thought. Dan had gone to MIT as an undergrad, too. He ran the calculation quickly, and the power requirement was about 0.05 of a watt. A fairly small battery or set of batteries would keep that wheel going for a few weeks.

"OK; 0.05 watt is the power required to overcome the friction. Let's figure out whether air jets coming out of the copper tubes could provide that much power. Pepper, you're the fluids whiz. Got any ideas how to calculate that?" Dan asked me.

"Well, I know how to calculate how much power is coming out of the tubes, how that relates to the speed of the air coming out of the tubes. And I'll throw in a 10 percent efficiency factor; i.e., one-tenth of the energy of the air jet coming out of the tube might actually go into turning the wheel. That's as reasonable an assumption as any we can make in the next hour."

I wrote down the equations with lots of wavy equals signs, meaning "approximately equal"; I'd learned something in Shapiro's class. "So that means that for the air jet to keep the wheel going, the air speed would have to be about 3 feet per second. If we put a cigarette next to the tube, the other 90 percent of the air should blow the smoke pretty visibly."

"That's good," Dan said. He was sort of taking on the role of our team leader, with Tim the really smart guy, and me sort of smart and sort of creative.

"Now let's consider other ways this thing can turn," Dan said.

"We need to determine whether the plates are driving the wheel or the wheel is driving the plates via the connecting rods," I suggested. "How about asking for a magnifying glass, and I'll get a good close look at the connecting rod at the wheel. If the wheel is driving the rod, the connecting pin will be on the bottom of its sleeve at the top of its stroke, and at the top of its sleeve at the bottom of the stroke. The opposite will be true if the rod is driving the wheel." I'd learned that trick from Professor Heywood's discussion of bearings in engines. "We'll need a magnifying glass, plus a spotlight for me to be able to see anything."

"Sounds good," Tim said. "We should also check out whether the thing gets any power from the lights in the room. Those little disks on the boxes on the frame could be solar cells."

I added, "Yeah, if that's how it works, then we can count revolutions of the wheel in a given time, then shut the lights out in the room for a minute or so, and then count revolutions of the wheel in the same time. If it slows down, we'll know that it's getting its power from the lights in the room."

Dan answered, "Right, let's do that test. It's a little on the obvious side, though; I mean, I bet he put those solar-panel-looking things on there just to fool us. But we should check it for completeness."

Tim said, "What about air currents? Maybe it's placed in the room so that the air from the air-conditioning is going up on one side of it and down on the other side of it. Or maybe the air currents from the heat of the bright lights hit the boxes on the rim so that the thing keeps turning. It's sort of a long shot, but hey, we're brainstorming here, aren't we? One wild and crazy idea could lead to a good one."

"We could put a big plastic bag over the thing," I said. "If they let us do that, and the air currents were driving it, it'd stop then. I mean that's within the rules, right? We wouldn't touch it. Barring that, how about we get some ice, a hair dryer, and an iron. We can move the ice and the hair dryer and the iron around so that we can try to break up the steady air flow that might be pushing the boxes around in such an orderly direction. We can introduce some entropy into the system that way."

"Okay," Dan said. "I'll put 'large plastic bag' on the list. We'll need some string to hold it up, and some scotch tape to seal it, and maybe some rubber bands just for good measure. Are there any other things we should ask for?"

"A large hammer," Tim said, "and a pepperoni pizza."

"No seriously, though. Are there any other mechanisms we need to test?" Dan asked.

"If the disks below are driving the thing, and they're running on some kind of capacitive repulsion principle—you know, like when you rub two balloons on your sweater and they repel each other—then we need to test that somehow. I'm not a physicist, though, and electromagnetic theory is why, so I don't know how to check that," I said.

Tim replied, "I remember something in freshman Physics, eight oh two, about an induced current in a piece of metal between two capacitive plates. If the plates are working as a capacitor—i.e., they store electric charges—and we put a sheet of copper in between the two plates, as the amount of charge varies in the plates of the capacitor, the amount of charge of the copper should vary, and we should be able to measure a current."

"Good," Dan answered. "So for that test we'll need a ring stand to hold the copper sheet, plus a current meter to see whether we can measure any current."

The show's producer entered and we gave him our list; Dan read it off the legal pad, while the camera caught him in profile.

"You'll be able to do your testing in about half an hour," he said. "Maybe now would be a good time for you to get some lunch."

"That's a good idea," I said. "Hello, room service? Three cheeseburgers and fries, please."

While we waited for the food, we chatted a little more about the machine, but then Tim suggested we needed some entertainment.

"Would you guys rather watch 'General Hospital' or 'Days of Our Lives'?"

The vote was two to one for "General Hospital."

"Tom?" Julie said on the screen. "I have to tell you something. I'm leaving you for Steve, the engineer you play golf with."

"What?" Tom answered. "But I'm an attorney at law. What could you possibly see in him?"

"It's just that he seems so . . . so . . . productive."

Music. Fade Out.

We finished our burgers and went in to test the machine.

Cigarette test, negative. Air currents test, negative. Lights out test, negative. Look under the table for cord and power supply test, negative. Look at bearing with magnifying glass test, inconclusive. Transistor radio test, positive! Tim scanned the machine the way Doctor McCoy scans sick people on "Star Trek," and the static made a louder buzzing noise every time the little box on the rim went past the box on the frame.

We didn't have time to set up the current meter in our forty-five minutes with the machine. That would have to come in our second session.

We went back to our room to discuss the results of our experiments.

"We know power must be transferred between the upper boxes on the frame and the plastic boxes on the rim, but how would the boxes on the frame know when to turn on and off?" Tim asked.

"Maybe the distance between the moving disks and the fixed disks on the bottom of the machine electrically tells a sensor inside the bottom box where the wheel is in the cycle," I proposed.

"The information could be transferred to the upper box on

the frame through a wire inside the frame. That wire could tell the upper frame boxes where the wheel is in its cycle. It could then turn on an electromagnet to pull the rim magnet and then reverse polarity to push the rim magnet away."

"That's fairly plausible," Tim said, "but what if the plates are doing the work? We still need to test that."

"We can do that in our next session with the machine," Dan said. "I'd like to know what's inside that lower box, though, too. Any ideas on that?"

"Maybe we can put a stethoscope real close to it without touching it," I said. "I might be able to hear whether there's any mechanical action inside the box that way. At worst, it might result in a nice profile shot of me on nationwide TV. I could send it to a talent agency."

Tim answered, "It probably won't tell you anything, but it might be worth a try. The main thing we should aim for is to get that piece of metal in between the plates. Anybody got any ideas of how to hook it up?"

"It should probably be in series with the ammeter," Dan said. "That's a little hairy, though. It's been a long time since I took sophomore physics lab."

"Yeah, it would really help if they'd picked a double E or a physics guy for the team instead of one of us. I mean we're kind of trapped by the narrowness of our fields," I said.

Dan drew a sketch of how to hook up the ammeter to the piece of copper. "I think we're ready for our second shot. What'll it be now? 'The Young and the Restless'? or 'The Edge of Night'?"

"I've been following 'The Young and the Restless,' " Tim said. "Can we watch that?"

The producer summoned us during a commercial break. Before we returned to the room for the second round of testing, Dan said, "Wait a minute. We've got to do something hacklike on our way in."

"How about whistling 'Whistle While You Work' in unison?" I suggested.

"I like that," Tim said. "Let's practice first, then walk in."

We did pretty well—the cameraman smirked slightly as we whistled past him. Nothing came of the follow-up tests. I heard nothing through the stethoscope, and the ammeter on the copper sheet on the ring stand between the lower plates told us nothing either. Dan looked like a roulette dealer in Las Vegas as he stood next to the machine. The pile of test equipment in the corner of the room did tell us something, though.

Oscilloscopes, many big electronicky-looking boxes. Holy home court advantage, Batman. The Berkeley dweebs probably had the whole physics and electrical engineering department technical supply staff on full alert for the day. And since this was the physics department made famous by Oppie (J. Robert Oppenheimer, A-bomb developer), their access to sophisticated nonintrusive diagnostic tools was far greater than ours. Maybe we should have come to Berkeley earlier and cut some deals with technicians.

Back at our room Berkeley had taped a happy smiley face to our door. How déclassé, we agreed. We taped a frowny face to their door.

"So what are we going to say, guys, and who's going to say it?" Dan asked.

"Tim's the smart one. He should do it," I said. "Dan, you and I've both worn red so we've gotten our fifteen seconds of fame."

"Are you willing, Tim?" Dan asked.

"Sure, why not. Let's figure out what we're going to say," Tim said matter-of-factly. He had professor potential.

I said, "Let's make a list of what we know for sure. That's what Nick the technician in my lab has always told me to do when I'm stuck on a mechanical problem in my thesis work."

"OK," Tim said. Dan wrote the list as we talked through it.

1. Upper boxes on frames have energy transfer, proved by transistor radio test.
2. Air currents in room aren't doing anything, as proved by ice/hairdryer test.
3. Fake photocells on upper boxes aren't doing anything, as proved by lights-out test.
4. Air jet tubes are just a ruse, as proved by cigarette test.
5. All power has to be self-contained in machine in batteries somewhere, as proved by look under table for plug test.
6. No major noise comes out of the lower box, as proved by stethoscope test.
7. No large current is being conveyed to and from plates, as proved by copper test.

When we finished our list, Tim said, "So we know the energy's going from the boxes on the rim to the boxes on the frame. We're still stuck, though, on how the boxes on the frame know how to turn on and off themselves at the right time to pull the wheel around. I mean, if he messed it up, the box on the frame could pull the box on the rim when it's supposed to push it and push it when it's supposed to pull it, and the thing wouldn't keep going."

"That might be what was happening this morning when it wouldn't start," I offered. "I still think it might be synchronized with the pistons below. There's a set ratio between the number of times the plates go up and down per revolution and the number of times the plastic boxes on the rim go by the boxes on the frame. Maybe there's a circuit inside the box that takes a pulse from the motion of the plates and tells the electromagnet when to turn on and off. There could be wires inside the machine that convey that information electronically."

"Sounds good to me," Tim said.

"Me, too," Dan said.

The producer knocked on the door. The three of us returned to the room and Tim presented the explanation, while Dan and I looked keen and alert for the camera as we sat in the background. Then we went out of the room and passed the Berkeley guys on their way in. The MIT undergrad physics major led the way, with a cocky, arrogant grin on his face. Team MIT was in trouble. Berkeley had put the frowny face back on our door.

Midway through "The Match Game," the producer came back to have us sit down and listen to Dr. David Jones's judgment on who had the better explanation of how the thing worked. I had that feeling in my stomach and my chest again, that hollow feeling you get when you're waiting to find out how you did on a test, what your SAT scores were, which colleges accepted you.

"Both of the teams have shown that this is not a perpetual motion machine. While both teams located the primary means of propulsion in the magnets in the plastic boxes on the rim and the electromagnets on the frame, the Berkeley team more correctly explained how the machine works, because they correctly isolated the entire control to a pulsed electromagnet contained in the box on the frame. The MIT team incorrectly implicated the rods attached to the side of the wheel, as some kind of 'control' mechanism."

Dr. Jones removed the boxes from the frame and opened one

for the camera. "As you can see, there is a small battery inside, and some simple electronic circuitry to provide the timing for the electromagnet to turn on and off."

Darn. Sorry guys. Sorry MIT. If only one of us knew some electronics. I really should take a class or two in that; it's the wave of the present.

Dr. Jones continued. "You notice, however, that once I've taken off the electromagnet boxes, the machine is still turning. You see, there is a separate propulsive mechanism that neither team addressed in their explanation." He smirked the same arrogant, cocky smirk that the physics guy from Berkeley smirked. The studio audience laughed dutifully for the camera. We dutifully shook hands with the winner and his colleagues and the inventor of the machine.

Afterward Dan and I sat in the Jacuzzi by the pool at the hotel. Tim dropped by and sat in the poolside lounge chair. Room service brought the refreshments—we were still on expense account.

"You know, we've really let the institute down; I mean, I feel really bad about it," I said.

"Yeah, me too," Dan said. "Could you pass the caviar?"

"We were close," Tim said. "Damn close. It's too bad Pepper and I took controls so recently; if we hadn't, maybe we wouldn't have tried to find a controller in the machine. And you know what else, when we tried to identify the work the plates were doing, I think we were on the right track for the other method of propulsion. I think it was some kind of capacitive device, where the electric polarity went positive and negative, so that at one point in the cycle it was pulling the plate toward it, while it was pushing the other plate away from it. We caught that; if only we knew more about electricity and electrical testing we could have proven it."

"Yeah," Dan said. "The thing that gets me, though, is that the only guy from their team who had any brains, who did any of the talking, was that astrophysics guy. The other guys seemed to be just going along for the ride."

Tim added, "And he did his undergraduate work at MIT. No wonder he was so good."

"Yeah," I said. "Three MIT engineers versus one MIT physicist. Forget Berkeley; it wasn't a fair contest."

C H A P T E R
═══ 15 ═══

Hackito Ergo Sum

Schedule:
Spring '83: 2.01 Mechanics of Solids (Hill)
2.94 Dynamics of Solids (Lincoln)
2.996 Thesis

February 14

Professor Hill solemnly stood before the solid mechanics class. There was an empty desk in the row behind me. "I've got some very sad news for you. One of your classmates took his own life yesterday."

I wanted to cry right then and there, but I suppressed it along with all the nineteen- and twenty-year-olds in the class. Why did he do it? What is it about this place that breeds the feeling of hopelessness, loneliness, and inadequacy that could push anyone over the edge? I remembered the Steve Watson experience; he was really smart and he *still* felt worthless. I remembered Eddy the janitor telling me to take it easy that first term, to have fun now and then so he wouldn't have to call the campus police to cut the sheet or the rope or the belt and issue mouth-to-mouth resuscitation.

Professor Hill was a kind and gentle man, who patiently answered my questions whenever I went to his office for help. He continued the sad prelude to the lecture. "Please. If you're unhappy, don't let it go that far. Come and talk to me, or talk to your hall tutor, or to "Nightline," or to a religious counselor, or to the psychiatric department, or to a friend if you have one. And don't forget one option that you have. You can leave the institute. It's not the only good engineering school in the world. In fact, if you go somewhere else where the professors aren't under such pressure to produce research funding you might receive a better education. Please talk to me if you need any help along these lines."

I enrolled in Professor Hill's class, a.k.a. Statics, and Professor Lincoln's undergraduate Dynamics class, two nine four. Statics is beams and trusses and bridges and things like that. Dynamics is beams and trusses and bridges that move, that rock back and forth in the wind. Dynamics is also lathes and robot arms and missile trajectories.

After two seventy I knew that A's were attainable in head to head competition with the undergrads. I figured the two courses would add two more A's to my transcript. And the classes would be my review for the mechanics section of the doctoral qualifying exams. At MIT you have to look for ways to MIRV things, to kill multiple birds with one stone.

March 10

In the cell. Chet and I prepared for the RCM firing at high pressure with the new starting mechanism.

"And I want you to mount the fuel injector, too," he said. "We may not be able to make a movie yet, but if we combust fuel we'll have some data to show the consortium."

"But, Chet, what if something goes wrong with the experiment? Why don't we leave the fuel injector off and I'll close the cylinder with a piece of Plexiglas? It's got the O-rings in it already and everything," I countered. "If everything goes well, we can do a second firing with the injector in place."

"I think it's a waste of time to do that, but if you insist, we can do that."

My pulse rate didn't rise quite as high as it had on previous firings. The pressure buildup was predictable; I knew at what pressures the clunks of the metal adjusting itself would occur.

BOOOM.

Hisssss. I dumped the pressure from the tank after the successful firing. I breathed regularly again. Chet and I went to the front of the machine, and Professor Heywood opened the door to the cell to see how the test went.

The window we put in at my insistence, without the fuel injector, was shattered. The piston, driven by the higher pressure and the higher force and the higher momentum, had obeyed not Chet's computer model, but Newton's and Murphy's laws. The piston's intended destination was about an inch short of the window; its actual destination was halfway through the window. Had the fuel injector been in place it would have been destroyed.

"I guess you were right on that one," Chet said to me.

"This will set us back a bit," Professor Heywood said. "We can fix the equipment. I'm glad both of you are all right. Mizugachi at the Hiroshima Institute of Technology lost two graduate students last year when their RCM exploded."

"Lost, Professor?" I asked.

"Half the building went with them."

Thank you for sharing that with me, Professor.

April 4, 1983

Fifteen years ago today, in Memphis, James Earl Ray located the Reverend Martin Luther King, Jr., in the cross hairs of the scope of his high-powered rifle and pulled the trigger. Fifteen years ago today, Professor Lincoln sat in my desk and was twenty-five like me. Fifteen years ago today he was more of a minority than he is now, as he received A after A and started on the path to tenure. He had a dream.

Professor Lincoln stood at the front of the room on the table on the lecture platform slightly above floor level. His suits qualified him to be one of *Playboy* magazine's twelve best-dressed men of 1980. His consulting fees netted him not one but two white Jaguar 12-cylinder XJ6 four-doors with full leather interiors and Bose ('51) speakers.

He finished the topic of the previous lecture. "And so resonance occurs when the frequency of energy input into a system is the same as the frequency that the system would rock back and forth if you gave it one push. See, it's sort of like when you were a child on a swing set."

He sketched a swing set with some Greek letters next to it.

He continued, "Now you as a child on the swing set were a pendulum. Your mother or father was a forcing function. If they held you up and let you swing without pushing, you would swing back and forth once every four seconds or so. That's your natural frequency, or what some people call your resonant frequency, once per four seconds. Now as a child you knew that the fun part of being on the swing set was to swing higher and higher. And the way that happened was that Mommy or Daddy gave you a push every four seconds or so, and the energy they input into you was in the right direction at the right time at the right speed to make you go higher and higher.

"In engineering, your problem will usually be to avoid these resonant frequencies. For example, if you were a bridge, and the wind made the air pressure on you vary at a resonant frequency, you'd soon shake apart. That's happened several times in the past century or two. On the other hand, if you become a musical instrument designer, your task will be to design systems that always resonate. But that's enough on resonance. Y'all put down your pencils, OK? For the rest of the lecture I'm not going to talk about dynamics."

The rest of the class put away their notebooks and pads. Lincoln assumed a different character.

"Y'see, Ah nevah wint tah college. Everuh day, before Ah come in tuh lecture y'all, the seenyuh white faculty, dey sets me down, and dey briefs me foe six houwuhs befoe ah comes out to talks to y'all."

There was a chuckle or two, and sort of a tense air in the class of eighty minus the one who left Professor Hill's class and the institute and Earth in February.

"But seriously, though," he continued. "MIT is a racist, sexist institution. You may ask yourselves, 'Why shouldn't it be; so is every other institution in this country, that means in the world,' but that's not the point. You are here now, and I want to give you some examples of the point I'm trying to make."

The chuckles disappeared and were replaced by stone cold silence.

"I've given you examples of how to solve Lagrange's equations. When I was about your age, I took the Physics department's equivalents of this class, and I took the Electrical Engineering department's equivalents of this class, in both cases at the undergraduate and graduate level. I even took two classes in the Mathematics department that formed the underpinnings of the material. During the summer between junior and senior year when I did research for one of my professors during the day, at night and on weekends, I did every problem I put my hands on. I made up my own problems and did them. I wanted to thoroughly master every aspect, every facet, every subtlety, every special case of how to apply these equations in the real world."

He paused. "I kept up the project to just before Christmas time, just after the end of classes, and when I was done, I wanted to share it with someone. I showed the book to my adviser, and he said, 'What you've just done is trivialize the equations to a set of mechanical solution procedures. There's nothing special to that at all. In twenty years a dumb computer will be able to do what you've done.' I ask you, do you think he would have responded that way if I were a homeboy like most of you?"

No, I thought. His adviser must have heard Shockley's (Ph.D. '36) allegation that blacks are genetically inferior. Racist scientists take their wizardly positions of power, and by virtue of the fact that they're smarter than the rest of us, they tell us lies that we are nearly powerless to debate, much less disprove.

Lincoln continued, "So I took that notebook binder, that one that I'd prepared during more than two years of nights and weekends, and I went to the bonfire in the Senior House courtyard, and I threw it in there and watched it burn while I cried. So you will have to make your own notebooks and pioneer those solutions yourselves."

Then he looked at me, straight in the eye, for an uncomfortable second.

"Now, I'd like to give you a more recent example. A few weeks ago, I lectured to you about flux linkage in an electromechanical system. One of you asked a question in that 'stump the professor' tone of voice, the kind that shows you're looking for a chance to get even, and since I'm black you thought I might be an easy hit. One of you asked me to derive the electrical side of the equation, the side that we mechanical engineers wouldn't normally have committed to memory. But even though I burned my notebook, I had internalized the knowledge, and as you may recall, I presented a complete, correct derivation."

I looked down at the floor, put my elbow on the desk and my hand across my forehead so as to avoid any further eye contact. He was talking about me.

"I'm not asking you all to change the world. I'm just asking you to consider the possibility of laying aside your prejudices," he added. "Now, it's a beautiful day. Why don't you all go out and take a walk for the rest of the class time. We can make up the lecture material on the next rainy day."

April 20

"Hey, Pepper, I want to talk to you about something," Eldon Tyrell said, drumming his fingers in a typing motion on the wall next to the door to my apartment. Eldon was one of the Atkinson freshmen, who lived down the hall from me. We both had a crush on Cindy, and he did fine vocal sound effects of, for example, a machine gun with a silencer on it and the buzzing virtual swords that Luke Skywalker and Darth Vader dueled with in *Star Wars*. I'd first met him when two juniors were trying to bully him out of his room during orientation week.

Eldon was an aero-astro major, which involved fluid mechanics, my forte, and we'd become friends—good enough friends that I'd confided my literary ambitions to him. He became an ally on that front, an informant.

"Sure, kid, come on in," I said in my best Bogart voice.

He sat in the chair next to the end of my desk, like the chair the client sits in in the private eye's office, a black wooden institute-issue desk chair, and I sat back in the green Naugahyde arm-swivel-chair on casters and put my feet up on the desk.

"Sho, whadaya got ta shay, kid?" I asked him.

"Wait a minute, the lighting's not right," he answered. "We need the art deco desk lamp you swiped from your office in the heat transfer lab sort of pointing away from the corner of the desk between us so we're half in bright light, half in shadow. There. And let me turn off the overhead light. That fits the mood much better."

"Sho, whadaya got ta shay, kid?" I asked him in take two.

"Here, let me show you this. I was just accepted. I'm finally in THA. It's so amazing; I'm really psyched. They just let me know yesterday. Here, look at this."

He put a sheet of paper on the desk in the bright part. At the top of the sheet was printed "Under the Eagle," and the left wing and head of a bald eagle completed the letterhead. The left margin said vertically, "Restricted," and the bottom margin said in fine print, "For security reasons, do not show this to anyone else in your dormitory. The Technology Hackers Association."

The high-quality printed text had several announcements. "Coming Hack on the buses that drive down Amherst Alley next to athletic field. Attack the dirty beasts with surgical tubing water balloons; no soap, please—we don't want to anger the bus company. . . . Possibility of pink water balloon throw at demonstrators. . . . Impossible Hack at graduation; the Dekes scooped us with the balloon at the H-Y game. Impossible Hack must be good."

I asked Eldon what the Impossible Hack plan was.

"I can't divulge details; I mean, I'm already telling you so much I should shoot you. Let's just say we're going to defeat the West German Secret Service security sweep. See, Helmut Schmidt, the former West German chancellor, is scheduled to speak at graduation in about a month. We're planning a hack that's going to cost a few of those guys their jobs. It's not going to be easy, though. We're dealing with the sons and grandsons of the Gestapo, and these guys are *good*. But I think we're up to it. I mean, our parents and grandparents won the war, didn't they?"

"Yeah." I stopped being Bogart, started being myself again. I took my feet off the desk and leaned forward in the chair. "What about the pink water balloons?"

"Well, that one I'm not too proud of. Some of these guys are really fascists. I mean, I don't agree with everything they do. You know how MIT has acquired all that land owned by Simplex, and how they're going to tear down all those rental units and make a whole lot of poor Cambridgeport residents homeless, and then they're going to build R&D office space that by the time they're through will probably be just an addition of square footage to a growing office space glut that will probably occur in the Boston market by then?" he asked rhetorically.

"Yes," I answered.

"Well, the THA brass wants to throw pink water balloons at them from the roofs of the buildings near where they're demonstrating," he said. "I'm not so sure it's a good idea. The demonstrators will probably figure MIT put us up to it and then they'll hate the institute even more. I mean that's how those warped, paranoid leftists look at things."

"Maybe as you advance in the organization you can change it from within," I said. "But aside from that, tell me more about your involvement. What was the application procedure?"

He offered to answer after I gave him a glass of ice water.

"These guys are incredibly organized," he said. "They gave me this form; I mean a printed form, just like you'd fill out for a job application, like for the government or something. It asked all kinds of personal questions, like what kinds of hacks I'd done in high school, what my political convictions were, and a lot of other personal questions, things I wouldn't want anyone outside the organization to see. It's sort of like Skull and Bones at Yale. The difference is that you have to be smart to get into THA, and you have to be a landed gentry blueblood to get into Skull and Bones. Anyway, I signed the application, so they've got me. If they find out I violated the confidentiality oath, for example, all they'll have to do is send my application form to my employer, and I'll be sunk."

"Don't worry, I'll change your name," I said. "The operation sounds like what I've read about intelligence organizations."

"You better believe it," Eldon answered. "They've got section heads and everything. There's even a minister of intelligence. They have files on when the janitors clean the classrooms and what the rounds of the CPs are. That way they know how to create a diversion. If they're going to do a hack, one team will create a diversion in an area away from the CPs' beat. X number of CPs will investigate the diversion, and the door that has to be picked or broken into will be free of heat. The minister of intelligence also goes around collecting other random information; he listens in on conversations, things like that. It's kind of sick but it's really fun. I could enjoy putting bugs into someone's house or tapping someone's phone."

"And take away some of the freedom you're working to protect?" I asked.

"Look. It doesn't matter. So what if all you find out is that the husband is being unfaithful and the wife doesn't know it. You won't do anything with that information. It's the old tree falling in the forest not making a sound idea. I could really have fun with this. I'd never kill anyone though. But gosh, I'm probably on a CIA career track and in five years I might be killing people and I don't believe in that."

I responded, "Don't worry about it. You won't kill anyone. Not directly anyway," I said.

"Directly or indirectly, I don't like it. It's against my religion. I think you're right, though. They probably subcontract all the hits. I'm pretty sure there is a pipeline from THA to the CIA, just like there is with Skull and Bones. For example, we have the OSS guide to lockpicking. The Office of Strategic Services . . . they were the precursor of the CIA."

"Yeah, but that's a public document by now. You can probably order it from the National Technical Information Service," I countered.

"Whatever. You should see it, though. It has all kinds of tricks in it. See, the brute force way to pick a lock is to put this thing they call a rake into it. But the problem with the rake is that you can shine a light into the keyhole and tell whether the lock has been picked. So there's this other little tool with a hook in it."

He took his keychain out of his pocket and showed me a short piece of metal that looked sort of like a can opener from a Swiss army knife.

Eldon continued the explanation. "You just pick one pin at a time, and no one knows anything about it. Some veteran CIA guys can pick seven pins in fifteen seconds. It's pick, pull, turn handle, pick, pull, turn handle, until bingo you're in."

"Don't the CPs find you guys annoying?" I asked.

"Not really. It's in our constitution that we can't do any damage. One time some group broke into the top of the Green Building and stole the air raid warning sirens. The CPs thought it was THA, but it was actually some sniveling frat boys. THA embarked on a little mission and returned the sirens the next day, with a note saying, 'Courtesy THA.' Plus, with doors and locks, we never attack them with pliers or vice grips. If the hack requires removing an entire door handle and then reassembling it later, that's what we'll do. That's just the way we operate."

"Have you hacked yet?"

"Yeah. I just went on a mission the other day. We hacked the dome in the library. It was just so amazing. We met in a conference room and reviewed all our tasks and what signals we'd send and receive to know that the coast was clear. We synchronized our watches and then when we were walking down the corridor the group leader saw just an anonymous hand around a corner as a signal at a couple of places, I mean with perfect timing. We went ahead and climbed to the top of the dome and had sort of a picnic up there. It was awesome, I mean what a view at three in the morning of the Charles and all of Cambridge and MIT. It was a starter hack. I don't know which dome hack was tougher, the one when they put a phone booth up there and the phone rang when the CPs went up to check it out, or when we put a live cow up there."

"It's cruel to put a cow up there," I said.

"Not really; see, cows don't walk downhill, so there wasn't any danger of the cow's hurting itself. Anyway, after we were done with the hack we met back at the conference room at the prearranged time to discuss the results. It was great. I mean it was so much fun it's scary. And just think; a lot of the CIA guys are just overgrown hackers and they think it's a game. Like they say, 'OK boys, time to do a little job for the prez,' and of course the prez would know nothing about it. I'm almost sure the Company recruits here."

I sharpened my pencil. "That's interesting," I said. "The CIA is the Company, MIT is run by the Corporation. I think I detect a trend."

"Yeah, but you better not write that."

"Why not?"

"Because you could lose your alumni athletic privileges. Or no employer will touch you. Or it might adversely affect your credit rating."

"Aw, come on, Eldon, people only worry about that kind of thing in the Soviet Union. We have freedom of speech here."

"Yeah, sure, we can print whatever naked bodies we want, but if you make people think you might be labeled a subversive. All I'm saying is be careful. And by the way, don't flame about any radical fundamentalist 'religious' groups. You don't want to spend the rest of your life moving from safe house to safe house."

"It's too late; I just did. Tell me more about THA."

"Sorry, I don't know any more. It's organized in a cellular network, so I only know four other people in the Association. It'll stay that way until I advance."

"And how do you advance?"

"By being good," Eldon answered. "It's not by seniority at all, not like in companies and trade unions. Like the minister of intelligence, he's only a sophomore now. Last year he spent all his time hacking. It was hack all night, sleep all day, and he almost flunked out. Come to think of it, he was pretty smart. He did his advancing as a freshman when all the courses are pass-fail. I wonder whether he planned it that way."

"How's he doing now?"

"He's doing really well. Actually, I'm not supposed to know who he is, but he opened a door for me and I recognized his sneakers. He's actually a friend of mine. I mean, I had no idea."

"Maybe you can follow in his footsteps," I said. "By the way, did I tell you the CIA sent me a recruiting letter?"

"Oh, wow. It really is true. They do recruit here. Do you know how they found your address?" Eldon asked.

"I put my résumé in the résumé book at the placement office. That's the only thing I can think of."

"Do you still have the letter? May I look at it?"

"Sure. It's here in my briefcase," I said. I put the case on the desk. My parents had given it to me for Christmas for upcoming job interviews.

"Cool," Eldon said. "I didn't know you had a briefcase. Can I play with it for a second?"

"Sure," I said and handed it to him.

Eldon became Q, the smart-sounding British guy in the lab jacket in the basement of the headquarters of Her Majesty's Secret Service. "Now you see, Bond, this briefcase is specially equipped for all types of emergencies. If you'd like to release the poison gas, release the latches one at a time. If you don't want gas to come out, release them together. Remember that. Poison, one at a time. No poison, together. Your camera is this brass fitting on the bottom; you'll have to remove it with the special tool on your keychain. If you lose your keys, the pop top from a soft drink can will do. The other brass fitting is the dagger. And, Bond, please don't lose it this time. It took us two months to prepare it for you, and you know how we hate to redo work."

I said, "You do that well. You ought to be an actor."

Eldon answered, "It's nothing; just straight out of the movie. Anyway, if I work for the Company, I'll have plenty of opportunities to be an actor. Let's take a look at the letter."

I started to open the briefcase.

Eldon said, "Don't forget. No poison, together."

I opened both latches at the same time.

The top of the letter had a smaller version of the eagle that was on the top of Eldon's letter from THA.

"Do you have the envelope, too?"

I gave him the envelope.

"That's interesting," Eldon said. "There's no return address on it. And it says 'Not to be forwarded out of the United States.' That must be so when you're on your summer vacation picking apples in Bulgaria the letter won't be forwarded to you. Otherwise, the Bulgarian branch of the KGB would figure it was in code, you were an operative, and they'd throw you in jail. We'd have to give up one of their guys to get you out, and that would be a waste."

Eldon read the letter, moving his lips really fast as he read, his eyes scanning line by line about five lines per second.

"Oh, cool," he said. "You'll be doing all the things that Q does. Look at this. 'High-technology collection devices,' read bugs. 'Photo-optical-mechanical devices,' read microfilm cameras."

"I don't know whether I'll follow through on it, though. There must be better uses of technology to protect our liberties and standard of living."

"Like what?"

"I don't know, counting light bulbs or something."

"Hey, I heard a couple of good light bulb jokes recently," Eldon said. "How many Tufts students does it take to change a light bulb?"

"I don't know. How many?"

"Only one, but they get twelve credits for it. How many graduate students does it take to change a light bulb?"

"I don't know. How many?"

"Only one, but it takes ten years. I gotta go now. Big eight oh two problem set due tomorrow. Hey, by the way. Don't tell anyone my name. In all THA mailings they use only first names and last initials; anonymity is key. And everything I've told you is classified. If you publish it before I graduate it could really mess up my future," Eldon said.

"I have a heady feeling of power, sort of like Bob Woodward," I said.

"Yeah, why don't you call me Deep Throat? Nah, that's too tacky. Oh, I know. How about Chromedome? Or Ghandi? Yeah, Ghandi, that's it. That'll be great. Just call me Ghan for short. Anyway, like I say, I gotta go. Remember. Not a word to anyone about who I really am."

"Okay, Ghan."

CHAPTER

——— 16 ———

Papa Flash

May 5, 1983

Steer Roast is on Derby Day every year. Steer Roast is Senior House's answer to homecoming weekend, when alums come back to remember the glory days and undergrads play one last time before exams.

It was a beautiful warm Saturday afternoon, and the courtyard was jammed with people, a couple of hundred at least, sitting at picnic tables, eating their beef or vegetarian lasagna and corn on the cob. A bluegrass group of former tutors played from the stage at one corner, and the Sport Death banner waved gently in the breeze from Runkle 4. Professor Edgerton, the strobe inventor, played the spoons.

The Senior House alumni club were free agents in the real world. From the dribs and drabs of the conversations, I gathered that many worked at start-up companies for good pay and stock options. Others did software consulting at home on their personal computers, like Dianne Mitchell, only for higher stakes. Others had low employee badge numbers and stock options at Sun, Lotus, Apple, or start-ups in Silicon Valley.

They loved Senior House, and after making $100K doing what they loved to do—hack—it seemed that their memories of MIT had become a little fonder, too. I hoped my memories of MIT would be fond some day.

Mary had come back to Senior House for the reunion and we sat next to each other at one of the picnic tables. She wore her Sport Death T-shirt.

"Does this bring back memories?" I asked her.

"Some."

"Good ones, bad ones?"

"Some of both."

A sophomore from Runkle wore a baseball catcher's outfit and carried an umbrella. He stood on the table next to President Gray's garden wall and waved his hands downward to quiet the assembly.

"And now for the moment you've been waiting for. As you know," he said, "last year I was selected the 'Most Obnoxious Freshman' of Senior House. By the powers of that office bestowed upon me, I hereby pronounce Howard Gelman M.O.F. of '83."

It was that geeky kid from down the hall, the first one to come to my study break in the fall, the one who predicted the Poisson arrival distribution of the others. Everyone scattered from his table and he ducked under it. The corncobs started flying in his direction. Not curve cobs, just bean cob fast cobs. The mob converged on his table and pelted his unprotected side from point-blank range with all the fervor of generic zealots at a stoning. He speed-crawled out the other end of the picnic table and dashed toward the Grays' garden wall, pelted all the way.

I wanted to make it stop. Mary didn't say or throw anything. Neither did I. Neither did millions of Germans.

The kid held up a folding chair to shield his face while the mob hurled the remaining projectiles. The sophomore in the catcher's mask said, "What would you like to say for your acceptance speech?"

I was amazed that he could respond at all.

"Well." Zing, pelt. "I . . ." Pelt ". . . can't accept the award without first consulting my lawyer."

Sunday night I talked to John Dorsey about the cobbing.

"I feel terrible about what happened to Howard Gelman yesterday," I said.

"It's a tradition around here," John said. "Usually the kid knows it's coming and has an umbrella or something as a shield. This year it went a little out of control. A psychiatrist friend suggested that they're throwing corncobs at their own self-images; since many of these kids were outcasts in high school, they take this chance to single out one and stone him or her. It follows from the pagan tradition of human sacrifice."

"I don't know. I still think it's sick. I can just see that poor guy writing a letter home. 'Dear Mom and Dad, Everyone in the dorm threw corncobs at me yesterday. I'm really popular.' "

May 22, 1983

"Uh, hello, may I speak with Doctor Edgerton, please?" I asked his secretary on the phone.

"Just a minute."

"Uh, hello, Doctor Edgerton. My name is Pepper White and I'm a student at the Sloan Lab, and I was wondering whether I could make an appointment to talk to you about some pictures. Do you have any time tomorrow?"

"What's the matter with now?" he answered briskly. "You busy?"

"Uh, I have a meeting with a . . ."

"You are busy. How about tomorrow at 9:30?"

"Okay, sir. Thank you."

May 23

I went to the fourth floor in Building 4, the hall lined with display cases that I'd admired on my first trip to the library to do my literature survey the year before. I had no idea then that my work might involve rubbing elbows with Doc Edgerton, the institute's legend in his own time. Doc Edgerton could have held his own with Eiffel (as in Tower), or with Edison, or with Bell. I wondered whether I could hold my own with him.

Doc was born in Nebraska in 1903, the year of the Wright Brothers' first flight. He went to the University of Nebraska and came to MIT as a graduate student in the Electrical Engineering department. Even though he was only MIT squared (M.S., Ph.D.), he'd become an assistant professor in 1932.

As a by-product of his Ph.D. research, he first developed the strobe photography techniques that were the basis for the company he founded with two of his graduate students, Germeshausen and

Grier. E.G.&G., Inc., grew rapidly, making Doc and his partners three of the richest men in Massachusetts.

But Doc was first and foremost an engineer, not to mention a midwesterner, so he remained friendly and open to whoever wandered into his office.

The fourth floor hallway, called Strobe Alley, was lined with large, clear photographs, all made possible by Edgerton's strobe invention: a bat frozen in flight, a somersaulting circus acrobat's trajectory, a football being kicked, Mickey Rooney with his arm around Judy Garland, smiling and singing.

On the other side of the hall cases displayed 1940s-style black metal electronics boxes with "EG&G" metal tags attached. Other cases displayed relics of ancient shipwrecks—urns, metal vases, things you'd see in a museum.

I went through the door with "Enter" painted on it and walked to a workbench where Doc was talking to a younger man in his mid-seventies. They were both standing up and held things that looked like rolls of wet paper towels in plastic bags. A four-foot-long yellow torpedolike thing lay on the floor, next to another box with EG&G marked on it. Doc started to put one of the paper towel rolls into the EG&G box; the box was a chart recorder to record data sent from the torpedo, also known as side-scan sonar.

"What can I do for you, son?" Doc asked.

"I called yesterday afternoon to make an appointment."

"Oh yeah. I remember," Doc said. "What's your problem?"

"I'm working on a rapid compression machine. It's in the Sloan Auto Lab."

"Yeah, I know the Sloan Lab," he said. "A young guy by the name of Draper did some work on a diesel engine there in the thirties. What are you going to do that he didn't do?"

"Well, we know more about what we're doing," I said.

"Suppose I call Stark Draper and tell him you said that?"

I didn't really want to go one-on-one with the inventor of the inertial guidance system that makes missiles land on target and put men on the moon. "I don't think that will be necessary. I just mean that we can control our operating parameters more precisely in the rapid compression machine than Professor Draper could in a real engine. I'm trying to make some movies of a diesel fuel spray, and I thought you might be able to tell me about some of the techniques available. We're using a high-speed movie camera, a HYCAM, and . . ."

"You're all set then. What do you need to talk to me about."

"I thought you could tell me whether there's anything faster than what we have or whether you have any cameras that go faster."

"You'll have to talk to my colleague Charlie Miller about that. He's the expert on movies," Doc said. "The fastest that technology goes is about 10,000 frames per second. How many frames you want?"

"Fifty thousand would be nice."

"Yep. You're just like everyone else, always trying to take pictures of more and more and you see less and less. Now if you take a single exposure with a fraction-of-a-microsecond flash, that might be educational. Then you could see some individual fuel droplets, get some good resolution. We like to take a 4-by-5-inch print and then blow it up to a couple of feet square and then you begin to see what's really going on. Would you like to try that?"

"Sure," I said. "I'd like to have the best pictures of a diesel fuel spray that've ever been taken."

"Good. This here's Billy MacRoberts," Doc said, motioning to the younger man in his mid-seventies. "He's my technician. Let's the three of us see what we can find."

The three of us went to the notebook where they recorded what equipment they'd lent out. It turned out that the equipment they'd lent me had been lent to Ben's research predecessor in 1981. The promised return date was May 25, 1981.

"It's due in two days," Doc said. "Oh. That's 1981, not 1983. Where is this Vilchis guy anyway?" he asked, referring to the name on the form.

"He graduated a year ago," I said.

"Let's go down there and see whether we can find that stuff," Doc said.

He escorted me to my cell. I showed him the electronics boxes we'd installed, and I explained how we'd shot the first high-speed movies of the fuel spray. Ben wasn't around and Nick couldn't find the stuff, so I asked Doc whether he wanted to see the movie I'd made the week before.

"Sure. Let's take a look," he said.

I set up the projector and tried not to be a klutz and mess up the threading of the film. It took longer than when I did it before but it worked the first time.

"It takes most of the film to reach where we see what's happening. The HYCAM has to reach full speed," I said.

"Yep. That's the problem with this high-speed photography business. Most of the film goes in the trash," he answered.

A minute into the film, the fuel jet appeared. It was well-lit, in focus, and clear. "You can imagine my anxiety the first time I ran this thing and waited to see whether I caught the injection," I said.

"That's a good picture. It must have been a thrill the first time you saw it." He said it with conviction.

Ben knocked on the door to the screening room and the three of us went downstairs to Ben's cell and found some little pieces of metal and glass that Bill had made. They were in the random junk section of Ben's storage cabinet.

"Yeah. This is the stuff," Doc said. "Let's take it back to the lab and get Billy to fix it."

One of the pieces of glass looked like a test tube, with melted plastic at the open end. Doc told a story.

"A couple of years ago Bill and I had one of these flashes set up, and we found that plastic wire wrapped around it absorbed most of the heat and almost prevented it from breaking. We put twice as much plastic around it, and it didn't break. That's engineering."

We walked back through Building 13, past the photo of Vannevar Bush ('16) at a drill press, wearing a velour shirt. "Where you from?" Doc asked.

"North Carolina," I answered. "But my father's from Beverly up on the North Shore."

"So you're a rebel," he said. "Billy and I are both Yankees, we've been here so long. But I won't hold your being a rebel against you. I've got a lot of family in North Carolina. One of my grandchildren is a CPA in Hickory, another's a doctor in Chapel Hill, another's a lawyer in Raleigh."

"Too bad none of them are making anything of themselves," I said lightly but received a cold look in return. "Just kidding."

By now we were back at Strobe Alley, and on the wall there was a picture of something that looked like a slowly melting golf-ball on top of a metal frame.

"Is that what I think it is?" I asked Doc.

"Yep," he answered. "That's a small atom bomb they were trying to get to work back in the mid-forties. We had to take that one with a rotating shutter and a magnetic polarizer. Those things let out a lot of light, you know."

Just a matter of fact. I answered, "When I did my thesis literature survey I came across an interesting paper entitled 'The Rapid Rise of a Buoyant Plume.' It was an AEC report and was written in 1945. I bet they were talking about the same thing."

"Sounds like it, dudinit?" Doc said.

We entered Doc's lab again. Bill was still loading water into the side-scan sonar paper towel rolls.

"The guy says he brought it back," Doc said. "Some guy named MacRoberts must have forgotten to write it down when he did."

"Or some guy named Edgerton," Bill retorted.

"Well, let's get this guy fixed up," Doc said, referring to me. "And get him out of here so we can get some work done. Come on, let's go into the other room and see what we can lend him."

We crossed the hall and went into the other half of the lab. It looked like the pictures from MIT I'd seen in Mrs. DaRosa's physics class in high school. There were strobe lights on every workbench, the famous spinning wheel with different circles on it that stand still as the strobe light flashes faster and slower. More and more electronic boxes from the preceding five decades.

The Sloan Lab felt archaic; so did this room, but it was high-tech. Maybe the Sloan Lab was, too. Along the wall next to the corridor there was a .22 caliber rifle mounted horizontally on one of the workbenches. There was a piece of cardboard behind it, spray-painted black like some of the things I'd spray-painted in my cell.

"Is this it?" I asked, knowing Doc would know I referred to his bullet series of photographs: a bullet standing still after it shears the jack of diamonds; a bullet just after it leaves an apple; a bullet and its shock wave as it passes through a candle.

"Yep," he said. "Usually we use a .45 caliber pistol, but it makes too much noise. The other day we did a demonstration for some high schoolers and we didn't want to blast their ears out. If you look over there you'll see we have to catch the bullet with something." He pointed to something that looked like a Clorox bottle.

"What's inside that?" I asked, thinking it'd be something like flak jacket material.

"Oh, that's just some sand we picked up at Revere Beach. It kills a lot of energy," Doc replied.

Bill pulled two of the black metal boxes off the back of the bench. They were strictly analog, predating the transistor and digital computers—they reminded me of pictures of MIT wartime defense research along the infinite corridor. Both of the boxes had the same little EG&G tags that everything else in the lab had. I tried to imagine working in a place where every object had my initials on it. Bill picked up another glass thing that looked like the broken test tube with not enough plastic wire that was in Ben's storage cabinet.

"Shall we see whether this one works, Doc?" Bill asked.

"Sure. Plug it in," Doc answered. He explained the operation of the flash to me while Bill connected the wires. "Billy's seen everything fail at least once, so he knows what to do about it when it happens. He should be able to fix up this thing for you in a jiffy. See, you got two capacitors; one 8,500 volts positive, one 8,500 volts negative, for 17,000 volts. That'll give you a nice kick if you touch it the wrong way. Need I say more?"

Bill finished connecting all the wires and he pressed the "manual" button. And POP there was a white flash so bright that I thought Bill and Doc should be blind by now from looking at that flash so many times.

"That's a fraction of a microsecond," Doc said. "Here. Take a look at this," he said pointing to the other little glass tube inside the test tube. "That thing there's what we call the stinger. The high voltage ionizes the gas in between the electrodes here, and then the electrical resistance goes down and the spark jumps across. It's just like a spark plug, only more powerful."

The tubes made a clicking noise and I asked Doc what it was.

"Corona discharge," he said. "Put enough voltage across a gap and those electrons will just die to hop over to the low-voltage side."

Maybe Herr Diesel wanted to hop over to the low-voltage side when he "apparently fell" into the English Channel and was never seen again. Maybe the kid in Hill's class succumbed to the intensity of the voltage as well. I wanted to put some of this on paper, but I'd left my notebook in my cell. "Do you have a sheet of paper I could take some notes on?" I asked.

"Sure. Here." Doc gave me a wasted Polaroid print with one corner torn off it.

"We got everything, Billy?" Doc asked.

"Sure do, Doc," Bill MacRoberts answered.

"Well, while we're here let's clean up this bench a little bit. We gotta get rid of these two-by-fours. This guy can tell we both grew up on the farm." Doc winked at me, referring to his early days in Nebraska.

They put a few things away and we crossed Strobe Alley again. "We gotta fix you up with a shield now so the flash doesn't go straight to the camera and that's all you see. Billy, can you make one up for this fella?"

"Sure thing, Doc." Billy cut a piece of aluminum, rolled it to shape in a sheet metal bender, and it fit perfectly on the test tube.

"He need anything else, Billy?" Doc asked.

"Just a circuit to prevent the power surge from going back to the trigger," Bill said. I wondered why they called it a trigger, the same thing that was on the oscilloscope in my cell.

"Why don't the two of you go back to the other room and see whether you can find one. I gotta go through my mail now."

Bill and I went to the other storage room again. Bill did a quick calculation of the strobe's instantaneous power output: 6 megawatts, or about the equivalent power of 100,000 light bulbs, but for a very, very short time. Coulombs, electric charges, volts, and electric potential were as real to Bill as inches and pounds were to me. We couldn't find the circuit so Bill sent me back to talk to Doc while he continued to look for the circuit.

Doc was still going through his mail. "Got something here from Koosta," he said. "You know, Koosta first came here in 1952. He was young and nobody'd ever heard of him. It was before the "National Geographic" specials. Heck, it was practically before TV. Anyway, I told every student in the class I was teaching then that if they didn't bring ten of their friends to the talk Koosta was giving it was going to be . . ." and Doc drew his index finger across his neck. "It worked. It was standing room only for the lecture, and the guy who booked 26-100 for it couldn't even get in the door it was so crowded." I was confused so I peeked at the letter. It was signed by Jacques Cousteau.

"Of course, Koosta's an old man now," Doc said.

"But has he lost his enthusiasm?" I asked.

"Nope."

"That's the important thing, isn't it?" I added.

"Sure is. You read French?" Doc asked.

"Yes, I do," I answered and started reading the text of the letter.

"It looks like they want me to fill out this questionnaire for some book they're doing about their ship's voyages," Doc said. "What's this question?"

"Um, I think they want to know how many times you went on the ship's voyages. If it's one or less they don't want you to fill out the form," I translated.

"Think eight'll qualify?" Doc quipped. "How about this question here?"

"They want copies of any photographs you may have taken while on board."

"We've got two thousand. Wouldn't they have a fun time picking through those to find the best ones?" Doc said.

While we were on the subject of the sea I asked him when he would raise the *Titanic*.

"We know where it is," he said as he pulled out a crumpled piece of paper from his wallet. "It's at 41 degrees 16 minutes north, 50 degrees 14 minutes west. I got that out of a book I was reading. That's an area 50 miles by 50 miles. That's just a point on the globe, but try finding a ship in that much water. It's not easy."

Doc continued. "We found her sister ship on the bottom of the Mediterranean some years ago, but that was in only 300 feet of water. The *Titanic's* in 12,000 feet of water and my sonar only works to depths of 3,000. He turned around and drew on the blackboard beside his desk.

"So you've got a lot of cable, and it's always going to be hanging behind the ship, making the hypotenuse of a right triangle. That's no easy trick, to have 15,000 feet of cable dragging behind you in the open ocean, then to coil it and uncoil it. And if you find it, then whadaya do? It's a whole 'nother can of worms to try and raise it from the bottom."

This Herculean, mythic task was reduced to geometry and seemed doable the way Doc talked about it.

Bill had found the circuit and brought it in to Doc. "I only could find one, Doc," he said.

"Well, give it here; I'll make him a drawing. He's a grown man; he can build the circuit himself," Doc snapped.

Doc sketched the circuit in a minute. I ran down the hall to make some copies, returned, and gave him the original.

Bill tied the cords from the power supply box with some small wires attached to the box handle. "It's a patented method I've developed to prevent people from tripping over the cords," he joked.

As Doc and Bill loaded my arms with the equipment, Doc issued the conditions of the loan. "We don't like to lend to people who aren't successful, so work hard now and take some good pictures," he mandated.

"I'll have some for you in a week, sir," I answered.

I turned the corner to Building 13 and Doc exhorted again from his office, "To the mark!"

May 25

I set up the Polaroid camera and Doc and Bill's flash. Chet walked in and said, "What are you doing? We're only taking movies here. What are you wasting your time for?"

"Look, Chet, I just want to give this a try. I wanted to see about making faster movies and Professor Edgerton suggested I try this instead. Who knows, we might learn something," I answered.

I felt a little more confident, a little more able to talk back to Chet since the time I was right about not mounting the fuel injector.

"Well, all right, but don't spend more than a day on it. You gotta make movies of combustion and take the pressure data and analyze it. We gotta get you outa here and into the real world," he said.

Look, Chet, I know you don't think I'm Ph.D. caliber, but let me enjoy following my intuition once in a while for the duration.

"You need any help?" he asked.

"The key is the timing. I need the fraction of the millionth of a second that the flash is on to occur within the thousandth of the second that the injection lasts," I said.

"Just use the timing boxes we have for the rest of the experiment," Chet said. "Put the strobe flash on one timing box and put the injector on the other timing box, and dial in the delay just as you did with the movie camera."

The high technology of mechanical engineering is in precise space. The high technology of electrical engineering is in precise time. The question remained, How many thousandths of a second delay should we put between when the injector starts and when the flash starts? The injector took about 42/1,000 of a second to inject from the time the timing box told it to start, so I suggested that number to Chet.

"No," he said, kind of arbitrarily. "Let's start with 40."

We dialed in 40. No fuel spray on the Polaroid film.

"Now try 45," Chet said.

Still no fuel spray.

"Forty-three." No fuel. "Forty-one." No fuel. "Forty-four." No fuel.

"Forty-two." A crisp sharp image of the fuel displayed itself on the Polaroid print. Each of the five jets looked like a tiny tuft of fluffy white cotton. It was beautiful, clearer than the movie. Doc was right.

CHAPTER

═══ 17 ═══

The Joy of Six

*"... of the tree of the knowledge of good and evil,
thou shalt not eat of it. ..."*

Genesis 2:17

Schedule:
Summer '83: 6.001 Structure and Interpretation of Computer
Languages (Siebert)
6.931 Basic Electronics (Zapf)
2.996 Thesis

May 27

Ari and I went to graduation to hear the speech by Helmut Schmidt.
It was a cloudy day for the professors in the procession with their
academic robes and their hoods from Stanford and Oxford and
Cambridge and MIT, and their scepters and their funny hats. It all
seemed so medieval, as if the wizards were displaying their power.

Schmidt marched past me, with four younger men in plain
black caps and gowns marching on all four sides of him. The four
younger ones didn't look like scholars; there wasn't the focus and
intelligence in their eyes. And instead of looking forward like the

people in funnier hats, they looked up at the rooftops, at the second, third, and fourth floor windows around Killian Court. Schmidt scanned the periphery as well.

The five looked tense. I wondered whether they were mentally reviewing the choreography if there were an attempted hit: Schmidt would hit the deck first, then two would jump on top of him to cover him, and the other two would whip out their Uzis from under their robes and open fire on the would-be assasin. Surely the security sweep had sterilized the area, though, and the bodyguards were only a redundant system.

They reached the stage without incident. A few of the older parents in the audience softly sang "The Star Spangled Banner," and I sang it loudly the way I had ever since I'd learned the words in Cub Scouts. When the anthem ended, a guy in the row in front of me said, "Play ball."

Midway through Schmidt's speech, the sounds came from behind the stage. "Click, thunk." The scroll fell from the frieze between the Ionic columns of Building 10. "NOTHING'S."

"Click, thunk." "IMPOSSIBLE."

Score one for THA. Nice work, Ghan.

Course Six is the Electrical Engineering department. This is where the power is. Paul Gray ('54), president, got his start as a professor in Six. Gerry Wilson, dean of engineering, was a professor in Six. And, of course, Doc Edgerton was in Course Six. Course Six invented radar, artificial intelligence, and computers. Course Six is high technology.

July 20

Software. Freshman double E's take six double oh one (a.k.a. six double no fun) to learn to program in LISP (*LISt Processing*, or *Lots of Insidious and Stupid Parentheses*). This is also where they begin to leave the rest of the world behind them in their ability to solve problems and to make things work.

I'd heard so much about Six at milk and cookies in Senior House that I wanted to experience it, if only vicariously. Anything that is not graded is vicarious at MIT, because you need the pressure of the other students and the quizzes and the graded problem sets to force you to absorb the mountain of data presented. The two week summer version would give me a big enough vicarious taste.

The underground guide to Course Six noted: "6.001 is not a programming course—it teaches you how to think about complexity." Perhaps it would fulfill Professor Mikic's promise to me in that first week two years ago.

Professor Siebert was a little younger than Gyftopoulos and Greene; he spoke forcefully, and seemed more like a Fortune 500 executive than a computer science professor. But his manner didn't hinder his ability to transfer the data.

"*Abstraction*," he said. "That is the word. When you go about designing a computer program, or designing anything for that matter, you need to make abstractions."

Right. What's an abstraction? And I thought I was making progress in this place.

Siebert went on to say that we might already be familiar with the term *black box*. A thing to which you give an electronic signal or signals is referred to as as a black box. A signal can be as simple as the voltage from a car battery or as complex as a radio wave. The black box operates on these input signals to give you an output signal. It's called a black box because you don't know how the black box performs the operation, but you do know what the operation is. The black box concept was developed in the early days of analog electronics, when they were, in many cases, literally black metal boxes.

Like those in Doc Edgerton's lab. I didn't have to know precisely how the capacitors and other electronic component devices inside the EG&G strobe boxes worked; I only needed to know what the boxes did and how to interface them with my experiment.

Abstraction is the word. From *abstractus*, "To drag away from." Abstraction is the act of considering something as a general characteristic, apart from concrete realities, specific objects, or actual instances. In the language of 6.001, an abstraction is also the general characteristic itself, the function or the operation.

So abstraction is the process of making abstractions, making black boxes. You divide a heavy, complex intractable problem or system into smaller, tractable pieces by abstraction.

Once you've dragged the smaller pieces away from the larger whole, and found the general characteristics, or the relationship between output and input for the abstraction, you can link the abstractions to attain a more complex abstraction.

Yes, but what about entropy?

"With every abstraction, you need to define an 'abstraction barrier,' i.e., the limits of the abstraction," he continued.

An automobile can be thought of as an abstraction. It has a weight and emissions and a length and a width that civil engineers and highway planners deal with. But the car itself is a collection of abstractions. You could call the engine an abstraction. The transmission is an abstraction, and the tires are abstractions. Each abstraction has performance characteristics that can be modeled by an engineering group.

Model. Key word. So an abstraction is like a model. And a model of a system may be composed of linked models of smaller systems, or subsystems.

"Now in design," Professor Siebert said, "the task will be to define the abstractions and the abstraction barriers."

You will also need to have clean interfaces between the abstraction barriers; this will enable more than one person to work productively on a large, complex system. It's the old divide-and-conquer approach. Any technology consists of linked abstractions, and the idea is to divide the abstractions in a manageable way.

This is what Chet and Scott and I had done with the RCM. I'd picked up the front half, the fuel system, the clear window design, the nozzle design, and the movie camera, while Chet and Scott had taken the rear half of the machine and all its attendant subsystems. Thus I could invent and tinker in the front half and feel like the old-time inventors, while Scott and Chet did the same in the rear half of the machine. Once our two systems worked, we would choreograph the whole process of the experiment with the timing electronics I had ignorantly assembled.

This level of subdivision has its limits. It works its way into the real world, where engineers and scientists are divided and conquered by allowing them only to know the cellular information they need to produce their assigned abstraction. As they climb the branches of the corporate tree, they are privy to more and more information, a broader view. They see that the whole thing is pretty easy once they know how to do all its parts, and if the noncompetition agreement they sign is not tight enough they form a spin-off company with some of the other abstractions. As John Delorean did.

It goes further. Turning a bolt mindlessly at a car assembly plant is an abstraction, easy enough to teach a robot. And a robot will never snort cocaine.

More Siebert lecture. "We encourage you to think wishfully."

When you're solving a problem, wishful thinking will help you define the appropriate subproblems. Wishful thinking is simply saying, "Wouldn't it be nice if I had a thing that did such and such a thing." Once you know what you want, it's easy enough to get it. Once you name a spirit, you have power over it. You just keep saying that question over and over again, looking for the answer, breaking the problem down into smaller and smaller pieces. Eventually you get to the point where you can actually solve one or two of the pieces, or one of your subordinates can. The trick with large systems is to choreograph or orchestrate it so that all the problems are solved at more or less the right time and people aren't sitting around waiting for some other abstraction to give them the information they need to do the next thing they need to do. This is what we mean by top-down programming. You make procrastination a productive part of the problem-solving process by not losing yourself in the fine details until later.

I remembered the bicycle museum in Belgium, where the technology development was displayed innovation by innovation. "Ainsi naquit la bicyclette": "Thus was born the bicycle," the label on the first example from the eighteenth century said. The men in top hats straddled steel two-wheelers in the diagram. There were no pedals, no brakes, no tires. In effect it was a running aid. So it answered the wishful question, Wouldn't it be nice if, when I ran, I weren't limited by the length of my legs, but rather could give the earth a push at regular intervals and compete with longer-legged people equally?

The second series had tires, which must have answered the wishful question, Wouldn't it be nice if my push-bike didn't hurt so much? followed by the penny farthing, which answered the question, Isn't it sort of stupid to be pushing off the ground when I can crank a wheel like all the big mechanical machines do?, followed by the two-wheeled, modern-day "safety bicycle," which answered the question, Wouldn't it be nice if I didn't have to crack my head open every time I fell off my penny farthing?

More Siebert lecture. "Now, in LISP, as in any language, we deal with primitives, means of combination, and means of abstraction, and also with idioms, or common patterns of usage."

LISP is a slow language, but once you know it, it's very easy to read and understand a program because the programmer's time is the expensive part and the electricity needed to fire the logic gates open and closed in the chips is relatively cheap.

"The key with large systems is communication," Siebert said.

You want to communicate with other members of your group now quickly and efficiently so you don't waste time explaining messy logic to someone else. Besides, the someone else may be you later on—after the weekend when you come back to the problem—and if your code isn't clear you'll spin your wheels trying just to get back to where you were on Friday.

"But we could talk all day," he said. "The machines in the computer lab are here to smarten you up."

The problem sets help you achieve mastery, and sitting at the machines trying to wrap your mind around the concepts presented is the best thing you can do to attain mastery. When you are at the machine, the machine is your teacher, your dictionary; the machine is your thesaurus; the machine is your version of E. B. White's *The Elements of Style*. Why? Because anything that is bad grammar or bad spelling or bad usage simply does not work, and you have to try again and again until it does work. Siebert said that there would be some tutors in the lab to help us if we really get stuck. They were sitting at the back of the classroom.

In the lab. The computers were Chipmunks, donated to MIT by Bill Hewlett ('36)–Packard. These things were sort of mega-personal computers, each worth $50,000 if it were commercially available. But, of course, these costs mean nothing because they are coming down by a factor of 2 every couple of years. They were all lined up in a big room in the EG&G building, Building 34. I don't know why they called them Chipmunks, unless it was a jab at the users of the machines, the chip monks. None of them was named Alvin, so that wasn't it.

There were fifty machines and not a lot of them were occupied so I sat down and tried to figure out how to log on. It was a little trickier than the Apple in Greene's computer room, because (1) there was no floppy disk to enter, and (2) the machine was already on. There was nothing on the screen, not even a little flashing rectangular cursor.

I thumbed through the guide to the machine, looking for an instruction that said, "Press any key to start" or "Type 'ENTER' to start." There were no clues anywhere. It wasn't written on the blackboard. It is so obvious, such common knowledge, such an idiotproof concept that everyone should know intuitively how to start.

After half an hour of reading and rereading the manual and looking through my notes, I asked the nineteen-year-old teaching assistant. Yes, it is humiliating to ask a mealymouthed sophomore for help, but age has nothing to do with ability.

"Hit the space bar," he answered.

Golly. I should have known that. The problem of the day was, Define a procedure (LISP for "write a program") that takes three (3) numbers as arguments and returns the sum of squares of the two (2) larger numbers. The problem was in the first chapter of the notes so it was by definition easy. No, it wasn't.

How to proceed? I stared at the little bar cursor on the black and white screen that flashed annoyingly, as if to say, "Come on, slowpoke, you're boring me."

Time for wishful thinking. But first, translate key words in the problem statement. This is what the people in the artificial intelligence lab make their LISP machines do when they feed them "word problems" from high school algebra textbooks (e.g., "John is one-fourth as old as his father. In ten years John will be one-third the age of his father. How old will John be when he's half as old as his father?").

The key words are *argument* and *return*. An argument is what other computer programming classes would call an input—for example, x in cos (x). *Return* is what the rest of the world would call "output." But this is MIT and we have our own terms here, and our terms are better than anyone else's.

So the problem statement means (1) take any three numbers; (2) figure out which are the two bigger ones; (3) multiply each of the bigger ones by itself; (4) add together the results of (3).

Now it's time for wishful thinking. Wouldn't it be nice if I had a magic box that figured out the larger two of any three numbers? Wouldn't it be nice if I had another magic box that would make the sum of the squares of whatever two numbers I put into it? Wouldn't it be nice? Maybe then . . . I couldn't remember the rest of the words to the Beach Boys' song.

I knew what I didn't know, if you know what I mean. If you precisely know what you don't know you can draw a box and call that a procedure and invent the details of it. The idea that Siebert stressed was legibility, communication to my colleagues now and myself later. They allow you to make the names of the boxes as long as you want, so I called one of the boxes "Make-sum-of-squares." I called the other box "Find-bigger-two-of-three." I called the spirits by name and had power over them.

I'd learned functions in high school, such as cos(x), "cosine of x," and LISP empowered me to invent functions with more than one argument. Awesome concept, dude. Powerful. Elegant. Clever. These are words that floated around the Chipmunk room. What I'd done on the Apple was cool, it was iterative, but it was really clumsy compared to this language—if I could ever become fluent in it. And as if that weren't awesome enough, LISP enables you to make functions of functions of functions of functions ad infinitum. It almost brought higher mathematics to earth.

My job, having named the spirits, was to tame them, to bring them into submission, to grab them by the hollow of the thigh as the angel did to Jacob.

To tame them is the same as inventing them, or programming them. So time to move the cursor.

DEFINE FIND-BIGGER-TWO-OF-THREE (A B C)

a, b, c, were symbols for the arbitrary numbers the program could take as input. I fished through the notes, through the manuals, through the solved problems from the year before to try to capture the pattern of how to write a solution.

The approach is to find a similar problem for which you have the answer and try to mimic it, try to change it a little bit, and maybe luck out and reach an answer. If the answer is like the one in the book you can fool yourself into thinking you're learning something. However, this is and was suboptimal (Course Six evidently had not heard Professor Wilson's definition of suboptimization as rearranging the deck chairs on the *Titanic*; their definition of suboptimal was "less than optimal"), suboptimal because the only thing you learn when you mimic surface patterns and how to change them is what they look like and how to sleaze some partial credit points out of the grader of the problem set or the test.

But the only way really to learn, to internalize the knowledge, is to concentrate, to focus, and to break the problem down into its simplest pieces and then build the solution up out of the problem's pieces. It's hard to focus, but if you can do that, the rest is easy. It's like the answer is a walnut and you have a walnut pick and you're trying to pull the walnut out of the shell. You can either scratch at the surface and pull little pieces off the top of the nut, bit by bit, and mix other little pieces of the shell with it, or you can work around the edge of the nut, looking for places to loosen it whole from the shell like an overripe fruit. Maybe this is what Professor Noam Chomsky meant by "surface" structure and "deep" structure.

I asked the mealymouthed sophomore for help again.

"I'm trying to define this procedure that will return the bigger two numbers by using 'greater than' signs," I said.

"The machine won't return two numbers like that," he said rapid-fire. "Well, actually it can, but we won't be telling you how. It would only confuse you. Why don't you try using the procedures 'min' or 'max'? They're in chapter three."

There I'd gone along with that narrow, limited, sequential way of looking at things and wrongly assumed that since the problem was in chapter one, all the material I would need to solve it would also be in chapter one. Not so at MIT. This is their way of tricking you into reading ahead.

And so I applied "max" once, then applied "max" to the remaining two numbers, squared the two resulting numbers and added them together.

It took several tries, though, and a paragraph in the Chipmunk manual was characteristically understated:

"Debugging: It will become apparent to you many times during a program's evolution that the program is not entirely right. Instead of blaming the program for these faults, strange creatures called bugs are blamed (back before the transistor, when computers were huge, when 'tubes' amplified signals, problems were caused by real bugs caught in the wires). In this way the programmer remains free of guilt. Debugging, like programming, is an acquired skill and an art."

Everything's easy once you know how to do it.

July 21

Siebert: "The mantra for today is 'recursion.' "

The way to think of recursion is that you have a set of dolls that they make in Eastern Europe, where one doll looks like the other one but is smaller and fits inside it. Now suppose there's something on the innermost doll that you want. Suppose further that each doll has a key to open up the next inner layer, and suppose further that your boss said to you, not only do you want the thing that's on the innermost doll, but also you want the dolls to be the same after you're done. So you use your key to open up doll number one, use doll number one's key to open up doll number two, then use doll number two's key to open up doll number three, et cetera, until you reach the innermost doll. Then you come back the way you went in until you have your result and a fully assembled doll set again. The beauty of recursion is that you structure the computer's solution to the problem in a way that lets you see the problem as nested subproblems of a similar nature.

Siebert said that when you want to write your programs, one useful technique is to write down all the steps in solving the problem by hand and look for the pattern in the solution. When you capture that pattern, try to say in English what you want the program to do. Then try to program it. Eventually you'll become fluent enough that you can just sit down at the machine and compose code without going through the intermediate steps. But it may save debugging time if you approach it as suggested.

I remembered the Belgian mathematics professor's saying that what a mathematician does is write something out with all the steps and then condense it into a form that no one else can understand. Maybe that's why math majors find six double oh one easy.

Siebert went on to an example of a "sort" routine. A sort routine is useful in doing things like putting lists in alphabetical order. Say you're trying to put some order in your filing system. Say you have one thousand items to categorize. First you pick ten or so categories, and go through the pile and put things in each of the piles. Then you go through the ten piles and make up subcategories for them, and so on, until you have everything in easily findable files.

Knowledge is power, information is power, but speedy access to knowledge and information is real power.

"We're helping you with techniques to manage complexity," he continued.

He said that these are simple techniques, but when you link them, your programs may begin to take on a life of their own. You'll input something and the output will surprise you but it will be real. Then you'll input something else and you'll be surprised again. You build so much complexity into a system that you cannot understand what is happening. And so any sufficiently advanced technology becomes indistinguishable from magic.

Yes, but the magician controls the magic, and I want to be a magician.

July 28

"Where are you from?" I asked the foreign-looking man seated in the Sloan Lab classroom, while we waited for the defense to begin.

"Building 32."

Ari had finished his Ph.D. research and had delivered the completed manuscript to his review committee. As is the custom dating from medieval Oxford, he would present his research in a public defense. His committee would then confer privately, decide whether the research were MIT-quality, and make him a doctor.

Ari's presentation was polished, affirmative, convincing. Chet, Scott, Ben, the foreigner from Building 32, and the rest of the audience left the room for the deliberations. Five short minutes later the door opened and the committee chairman said, "Congratulations, Doctor Solomon."

July 30. I helped Ari load the boxes into his car. It felt as if the older brother I never had were going away to college.

"You know what they did to me?" he said. "All the figures in my thesis, the ones I thought surely the grant would pay for, the bill from the Graphic Arts department here came to $6,800. And I have to pay it or I don't get the degree and I wasted three years of my life."

"Well, Ari, you know what they call that."

"What, my friend?"

"The Institute Screw."

"I will miss you, my friend."

"And I you, Ari. And I you."

Schedule:
Fall '83: 2.31 Strength of Materials (Ghandi)
           6.111 Digital Electronics Lab (Troxel) (audit)
           2.996 Thesis

Hardware
September 10

"Hello Goodbye"
—JOHN LENNON–PAUL MCCARTNEY

Six one eleven. Course Six's version of two seventy, only a hundred times harder. This is the course wherein the first video game was invented in the early 1970s. I'd seen kids at Senior House at all hours of the night, every night, Friday and Saturday included, poring over their nerd kits, the briefcase-size boxes, poking wires into them next to the chips. I wanted to find out what they were up to.

The underground guide to course Six said, "6.111 is a practical 'hands-on' lab course on the design and debugging of digital electronic circuits. How well you do in this course depends greatly on being able to get the various labs to work. Consequently, the ability to debug, though never specifically taught, is of prime importance. . . . The difficulty of the material and the associated labs increases rapidly as the course progresses; so rapidly, in fact, that the lectures tend to fall behind [understatement]. . . . Unfortunately, TAs are in high demand, so waits of over an hour are common just to be checked off, to say nothing of getting help [you're on your own, kid]. . . . Of course, the final third of the course is devoted to the infamous final project, which usually grows to fill all available free time [understatement]. Take 6.111 with nothing else." Six one eleven is the ultimate fire hose course.

I walked past a classroom on the way to the lecture. The professor had drawn an electric field on the blackboard and had set up circuitry to generate that electric field in the front of the room. He had a transistor radio tuned to noise, as Tim did with the perpetual motion machine, and traced the outline of the field, whose shape was as in the diagram on the blackboard. The invisible made visible. Mens et Manus—Mind and Hand.

Professor Troxel was erasing the blackboard as everyone went to his or her seat. It must be sort of humiliating, I thought, to have tenure at MIT and still have to erase the blackboard from the class before. Of course, the professor from the class before could have erased his blackboard notes from his lecture, but he had to erase the ones from before him and dammit one stint of blackboard erasing is enough.

I was just auditing the class, and it was kind of a nice gesture that he allowed me to sit in, and I was a graduate student from another department and no way could I be accused of brown-nosing if I helped him, so I took care of half of the boards.

The lecture began. "There's no text for the class, because none covers everything we'll be covering," he said. "Today's lecture is partly on Boolean algebra, partly on laying out the combinational logic for the first lab."

Boolean algebra is the language of combinational logic. George Boole was an English mathemetician, who, around the time Rudolph Diesel was in Kimbies, developed logic operators that could receive two statements, true or false, and output a third statement, true or false. The simplest was an "and" gate, which said, "If a is true and b is true, then c (the output) is also true. If either a or b or both a and b are false, the output is false."

Boole had no idea that the system he developed over a century ago would become the bread and butter of electronics designers. And so the advanced mathematics of today may be the bread and butter of whatever designers a century from now. And so it recurs. But then Dr. Bardeen (Princeton, Ph.D. 1936 [sorry, MIT]) discovered the semiconductor. I'd seen his lab notes on display at the microprocessor exhibit at the Science Museum in London. They were fully as messy as my notes in the RCM cell, but they won him a Nobel Prize.

The semiconductor is the heart of a transistor. My first association with transistors was with the transistor radio my mother's father gave me when I was seven; its black plastic-smelling case came out of the box and I asked my father why Lloyd, the manufacturer, had two l's.

A transistor is like a light switch. Turning on a light switch completes a circuit and lets electricity go to the light. A transistor does the same thing, only instead of putting your finger on a switch, a teensy tinesy bit of electricity is like your finger, and it switches the transistor on when it goes to the transistor. But unlike a light switch, where, no matter how dextrous you are, you can only turn it on and off three or four times per second, you can turn a transistor on and off about a million times per second. That much I'd managed to pick up in my summer electronics class, even though the jerk gave me a C.

If you can turn on and off, you can say yes and no, if you define yes as on and no as off or no as on and yes as off. And if you say yes and no fast enough and are clever in the logic you link, you can create a machine with "intelligence."

Troxel blasted through all of Boolean algebra in the first half-hour of the lecture (lesser schools spend entire semesters on this subject), at which point a pizza delivery person opened the door to the lecture hall. "Pizza for a Mr. John Doe," the guy said.

Troxel stopped dead in his tracks for a few thousandths of a second, a long time in his world of trillionths, and said after the laughter died down and the kid in the top row paid the deliverer, "That'll teach us to schedule lectures during lunchtime."

He ended the lecture with an overview of the course. "You'll find that in logic design, as in any design, there's more than one way to state a logical relation; i.e., there are synonyms. These synonyms have subtle differences in meaning, as in English. English is expressive but not exact, which is why lawyers make so much money. Using the logic that says closest to what you want to say will help you communicate with your lab partner now and with yourself later."

That sounded familiar. Siebert had said that in the summer. I wondered whether there were some kind of conspiracy in the department.

"But this isn't law school, and it isn't medical school. We won't have you memorizing what certain chips do. You can look that up in the TTL *Data Book*, the way every digital designer in Silicon Valley does. A lot has been put into chips already, and you'll have to discover what chip to use by looking through the data book. And as you go along, you'll gain experience and develop intuition about what's going to work. You'll develop your personal Book of Tricks, to which I'll add a few of my own during the lectures.

"And I strongly encourage you to work through the first three labs as quickly as possible, so that you will have time to complete lab four, which will take up your entire nerd kit, if your design is not suboptimal. Significantly suboptimal designs for lab four simply won't fit on your circuit boards.

"And then, of course, there is The Project. You should start thinking about a lab partner now; the maximum group size is three, and two is probably ideal. More than three and it becomes a management project, not an engineering project. Choose your partner carefully, though.

"I encourage you to do well in this class and on the project. If I were to make a hiring decision based only on this course, I'd hire you immediately without an interview if your grade is an A. If you had a B, I'd interview you and ask you about your six one eleven project. And if you had a C you wouldn't get in the door. Good luck."

This is a good course just to audit, rather than to take for a grade, I thought. I don't need any more C's.

CHAPTER

——— 18 ———

Results

*". . . most real-life problems are for killing peo-
ple. . . ."*
—Anonymous comment overheard in MIT
corridor

October 20

Meanwhile, back in the engine lab . . .
"Film loaded," I said.
"Check," Scott my lab partner said.
"Camera focused."
"Check."
"Fuel injector armed."
"Check."
"Computer data acquisition system initiated."
"Check."
"Oscilloscope initiated."
"Check."
"Lab lights out."
"Check."
"Flashlight on."
"Check."

"Raise tank pressure."

"Fifty psi, 60 . . . 70 . . . 80 . . . 90 . . ."

The cell door opened unexpectedly, suddenly, caught me off guard, made me jump. "Who the hell is that? Can't you see we're doing a test?" I barked.

It was Nick.

"Uh, g'mornin', uh, Cap'n," he said, taken aback at my outburst. He looked hurt, as if he'd lost a friend. He looked the way I must have just before I broke into tears in Gyftopoulos's office two years before. But he held it at that; twenty years at MIT had toughened him. "There wasn't any sign on the lab door'n all so I figured I'd sotta check in on you an' see how you were doin'. Sorry if I messed up the experiment."

I wasn't through. "Well, dammit, Nick, next time knock, will you? Now we have to start all over. Besides, if you'd opened the door when the camera was running you would have ruined a test."

Nick's expression sank further. "Sorry, Cap'n."

The abuse the institute had dealt me, the damage it had done to my self-esteem, had piled up like the pressure in the tank; it needed to be vented, and Nick was the nearest victim.

Scott opened the valve and dumped the air from the tank. "It's no big deal," he said, trying to patch things up. "Everything's armed. We can just start the sequence again. We'll finish all the tests we need to do today."

"Gee, Nick, I'm sorry," I said. "I just kind of lost it there for a minute."

" 'S all right, Cap'n. I've seen it happen to a lotta students here. It's like one of the professors said to me once. They put the heat on you to harden *you*, just like they do to steel."

So now I'm a product of this place, I wondered. Quicker, smarter, arrogant, impatient, directed, inhumane. I've got to get out of here. But if I'm a tough, arrogant jerk to Nick, who's used to these people, who will I be to the rest of the world? I wish I could stay here forever.

"There's a sign down in one of the idle cells, Cap'n. I'll go bring it for you," Nick said, and he returned with a framed white sign, like the one on the door of the cell, that said, "Test in progress; do not disturb."

"Thanks, Nick," I said.

Chet rounded the corner into the cell.

"So how you guys doing?" he asked.

I answered, "OK. We're about to do a series of tests. We're aiming to do the swirl case and the no swirl case today." Swirl means the air is spinning in the engine, like a whirlpool. That's supposed to mix the diesel fuel with the air better so it burns better. No swirl means it's not.

Chet said, "Well, if you get those two cases to work, you'd better keep going. You know when an experiment with this many pieces works all at once you gotta keep the momentum before something breaks. A lotta my friends spent three years building their experiments and one day doing the tests. I'll hang around and be a cheerleader. We also oughta vary the air temperature and see how that affects the ignition delay. If you get five temperatures, you can make a graph and that will be your thesis."

The light at the end of the tunnel wasn't a train coming the other way anymore. I could have the data today. Some pretty movies to wow the reviewing professors at the qualifiers, some analysis of the films. Master's from MIT. I remembered the sound of it from the guy at West Virginia U talking about the guy who'd been there the summer before who had a master's from MIT and how smart he was. Of course, now my sights were higher, and M-I-T, P-H-D, M-O-N-E-Y was on my lifetime to-do list. Whenever you near a milestone you look ahead to the next one.

All systems were go in my miniature version of the space program. The injector now spurted consistent amounts of fuel on every injection. (I'd figured out how to modify the insides using the pieces of junk that George the technician at United Technologies had given me.) Its spherical nozzle went in the right direction now. George's shop didn't read my drawing right the first time, so I'd taken a golf ball out there and marked it up like a giant nozzle and shown it to the machinist to make sure he knew what I was talking about the second time.

And we'd tested the clear window I'd designed, and we knew it would withstand the pressure of the combustion. That was my end of the machine.

For his part, Scott had finished the new starting mechanism, and the electronics to sequence the experiment were set to make everything happen at the right time. We knew just how long the film would take to reach a viewing rate of 3,000 frames per second. We knew just how long the piston would take to travel the 18 inches from one end of the machine to the other. We knew the mechanical delay times in the starting mechanism and the fuel injector. With all this data, we'd constructed a map, a sequence of the experiment, much as a choreographer would block out a dance, or a composer would arrange a score.

We'd dialed in the appropriate delays, all thousandths of seconds, in the little black electronic timing boxes. God willing, the delays would be repeatable, the film would catch the combustion, the computer would catch the pressure data, and I would find something inspired to say about it all.

"Lab lights off," I said.

"Check," Scott said.

"Flashlight on."

"Check."

"Raise tank pressure: 50 psi . . . 60 . . . 70 . . . 80 . . . 90 . . ."

The machine creaked and made the 90-psi thunk, but I knew at what pressure it would make each noise so my pulse rate only increased half a beat per minute for each psi of pressure, down from two beats during the earlier firings.

I continued to let the air in the tank. "100 . . . 110 . . . 115, 116, 117, 118, 119, 120 and steady," I said.

The creaking stopped. The machine was at equilibrium at its high state of stress.

"Check."

"Say a little prayer."

Pause. Silence.

"Check."

"Fire!"

ZZZZZZIIINNNNGGGGG. The film rolled. *Click*. The shaft released. Boom. Flash. Ignition. We have ignition, Houston.

All in half a heartbeat. "Okay, turn the lights on," Chet said. "Write down the readings on the pressure gauge in the tank and on the fuel injector. You might need that information later. You probably won't, but if you don't write it down it's lost forever. I think we got a good test. I think it's going to be a good test day."

I recorded the pressures in the lab notebook and dumped the pressure to the tank. We opened the door and Nick was standing outside.

"Sounded like a good one, Cap'n. Everything sounded just right. Yep, I bet that one took the building another thousandth of an inch apaht or so. We better keep an eye on that crack in the wall."

"Thanks, Nick. Five more to go and I'll have a master's degree."

Zing. Click. Boom. We repeated the sequence five times, with swirl, without swirl, with different air temperatures. The computer worked every time. The flash worked every time. But did the film work every time?

I loaded the undeveloped film in my backpack and cycled across the Harvard Bridge (the bridge next to MIT spanning the Charles), from the Harvard Bridge down Commonwealth Avenue past the exponentially appreciating condominiums and on to the film developing lab in the South End.

It seemed like yesterday, last spring when I'd done the same route with the film of the fuel injection into air. The pink magnolia flowers were blooming then, their fragrance overpowering even the diesel bus fumes ahead of me.

Now the leaves were changing and I smelled only the diesel exhaust. But if the test were successful, I would soon see that exhaust in its formative milliseconds. I would see what Rudolph Diesel could only imagine. If I could see the exhaust, perhaps I could find a pattern in it, an insight, a new way of looking at it that would maybe, just maybe, find its way into future generations of diesel engines. In the Eiffel tower of technology, I would be a rivet.

October 22

Most of the Calorics had graduated, but Senior House had an intramural soccer team in B-league, one notch above C-league. Everyone on the team was a skinny nineteen-year-old, but at twenty-six I was wiser.

"Come on, you fat old man," they said. "Run. Move."

I played smart. I was at the right place at the right time at left wing and the goalie was flatfooted when I rocketed the shot to the back of the net. Score one for me.

After the game the Senior House crew returned across campus to Walker dining hall and I went to eat in Lobdell, closer to the lab, by myself. More and more I ate by myself. Friends from the first year were gone and I'd slackened in my efforts to make new friends. All that mattered now was the thesis, and after that the doctoral qualifying exams.

Cindy Brooks sat at my table. After a few minutes of conversation, she said, "You're kind of a loner, aren't you?"

October 25

The placement office is in Building 12, on the same level as the infinite corridor. It makes it easier for the recruiters to find the place. I'd signed up to talk to the people from Schlumberger, the oil exploration company.

I had no interest in exploring for oil; in my heart of hearts I would prefer to explore industrial plants for ways to lower the need for oil. But these guys made about fifty thousand 1983 dollars in their first year, plus bonuses, and their taxes weren't as high because they worked overseas in places like Malaysia and Indonesia. In three years you can buy a house for cash and then do what you want. A master's from MIT qualifies you for this kind of job.

The placement office was skylit, had several tables with corporate brochures with pictures of mostly men in shirtsleeves and ties and women wearing lab jackets, and headings like "Expand your horizons at Data General" and "Let your career grow with Du Pont."

This day, in addition to the normal interviews, the sophomore Six-a's (Course Six majors; *a* means co-op) were interviewing for their co-op positions. These electrical engineers would spend part of their undergraduate years working in industry, defray the cost of their education, provide cheap skilled labor, and obtain "real-world" experience before graduation. The Six-a's all wore the same dark blue suit, white shirt, red tie, and black shoes and socks; I wondered how the interviewers could tell them apart.

I signed in for the interview as Mr. Theunissen, in a light blue suit, walked out of the back area of interview cubicles and put his hand out. "Mr. White?" he said.

"Yes," I said and shook his hand firmly, as recommended in the placement office guide to interviewing.

"It's a pleasure to meet you. Please come this way." He led me back through the long narrow corridor with the little interview compartments on each side, with doors for privacy. The walls weren't very thick, though, so we could pick up bits and pieces of the interviews as we passed to his space. "Why weren't you at the slide presentation about the company last night?" he asked. "Attendance was mandatory."

What slide presentation? He's trying to catch me off guard. He's no Chet Yeung, though. Nor is he a Heywood or a Gyf-topoulos.

"I had a test this morning, and I really needed to study for it," I answered. "Do you have a video or anything I can borrow? There are VCRs in the library."

He smiled, made a little note on his pad. "No, I don't think that will be necessary. If you come visit us in Houston, you'll find out all you need to know about our business. Why are you interested in working for Schlumberger?"

"I hear you guys make tons of money," I said.

He smiled more this time, almost laughed, and made another note. "You know, that's the first time anyone has ever answered that question that way," he said. "How much do you think we make?"

"Oh, I don't know, maybe $50K or so. I figure after a few years with you guys I'd be set for life."

"Yes, you're right; it's at least fifty thousand in the first year, and then within the first five years at the company it reaches up to one hundred thousand; then, as you move up in management, the compensation package becomes more and more attractive."

I smiled, made a little note on my pad.

He asked a question, "It says here you speak French. Would you mind if we conducted the interview in French for a few minutes?"

"Bien sûr; et italien?" (Sure, how about Italian after that?) After a few minutes and friendly marks on his notepad we returned to English.

"I see you spent some time in Belgium at the von Kármán Institute. Would you care to tell me a little about what you did there?"

This is the part of the interview where they want you to show how you can communicate technical concepts; it might be important in a meeting with a king or a sheik or an oil minister someday in the future. The consortium meeting presentations had prepped me for this. "Well, I spent a lot of time dealing with air flow speed measurement techniques such as hot wire anemome-try." A big word or two couldn't hurt. He'd probably never heard of hot wire anemometry anyway.

"That's very interesting," he said. "In fact, my thesis at the École Technique Supérieure in Paris involved exploring the electronic limitations of hot wire anemometry."

Uh-oh. I'd broken interview rule number one. Never throw out a buzzword that you can't back up with a full explanation, a derivation of its tree of specialized knowledge. I wished they'd put that in the interview handbook instead of tips on tie colors.

It was two and a half years ago I did that. It was before I'd learned about internalizing the deep structures of things, and I was busy enjoying my year-long paid vacation in Brussels. "Uh. It has to do with the air flow cooling off a wire. As the fine short length of wire cools, its resistance decreases. The wire is in an electrical circuit, and the decrease or increase in electrical resistance is sort of like an input to the circuit. It changes the output to the circuit, and that's how you know how fast the flow is going." That should do it, I thought. A general discussion is sufficient for a job interview, isn't it? This isn't a doctoral qualifying exam.

He wanted more. "Would you mind sketching the circuit that the anemometer would fit into?"

"Well, gee, it's been a while and, uh . . ."

"You can take a couple of minutes if you'd like. I'll just read my newspaper," he said, removing his copy of Le Figaro from his briefcase.

I tried to remember the explanation from my summer electronics class of how a Wheatstone bridge measurement circuit worked. I'd understood about 80 percent of it then, just enough to pass the class. It was a little hard to concentrate, though, with him behind the paper, occasionally flipping the page.

"This is the best I can do for now," I said finally. I showed and briefly explained my sketch. "And so as the resistance changes in this leg, it makes a voltage difference between these two points in the circuit and that's what you see on the oscilloscope; I remember there's a trick to setting up the equations for the circuit to solve for the voltage, but I can't remember that right now. Maybe I could mail it to you this evening."

"That won't be necessary. I think that's enough for now. We would like you to take an application form and send it in to us as soon as you can. I'll show it to some of the other recruiters and we may invite you to Houston for some further interviews," he said.

I think I passed.

That night, in my office. Whirrwhirrwhirrwhirrr went the desktop film viewer as I scanned the high-speed movie of the first combustion test. It was blackness, blackness, blackness for hundreds of frames. I was expecting mostly darkness: the camera needed to accelerate for most of the test; that's why it was the first thing to be turned on.

Frame 800 showed an image. I slowed the film viewer. 801 was brighter, 802 brighter still, 803 brighter still, each frame a three-thousandth of a second. The three flashes that I'd found at the used camera store in Newton started to light the combustion window. 804, 805, 806, 807 were at full brightness, but nothing was happening in the cylinder. I hoped we caught the injection of the fuel. I hoped our synchronization of all the delays was correct.

810, 811, the diesel fuel appeared at the nozzle tip, a liquid starfish-shaped set of jets radially emanating from the center. We have injection, Houston. 812, 813, the jets traversed the cylinder. Fourteen more frames, fuel kept flowing into the hot air in the combustion chamber. Come on, big guy, you can do it. The fuel jets became thicker for a couple of frames. 828, 829 then returned to the regular flow of the previous fourteen frames, then another pulse of thickness for a frame. The little parts inside the injector were bouncing up and down as the plunger compressed the liquid and the liquid went out and the plunger compressed it again and the liquid went out again.

Let's go, guy. Burn.

Frame 831. We have ignition, Houston. Little orange lights started at the edge of the cylinder, and then like a house afire the orangeness became bright yellow, then almost white as the flame engulfed the jets from the outside in—a bright flaming starfish. Please refer to Figure 1. Next slide, please.

The starfish flamed and burned and flamed until . . . frame 839, as we can see, the soot particles are forming around the outside of the flame and . . . the starfish is no longer there now, just a glowing ember of primordial galaxies forming and glowing and darkness yielding the last breath of the starfish's life gasping, glowing embers fading fading back into fading darkness . . . this is the no swirl case. There is residual soot formation as less of the fuel vaporizes prior to combustion and more of the fuel is effectively baked, not burned, in an air-starved environment.

Next slide, please. The swirl case.

The starfish burned and disappeared, without the lingering, burning embers. A result to report in my thesis. Similarly for the other swirl cases at different air temperatures. Now to look at the pressure data. I looked at the computer-generated graphs. The cylinder pressure rose, stayed fairly constant as the piston reached the end of its travel and was locked in place, and then the graph steeply shot up again.

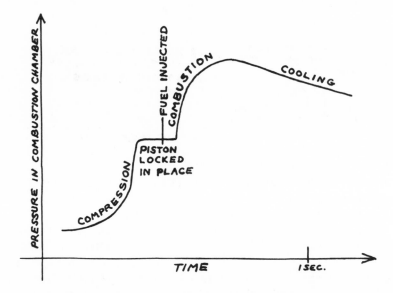

All the graphs looked the same, sitting side by side.

What to do? The consortium meeting is in three days. I stared at them all, looking for a pattern. There has to be a pattern. The first definition of thesis is a proposition advanced and maintained by argument. If there is no proposition there is no thesis. If there is no thesis there is at least no master's degree, and certainly no Ph.D. There must be something more to say about these narrow lines generated by a computer printer. What to do?

Trace them on transparencies.

Okay, I'll trace them on clear plastic. Now what?

Mark where the injection starts with a little arrow.

Easy enough. What else?

Pile the transparencies one on top of the other, and slide them

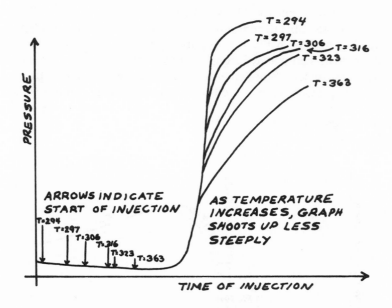

around until the steep part of the start of combustion lines up at the same place.

The still, small voice was not in the fire.

T plus 19,000 hours. We have thesis, Houston. We have thesis. Mission Control clapped and cheered and the engineers hugged one another and shook one anothers' hands and patted one another on the back and looked up at the large-screen television and tears welled up in more than one pair of eyes. The *Eagle* has landed.

The longer the time between the start of injection and the start of combustion (a.k.a. the ignition delay time), the longer the steep part of the graph lasts. This, of course, is obvious if you think about it, because the longer the ignition delay time is, the more stuff is mixed to easy burnability. More stuff's being easily burnable means the burning will happen faster, and the pressure will rise faster as the flames engulf the more easily burnable stuff almost all at once.

That's the proposition, and I'll be able to construct the arguments with further analysis of the existing data. But other questions about the combustion lingered.

How much swirl is good swirl? I've seen that swirl mixes the fuel well, but is there a point beyond which adding more swirl doesn't do you any more good? What is the global point of these experiments? If I were designing an engine for a bus, would the point be to minimize the pollution per mile? If so, would I reach a point where the cooling of the cylinder's gas from the swirl's flow decreases the power of the engine even though it reduces the emissions? Perhaps there's an amount of swirl that accomplishes the mixing without dumping too much of the combustion heat through the walls of the cylinder. To find answers will require more experiments and more understanding of combustion modeling. Another couple of years of research beyond the master's level. Peregrine White, Jr., Sc.D. It has a nice ring to it.

October 27

Atkinson. Dianne was on the phone in the second floor hall. "Look, Mitch, if you want that piece of software in four weeks, it's going to cost you. My people have problem sets and labs and exams and other stuff to do, y'know. And they need to sleep now and then." One of the other lines lit up.

"Can I put you on hold for a minute? Thanks. . . . "Hi, Steve. Say, can I get right back to you? You're three hours behind us, right? I'll call back before six o'clock your time. Ciao." Before she hung up the third line lit up. "Bill. Buddy. Yeah, it's coming along. Say, can I call you back in ten? Thanks."

"So, anyway, Mitch, my people should be able to deliver, but it's going to be at premium rates, and what with overhead and all. . . . It's a deal? Great. I'll have a courier drop the contract by first thing in the morning."

After she was off the phone, I said, "Business seems to be pretty good."

"Yeah, I'm hangin' in there. Say, I'm going to an introduction-to-real-estate seminar tomorrow. Care to join me?"

"Sure."

Next day on the way to the Boston Marriott:

"So how'd you get started in the software biz?" I asked.

"Well, I bought an Apple with my baby-sitting money when I was thirteen and I began to hack. You know how you hear these stories about musicians and how when they're in high school and all the cool people are working part time at the mall'n stuff and *they're* in their bedroom listening to records and memorizing solos and doing scales? Well, I was like that, only the computer was my instrument. Sometimes my mother and stepfather worried about my spending so much time alone in my room, I think.

"So, anyway, it was fun and I started subscribing to magazines and I answered an ad for a free-lance software person, and I just kept getting more work in high school. I kept up with my clients when I came here freshman year, and for a hack I put my résumé in the placement office résumé book. OK, I misrepresented my age and pretended I was a senior, but they never checked so freshman year I was flying around the country to plant trips—y'know, interviews at these companies—and they'd always make me job offers but I'd politely decline and hand them my business card and say, 'But if you'd like any work done on a contract basis . . .' Instead of Senior House, 4 Ames St., Atkinson 202, I listed my address as 4 Ames St., Mail Stop A202. Once I show I can deliver on-time and on-budget these people don't even care where I live. I haven't even met half of my client contacts. It's all by phone and FedEx floppy disk mailers."

"Why do you want to go to a real estate seminar? Sounds like you're doing really well already."

"Taxes are killing me. I gotta shelter some income. Besides, my stepfather is a jerk. I mean, he thinks that since I'm making a few bucks he shouldn't have to pay my college expenses. And I say I shouldn't be penalized for my initiative. It'd get him where it hurts if I come back at Christmas and tell him I just bought a twenty-unit apartment building."

Johnny Venture stood at the front of the Marriott Long Wharf conference room and said, "You wanna be Riiiich?"

"Yessss!" the crowd of over two hundred said.

"You wanna be Set for Life!"

"Yessss!"

"For seven hundred and fifty dollars and two days of your time you can be well on your way to financial independence. Does anyone have any questions?"

"Yes," Dianne said. "Can we take the course with no money down and a balloon payment in five years?"

On the way back to Senior House I asked her whether she would sign up for the course.

"I think I'll sign up for it and take earplugs and a little notepad to the complimentary first morning session. As the guy's explaining depreciation I'll read the course binder and make note of any helpful hints. Then I'll go to the Sloan B-school library for some follow-up reading. I can't believe what suckers the rest of these people are."

"Oh. Right," I said. "Well, I wrote them a check when you made one of your phone calls."

October 30

Consortium meeting. Philip Hughes, the Aussie from Caterpillar, asked, "Is there any significance to the width of the lines on your graphs? Does it have to do with expected experimental error?" He was referring to my transparencies.

"It has to do with the width of my magic marker," I answered. They liked the joke and laughed. The sponsors had become almost colleagues, peers, friends.

Phil continued, "Do you suppose you could slide the transparencies so that, rather than lining up the start of combustion, you line up the arrows indicating start of injection one on top of the other?"

"Sure," I said.

Just a slightly different way of looking at something can yield significantly amplified insight. Professor Keck, a colleague of Heywood's and as much a physical chemist as a mechanical engineer, recognized the pattern immediately.

"It looks to me," he said, "as if you can separate the diesel combustion into two distinct phenomena. There is the chemically controlled nearly instantaneous combustion, where the only limit on pressure rise is the speed of the combustion reaction, which, based on the exponential branching of the chemical reactions, is very fast. And then you have the mixing controlled combustion envelope, the curve on the top. Here the rate of combustion can be no faster than the fuel and air mix to the chemical proportions necessary for combustion."

Professor Keck continued, "With your higher-temperature experiments, you have shorter ignition delays, and hence more of the combustion is mixing-controlled. In the lower-temperature cases, you have longer ignition delays, and more fuel is ready to go when combustion is initiated. But the mixing rate is close to the same in each case, so the longer ignition delay experiments

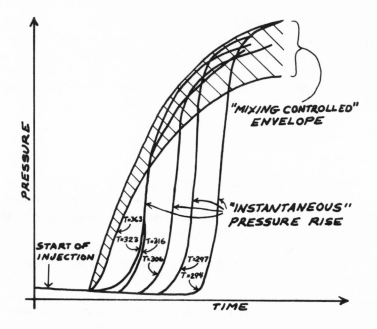

instantaneously catch up with the mixing-controlled curve when combustion is finally initiated."

Thank you, Professor Keck. Thank you, Philip Hughes. You just wrote the "Conclusions" chapter of my thesis. As you raise the temperature of the engine's fuel and air, the fuel starts to burn sooner.

November 15

"They're going to fly me to Houston, Nick. Schlumberger wants me to come down for a plant trip," I told him.

"Hey, Cap'n, that's great. Congratulations. One of the students from the lab went to interview with them a couple of years ago. A real tough interview, he said. They asked him all kinds of technical questions, like how does a spahk plug work, and they even gave an electronics test in the afternoon," Nick answered.

I'd probably better brush off my notes from last summer, I thought. And I'd really better find out how a spark plug works. Here I've told the guy I'm Joe Diesel Engine on my résumé, and

I work in an engine lab. It wouldn't look good for me not to know how a spark plug works.

"Say, Nick, how *does* a spark plug work?"

"C'mon over to the blackboard, Cap'n," he said.

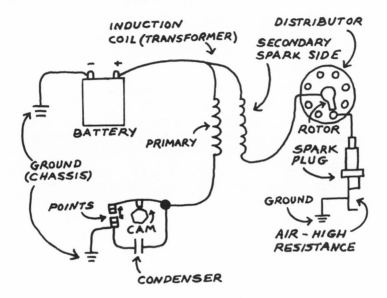

"See, heeyuh yuh got the batt'ry, that's at 12 volts. An' that's connected to this transformuh heeyuh, the ignition coil. Then you got the contact breaker, that's just a switch that opens an' closes at the right time when the rotatin' cam shaft pushes it up an' down. On the secondary side of the transformuh, you got the distributor's rotor arm that makes the electric current go to the spahk plug when the piston's at the right place. Got it?"

"Uh huh."

"Good. Now when the contact breaker closes, current from the batt'ry heeyuh goes through the contact breaker back to ground. When it does that, it stahts a magnetic field in the primary side of the coil. Once the field gets big enough, the contact breaker opens up again, and *pow!* The field in the primary side collapses. The current soughta gets sucked into the condensor heeyuh, and makes the volts in the secondary field go way up, to 20,000, even 35,000 volts. That's enough volts to make the current jump the gap in the spahk plug, an' it lights off the fuel in the engine."

It was just like Doc Edgerton's strobe light, only a little less powerful.

"This is great, Nick," I said. "Do you mind if I make a little sketch of it?"

"Showah. Put it on a little piece a paper an' put it in your wallet. It might come in handy someday."

November 17

It was a night flight to Houston, and the airplane felt different now that I knew how jet engines worked, and I knew about statics and O-rings and the stress on the rivets and how many times the wings could flap up and down before they fell off. But I didn't have time to take the bus.

I remembered the steep descent into Boston from Brussels. Had I changed since then? Was I the professional that Professor Mikic said they would make me? The two businessmen in the seats beside me discussed who would head up the valve division of their company after Higgins retired. The most likely candidate had a big house and a pretty wife.

November 18

There were four other interviewees, all from good schools: Princeton, Stanford, Cal Polytech, Notre Dame. Two of them looked like football players, which might give them an edge; it's rough work, working on oil rigs. I wondered whether my preppy horn-rimmed glasses and pin-striped suit would help or hurt.

The morning was a briefing session about the job. Movies of crews running core samples of the earth, drilling for tens of hours at a time while the youthful, sleep-deprived field engineer no older than I punched commands into the computer and gave orders to the Arabian men on the deck. Movies of the field engineers relaxing and chatting next to the pool on their two weeks' recuperation at the company resort in Oman. It looked exciting. Hard work, good money, set for life in five years—what a deal. I jotted a few notes in the little notebook that fit in my suit jacket pocket.

The morning was nonevaluative, except for the fact that Theunissen and the other interviewer, a British guy with a Ph.D. (maybe he feels underemployed, I jotted in my little notebook), both looked as if they were sizing us up and taking mental notes as we asked questions and tried to look enthusiastic.

"Now, what do you think the single largest source of accidents is for the field engineers?" Theunissen asked after the second movie. The danger must make it hard for them to hire people, even with the high money.

I suggested, "It looks as if there's a lot of heavy stuff on those rigs. I'd imagine occasionally something lands on someone's foot or ankle and mashes something." It seemed plausible enough, I thought. Oil rigs don't blow up every day.

The British guy jotted down a little note. Theunissen said, "Actually, it's automobile accidents; so if you're a safe driver, you should be fine."

Sure. Do you have a copy of the report that came up with that conclusion? Could I glance through it for a second?

For lunch we went to The Sagebrush. This was, after all, Houston. I rode in the front seat of the British guy's yellow Mercedes with brown leather interior and electric door locks.

"Hello, Sundance," Theunissen said to the waitress. "I'll have the usual; two Bloody Marys." Then he turned my way and said, "Go ahead and order; drink up, it's on the oil industry."

"I'll have an orange juice," I said.

His left eyebrow went up to his hairline. "What? Don't you want anything stronger?"

"I don't drink," I answered.

Stanford ordered iced tea, Princeton milk, Notre Dame ginger ale. I wondered whether it was because they didn't want to drink or whether they wanted to be sharp for the test. On the way to the car after lunch I jotted some notes on my little pad.

The test was a piece of cake, what with the couple of hours of preparing I'd done. It was all stuff from the first two weeks in the summer electronics course, plus a little stuff from the first fifteen minutes of six one eleven. Cal Polytech, a double E with straight A's, looked particularly intent on doing well on the half-hour quiz.

Theunissen and the British guy handed them back ten minutes after we were done. I had twelve out of fifteen points. Cal Polytech had eleven, the others were all below ten.

Ha. So I'm not such a dummy after all; it's just that at MIT you always feel dumb by comparison to the environment.

And now for the oral exam, the final interview with Theunissen. I was ready for the lead-off question. He said, "Now, I suppose being a good American you own a car and being a good engineer you do your own work on it. Can you tell me how a spark plug works?"

I pulled the little sheet of paper out of my wallet. "You know, I heard that was one of your questions. Do you mind if I use notes?"

His eyebrow soared again. "Who gave that to you? Which one of the other candidates leaked that to you?"

"None of them, really," I answered. "The technician in my lab told me it was a standard interview question for you guys."

"Okay," he said incredulously. "Look. I know you're a smart kid. I know you can do the work. Do you want this job?"

I wondered whether it were the corporate interview manual talking or Theunissen himself.

"I want the money," I answered.

"You already told me that. I appreciate your honesty. But do you want the job? What would you do if you could do anything you want?"

Another loaded question. But answer honestly. That's what Dean Hooker at Hopkins told me when I was about to go to my interview for a Rhodes Scholarship (I didn't get it). Answer honestly, say the first thing that pops into your mind, and you'll stand out. Most people try to tell the interviewer what he wants to hear and a good interviewer can tell when you're doing that.

"Well, you know, I'm kind of an environmentalist, and I appreciate what you guys do—I mean I drive a car sometimes, too—but I'd really like to work on making the other end of the pipeline, the user end, more efficient. Maybe do some consulting in factories, invent some products that are more efficient."

It seemed to be more and more of him, not the interview manual. "So why don't you do that now?" he asked.

"It helps to have a nest egg. I figure I could work for you five years, see the world, and then do that."

He answered, "You know, that was my plan originally, but after five years, the pay was great and they offered me a huge bonus to move into management, so here I am. Do you have any other concerns about the job?"

"How often could I come home? My father's been ill, and I'd like to be able to see him more than once every two years before he leaves us."

Theunissen raised his eyebrow only slightly on that one. "We can get you home once a year on the company. Beyond that you're on your own."

Right. What's the round-trip airfare from Raleigh-Durham to Kuala Lumpur?

He continued, "Well, we'll probably make you an offer. Have a good flight home."

In the cab on the way to the airport, I reached into my coat pocket to make some further notes in my little pad. Uh oh. I left it on the table. They'll find it, compare the handwriting with the tests, and see my innermost thoughts and observations about them.

Sometimes the decision is not yours.

CHAPTER

——— 19 ———

No It Isn't

Swirling Waters . . .
  (the Charles)
Cool Charles wading, senses invading
  fresh splashes wake from clashes before
ashes
waste deep now,
  don't know how,
    it will end.
  chest deep, eye deep,
    wish I had
      a friend
All my battles so hard fought,
  All my efforts lead . . . to . . .
                    nought . . .

November 19

Somebody'd pinned the poem on the wall across from my apartment. And I thought I'd earned my free room and board last December with the Watson incident. But nooooo; the institute environment does not relent.

I called John Dorsey. "See whether you can figure out who

put it up there," he said. "Try to enlist the help of some of the other students, too."

Downstairs the gin game was going on in the hall. Eldon was one of the four players. "I don't know whether I'm going to make it through the term," he said.

Ah, a suspect. "Why not?" I asked.

"I've always wanted to be an astronaut. To be a mission specialist you need a Ph.D., not to mention being able to run a sub 2:30 marathon. But to get a Ph.D. from here I'll need more A's than B's and I'm pushing C's in two of my classes and I'm only a sophomore. If I get two C's, it'll be swing or swim," he said.

"What do you mean?" I asked him.

"You know, swing . . ." and he jumped up and caught the steam heating pipe with one arm and let the rest of himself go limp and his head fall limply forward.

"You do that really well, Eldon. I still think you should bag engineering and head to New York for some auditions."

"Wait, I'm not through," he said emphatically. ". . . or swim." He let go of the pipe and lay prone on the floor with his arms and legs stretched out the way they do in the East River.

Time to change the subject. "Do you think the Patriots will make it to the playoffs?"

"Who cares?" Eldon said. "What is this, national non sequitur day or something?"

"Yeah," Cindy said. "I've been reading a book about depression. It says that whenever people talk about suicide, in any way, you should let them talk about it. They want to talk about it, like, they're asking for help."

"Okay," I said. "Keep talking, Eldon."

"Well, you know there are magazines that advertise how to do it. There are books. There are mail order kits."

I tried to reassure him. "Look, can't you go to one of your professors and have him help you understand the material better? You can still probably pull a B out of each of the classes and go for the A next term."

Eldon answered, "I tried that. But the guy had this attitude about him, like he kept asking me questions, and it was like he enjoyed making me feel stupid. Then I went to another professor and the same thing happened. I figured I'd stop at two strikes. It's like 'If you can't figure it out for yourself, kid, you don't belong here. Nobody's going to take you by the hand when you're in the middle of that big room full of drafting tables and computer terminals in the real world.' "

"Did you write that poem?" I asked him.

He did Katharine Hepburn. "Poem, what poem? I have no idea what you're talking about. . . ."

"Come on, Schweetheart. Admit it." I went back to Bogie.

"No, seriously though, I don't know what you're talking about." It wasn't Eldon.

Dianne went into her room and brought out a nylon noose. "I picked this up as a hack my sophomore year. I carried it around on April Fools Day. Really freaked out the tutor; he took it away from me and gave it back at the end of the year. Just look at it. High-quality nylon—it'd probably carry 500 pounds."

Eldon perked up. "With that, two or three of us could get together and have a gang hang."

"Come on, guys. Let's be happy. This place isn't so bad," I said.

"Oh, yeah?" Eldon answered. "Well, how about my day today? I already told you I'm well on my way to two C's. That was based on the two tests I got back today. Both were 15 points below class average. My mother called tonight and she said how proud they are of me and how happy they are I'm so successful and how it's rough working at Sears nights to pull together the money for tuition but it's worth it. Then on the way back to the avionics lab three people I knew or thought I knew on the infinite corridor didn't say hi; their eyes were just beaming forward."

"They were probably just preoccupied with some problem set or something," I said. "We all have bad days."

"Yeah, I guess you're right," Eldon said. "But sometimes it feels like MIT is a dragon I have to slay."

November 22

The tutor meeting was to prepare for "The Day After," the made-for-TV film about being nuked.

"Now I want you all to be on the lookout for any warning signs after it's aired," John Dorsey said. "You might want to have some kind of discussion group about it. Let the students talk through it. The film contains material that may be offensive. Viewer discretion is advised. The institute is worried that it might depress people, that there may be mass suicide. We have to take steps to prevent that."

I spent the evening of the movie reading, not watching TV. On the way back from the student center library, there were signs up and down the infinite corridor. WHY IS THERE NO HOPE? one said. WHY IS THE INSTITUTE HOPELESS? I wondered whether it was somebody's idea of a sick joke, a way to push the reader into a life-threatening depression. I ripped down every one I could put my hands on.

I hosted a milk and cookies break after the movie. "It wasn't that great," Dianne said. "The character development just wasn't there."

"Yeah," Eldon said. "And the special effects were like totally fakey. If they wanted to be really effective they should have shown the real films from Hiroshima and Nagasaki. When the real thing happens the destruction will be a lot worse than they showed in that movie."

"*Would*, Eldon, *would*. Always use the conditional when talking about these kinds of things."

November 23

The Tech, the student newspaper, ran a story about the firing of Dean Hope, a black woman. That explained the signs.

November 24

My office mates and I were telling dirty jokes. The door to the hall was open. Sometimes you forget that women are in the lab, too; that what you say might kill someone. But the jokes were funny, and I felt like one of the guys when the other guys laughed at mine. The conversation drifted toward ranking the looks of the various women in the lab, and in the Mech E department in general. Women do this kind of thing when they're together, right? It's natural, right?

One of the guys said, "Yeah, Mary's got a nice body but her face isn't that great." We all sort of chuckled. She walked by the open door, didn't look in. I wondered whether she heard it. It was the last time I saw her.

I don't know why she did it. Who knows whether it was that last little comment? Who knows whether it was the fact that I didn't say anything in her defense? We'd sort of drifted apart since the first term. I'd say hello and she'd give me that Senior House forced smile that is really a parody on a smile because how could anyone possibly be happy at this place? But she had her friends in the outdoors club and rumor had it she had a boyfriend, so it wasn't my responsibility to ask her why she wasn't talking to me much anymore. We're the masters of our souls, right? It wasn't my fault. It wasn't my fault. It wasn't my fault, was it?

It wasn't the pressure. She was too smart to let that do it. Maybe it was the loneliness. But she had a boyfriend. Perhaps it was the hopelessness spurred on by MIT's overmechanistic worldview, in which logic and reason are gods and spirituality, soul, and humanity are dismissed as irrelevant at best and nonexistent at worst.

The following morning Chet asked me into his office. He closed the door behind me.

"Have a seat," he said. "I've got some very bad news. Last night Mary took her own life."

Where'd she take it?

But seriously. "How'd . . . How'd . . . ?" I asked.

"They found her in her Chevette this morning. I've checked with everyone. Campus police, her landlord, Cambridge police, the dean's office. I keep getting the same story, but I can't believe it happened. It's Mary all right," Chet answered. His eyes blinked a little. "She put some tubing from the tail pipe of her car into the passenger section. She was parked over on Albany Street. And she just sort of fell asleep."

Let's see, I wondered. If the car is idling at, say 800 rpm, and the displacement is, say, 2 liters, then the volume flow rate into the car will be 400 liters per minute, times the percentage of carbon monoxide in the exhaust gas. We'll have to set up a differential equation for the concentration of carbon monoxide in the passenger section of the car, assuming equal inflow rates and exhaust rates. It's sort of like filling up a leaky rigid balloon with a hole in the other end. We'll have to make another assumption about the breathing rate of the passenger. Figure a 2-liter lung capacity and 20 breaths per minute, that means 40 liters per minute of passenger compartment gas. Now to model the rate of carbon monoxide uptake into the lungs we need to . . .

Nerdalert. Mary's voice was almost audible, like the time she said, "Nerdalert" when somebody's watch beeped at the top of the hour in Thermo class. That's it. I'm done. They've got me.

The knot in my stomach tightened. I couldn't believe it, either. By the time you're twenty-six you may have heard of death, maybe lost a few pets, but if both your parents are still alive and no one you know really well has passed away, you still feel kind of immune to it.

"The memorial service will be next Sunday night," Chet said, "in the chapel. Hey, kiddo, by the way, I've had my criticisms of your work, but the reason is to help you learn so you can go out of here and be competent and do the good professional work that people expect out of people with MIT degrees. You've really come along in your experimental techniques. You're good at solving problems."

He paid me a compliment. I couldn't believe it. Chet paid me a compliment. And what he said must be true, because Chet is incapable of lying, even under duress.

I went downstairs to take some Polaroids for the apparatus section of my thesis. Nick was at the drill press.

"What's New?"—the Billie Holiday version—played on the radio.

Nick put his hand on my shoulder and said, "That's a terrible thing that happened, just a terrible thing. Don't ever let anything like that happen to you, OK, Cap'n? The Lord just wants you to keep doin' the best you can; that's all that matters. You'll have some bad times but you'll make it through. It happens too fast by itself."

I didn't cry then. I was tough; I could take it. I could take anything the institute could dish out. I delivered the Polaroids to Charlotte Evans; she was typing my thesis for me and helping with the figures for $3 a page. She had just heard the news from Chet as well.

"The poor thing," she said from behind her desk. "I feel just awful about it. Do you have any idea why she did it?"

"No, not really. We didn't talk a lot recently. I feel kind of bad now, like I should have asked her whether something was bothering her. But we drifted apart and now we'll never drift back together, not here anyway."

Charlotte said comfortingly, "Now don't you go blaming yourself. Everyone is responsible for his own actions and no one else's. Besides, a lot of people have a hard time this time of year, what with Christmas coming up and all. You can't get near a psychiatrist these days they're so heavily booked. Christmastime and springtime, a lot of people get depressed, especially if they're single."

I raised my hand and said, "Guilty." I wondered how she knew it was hard to schedule time with a psychiatrist.

Charlotte got down to business. "So I've typed the introduction and the description of the experiment. And I've typed the blank headings for the photos of the lab. Here's the manuscript for you to read through and proof." She handed me the full manila folder.

"Thanks, Charlotte. I can almost taste Chet's signature."

"No problem. That'll be eighty-one dollars. I'd prefer cash if you have it."

"I'll have to go to the bank. I'll be back by five."

"Good," she said as I left the office. "And Pepper," she added, "don't work too hard."

"There's no such. . . ." I paused from my standard response. "Uh, OK. I'll try not to."

Three days later. Two women who looked a little like Mary, only older, looked lost in the corridor near my door. I remembered feeling lost in the corridor near my door. They could have been my older sisters. Their eyes were still red.

"Do . . . do you know how we can get into this office?" the older one asked. "Mary Patterson was our younger sister, and we've come to go through her belongings."

"Uh, gee, I don't know. I can run downstairs to the lab to see whether any of her office mates are around." They weren't.

"Let me call campus police and they can come and open up the door for you," I said. "By the way, my name's Pepper White."

"Oh, so you're Pepper," the older one said. "Mary talked a lot about you; she said she really liked you, and she told us about some of the things you'd done."

What is this, a variation on the *It's a Wonderful Life* theme? Look, I feel bad enough as it is without knowing that she thought of me as a good friend even when she didn't say hello to me. This place is a salt mine and there's no time to do anything but mine salt, much less try to pull someone who sent me a postcard from her vacation in Acapulco and signed it "Love, Mary," who gave me the originals for the notes for the Thermo and Fluids classes I missed two years ago and made photocopies for herself, who went out on a couple of dates with me, out of a depression. It wasn't my fault, was it?

I said, "Uh, yeah. We all miss her very much."

"Our father's a physicist," she said. "We'd like to go through her notebooks to give him some examples of what she was working on."

The campus policeman arrived and opened the door. We assembled the cardboard boxes they'd picked up from U-Haul, filled them with Mary's notebooks, carried them to the rented van.

"What about the fish tank?" I asked them.

"We'll leave it for now," the older sister said. "Could you make sure someone feeds the fish and cleans the filter for a couple of weeks?"

"Sure," I said. "Say, I'm uh . . . really sorry about what happened. Have a safe drive home."

"Thanks. Bye."

That night. The radio in Ben and Mary's office played loud rock music from WBCN and the office door was open.

"Yo, Ben. Could you turn that down a little bit?" I asked him.

"Huh?" he said, looking up from his problem set. "Oh. Yeah. Sure. Sorry it's so loud. I guess I want to sort of ward off any evil spirits that might be in the area; I mean it's kind of spooky here late at night now with Mary gone. Every time I walk into the office, I expect to see her at her desk or walking the other way, and she's never there anymore. I still can't believe it happened. The only thing that's left is the fish tank. I wonder whether the fish know what's going on," he said.

"Oh, that reminds me. Do you know where she kept the box of fish food? I promised her family I'd take care of them for a while," I said.

We both sprinkled the food on the water and the fish scurried up to the surface to eat.

Ben continued. "It's like I'm trying to imagine her pain, you know, how she felt, what made her do it. She was so smart, too. That's the scariest thing. She read the *New York Times* every day, knew everything about what was going on in all these little countries around the world. It's like I wonder whether she knew something we don't know."

I answered, "Who knows, maybe we'll see her again on the

night shift and we'll be able to ask her. For now it's past my bedtime. If you want to turn the radio back up, go ahead."

"Thanks," he said. "Take it easy."

Before bed I took the bulletin board's handwritten poem out of my filing cabinet at Senior House and compared the handwriting to the first-semester Fluids notes that Mary gave me. The handwriting in the notebook didn't match the handwriting on the wall. It wasn't hers, but whose was it?

I lay in bed with "Soft Hits" playing on the radio and gradually drifted off to sleep.

It was night and Mary was standing in front of the chapel, across from Kresge and the student center.

"Hi, Pepper," she said.

"Hi, Mary. What's new?"

"Oh, not much, how about you?" she said.

"Me neither. Gee. You haven't changed a bit."

"What do you mean?" she asked, reaching toward me.

"Wait a minute," I answered. "You're dead."

"Huh? Oh. Yeah. Sure. Adieu. . . ."

And as when Mr. Spock and Captain Kirk are beamed up to the Starship *Enterprise*, she shimmered for a few moments and disappeared.

My head jerked up from the pillow. Linda Ronstadt sang the soft hit with the Nelson Riddle orchestra:

. . . but seeing you was grand,
and you were sweet, to offer your hand . . .

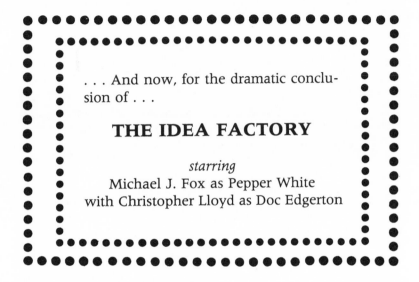

. . . And now, for the dramatic conclusion of . . .

THE IDEA FACTORY

starring
Michael J. Fox as Pepper White
with Christopher Lloyd as Doc Edgerton

C H A P T E R

—————— 20 ——————

Quality Control

"The wind bloweth where it listeth, and thou hearest the sound thereof, but canst not tell whence it cometh, and whither it goeth. . . ."
—John 3:8

". . . and the wind . . . cries . . . Mary"
—Jimi

December 18

I asked Professor Heywood to recommend me for the doctoral qualifying exams.

"Hmmm," he said. "And just what is it that you'd like to do with a Ph.D.?"

My friends could call me Dr. Pepper. Besides, the exams should make for a really good chapter in the book.

"I want to consult. I want to advise industry on how to save energy. That's why I came here in the first place, and I think the Ph.D. would help," I answered. "It would give me a certain credibility."

"Yes, it would," he said. "But it may not really be necessary for what you want to do. In fact, it may be much more advantageous for you to go out into industry now and see how things work in the real world. The three years or more you'd spend on a Ph.D. would involve that opportunity cost."

"I don't know; I'd still like to give the qualifiers a shot now. If I don't try now, I'll never do them. Besides, you have to admit it would be a great opportunity to review what I've learned here."

"How are your grades?"

"Uh, er, I, uh . . . well, I have three C's, two A's, and the rest B's. But two of the C's were my first term and the third was in a summer electronics class so they shouldn't really count, should they?"

"Everything counts. You'll be going in with two strikes against you. But if you really want to do it, I'll write the letter. You'll have to do remarkably well on the oral, written, and presentation components of the examinations, so I advise you to prepare well."

"Thank you, Professor."

That afternoon, Chet shook his head.

"You really want to go through with it?" he asked.

"Yeah, Chet. I have to try. I know it's a long shot, but darn it this is America and we love an underdog, and we love to be underdogs. I'll be humming the 'Theme from Rocky' all month."

"Well, I'll sign your application. But be careful. Study hard, and know what you're talking about; otherwise they'll eat you alive."

"Okay, Chet. I'll do my best."

The qualifiers are the barrier they put between graduate students and the ability to be called "Doctor So and So." The examinations exist for several reasons. First, they give the sadistic elements of the professors' characters an opportunity to express themselves. Second, they separate the chaff from the wheat of the graduate student body. See, if they made it easy for everyone to pass, more incompetents would be called "Doctor So and So." If they let anyone pass, he or she might finish a Ph.D., glibly sleaze through an interview for an assistant professorship at Princeton or Stanford, and, when teaching Intro Thermodynamics, be eaten alive by some bright nineteen-year-old. And that would be more devastating than being eaten alive by some MIT professors, so the cruelty is kind.

The examinations are in four areas. Friday is the written section. One hour of testing in each of four areas of specialization. Each student has some choices in the test subjects, and I chose the basics: Fluids, Thermo, System Dynamics and Controls, and Mechanics. Then the weekend comes just to make you sweat. I mean, I'd rather have it Monday, Tuesday, Wednesday, and then you disappear and go skiing and find out whether you passed, but it's their ballgame and they make the rules.

On Monday they examine you orally. They present you with a problem; you have twenty minutes to look at it and try to solve it or at least think up something to say about it, and then you present your solution and/or answer their questions for twenty minutes. To discourage cheating, the forty-minute periods are consecutive, with no time allowed to go from one room to the other. Thus you run from examination room to examination room, to have as much of the twenty minutes of preparation time as possible.

And on Tuesday, you present your research work to date. This enables them to evaluate whether you are able to "do research."

December 31

Twenty days to go. New Year's Eve. No one in the Sloan Lab except Mr. and Mrs. Tung, the Chinese couple across the hall with the foul-smelling seaweed they cooked on their hot plate. Their New Year's Eve was in February.

Solo. This is how it ends. By yourself. Do it yourself. Plow through the problem sets alone. Alone with Newton, with Lagrange. Alone with the authors of the textbooks. Pattern recognition, no time to look deep into the problems, just time to pick up as many tricks from worked-out solution sets as possible. Try problem; get stuck. Look at solution set for hint. Continue. Get stuck again. Look at solution set again.

By the second or third of the same type of problem the pattern becomes clearer. And then you hope the problem on the qualifiers will include the trick you have internalized.

At 10:30 even Mr. and Mrs. Tung had left; the only noise left was the filter from Mary's fish tank loud through the locked door of her office. On the way back to Senior House the institute was empty. The infinite corridor, normally populated at all hours, was empty for all of its 319 paces. So was every other corridor. Only a nerd's nerd studies at 11:30 on New Year's Eve.

1984. More Dynamics (Lincoln's class, B plus), plus review of Statics (Professor Hill, B plus plus, the highest B in the class, not an A). I skipped from book to book, closing the conceptual gaps. In Statics, the weight sits on the beam. In Dynamics, the weight moves up and down. In System Dynamics (David Miller, A with the navy guys), the weight moves up and down and you call the beam a spring. The same weight, the same beam.

January 2

The *Globe* article on the front of the Living section with the funnies in it said, "We learn to strive for and 'need' external symbols of our worth, instead of enjoying the process of learning, accomplishing, and mastering, which is a more natural human gratification." That's MIT in a nutshell. The grades are the external symbols of worth. Objective, quantitative, like an SAT score, like an IQ, a salary, a bank balance, a Dow Jones average, a lottery number. It's all such a crock.

I set out to learn and master more of Fluid Mechanics. This was the last time the external motivation of the qualifying examinations would make me internalize more deeply how fluids behaved. It became clearer to me why Peppermint Patty's tea leaves went to the center of the cup. The smokestack plume I'd wanted to understand had not only boiler exhaust but two counterrotating vortices. It took on the abstract beauty of chemical equations and vector calculus.

January 3–5

More Fluids, and some Solids. It was all physics underneath, balanced forces, balanced moments, continuity. The physics of everyday life. Vortices at the edge of buildings. Bridges shaking when trucks drive by. Skyscrapers buffeted by the wind. A solid breaks when the force applied is too big; a fluid continues to deform, to adjust to the force.

I met Professor Hill on the infinite corridor.

"Yes, I really enjoyed the opportunity to review everything at once, back in the '50s when I took the exams," he said. "You'll find that just three or four equations govern a heck of a lot of phenomena."

January 6

Party at Chet's house. Chet didn't have a lot of furniture in his three-bedroom Cape in Lexington. Perhaps he would marry and fill it with kids and furniture once he was tenured.

In a circle of conversation, Chet said, "The qualifiers are a good measurement of your knowledge relative to your peers, but they're not a good absolute measure. A lot happens at the results meeting, when the professors get together and duke it out or decline to duke it out for their students. It's supposed to be entirely objective, quantitative, but there is a fair amount of subjective evaluation that goes into it."

"So, Chet, are you going to fight for me at that meeting?" I asked.

"I'll be giving a paper in Detroit that day."

On the way back from the party, in Ben's car, the radio played Brenda Lee. She sang, "Breeaakk it . . . to me gintleeee . . ."

January 7

Depression. Staring out the window. Inability to function. Inability to think. It comes with this territory. They pick you up like a bolt, examine you for flaws from all angles. If you are good, they put you in the bin with all the other high-priced bolts. If you don't meet the specs, they throw you in the scrap heap. In either case, they don't treat you like a human being.

January 8

Bicycle ride to escape. Lincoln again, Sudbury. England-like gray, snowy, wintry dead landscapes. I input a sinusoidal forcing function to the bicycle through my knees going up and down like pistons; my lower legs were connecting rods to the shaft on the two-cylinder engine. My weight stored the energy and converted the alternating input into a direct output, fifteen miles per hour.

The soda machines at the gas stations along the route haunted me. In two weeks I'd have my shot at being "Dr. Pepper."

January 9

Ben and I got together to review Controls. Ben was turning out to be a star student, what with straight A's and all. Normally no one studies together for the qualifiers, because one of you probably will end up teaching the other and if you do that then you'll be at a disadvantage and you'll have wasted some time that might have given you some insight that would help on one of the tests. But there were a few exceptions to this rule.

"I tell you," Ben said, "ever since I was accepted here and they included in the acceptance letter the packet of sample questions from the previous qualifiers, I've been thinking about them. It's been over two years now and they're only ten days away. It's hard to believe. I haven't been sleeping well recently, and I must spend an hour on the john every day. I mean, if I don't make it, it'll haunt me for the rest of my life, like every time I turn on the TV set or pick up *Time* magazine there'll be some guy from MIT giving his authoritative opinion on something and I'll say to myself, 'That could have been me if I'd just worked harder.' "

T minus ten

Songs ran through me. "I don't care what they do to me, they can't take away my dignity," and "Makin' it / No more fakin' it, this time in life I'm makin' it." What a culture we have.

At the cafeteria, I sat with Carlos Lopez and some of the other remaining guys from the Heat Transfer lab soccer team, the guys I'd maintained close friendships with through our ten minute hallway chats every three or four months for the past two years. I told them about the song line about my dignity.

"You're wrong about that," Carlos said. "Your dignity is the first thing that goes. It's sort of like that scene in *Deliverance* where the guy's getting raped and the redneck says, 'Squeal boy; squeal like a pig.' This is the last time the professors have any power over you. After the exams, pass or fail, you're your own person. They know that, so they want to nail you."

Oh, come on, it can't be that bad.

"By the way," Carlos continued. "You got your kneepads?"

I said, "Yeah, I'll need them so I can kneel before them and beg them, 'Please, please, let me be in your club. I want people to seek advice from me and think I'm one of the smartest people in the world . . . even though I'm not.' "

"Hey, I like that," Carlos said. "Especially the punch line."

T minus nine

Nick was at the lathe. "Yeah, Peppah, I hope you make it. Maybe you'll be a lifer here. It happens to a lot of people. They keep passing the tests and before you know it, boom, they've got tenure. They've got a good life, those professors. Secure base pay, four-day-a-week job, eight months a year, the rest of the time starting their companies and consulting and writing their books. They're their own men. I can see why you want to try to be like them. By the way, did I tell you they're lettin' me go?"

"That's great, Nick. Where are they letting you go?"

"No, you don't understand. They're layin' me off."

"They're giving you the axe?"

"It's pink slip time. Just like from the tire plant in Watertown. I can't complain, though. I been here twenty years and the pension'll keep me an' my honey bear in the house in Ahlington. I'll come in one or two days a week, though, sort of like a whadaya call . . . consultant."

"Gee, Nick, the place just wouldn't be any fun without you," I said.

"Don't worry, Cap'n. We'll always have the rapid compression machine."

T minus eight

Philosophy time. Forget passing or failing; learn what I can learn. Ask professor in controls group about Stability. Stability in the Dynamics (Lincoln, course two nine four) sense tells you things like whether or not your car will flip over going around a turn too fast. Stability in the Controls sense (two fourteen) tells you things like whether the robot arm you're working on will bounce back and forth and break itself apart.

Since the Controls class was called "System Dynamics and Controls" and the Dynamics class was called "Dynamics," I thought there must be a connection between the two different meanings of stability. The anonymous tenured professor hemmed and hawwed and in fact he didn't know. He escaped with "I'm deliberately being evasive. I think you should work these things out for yourself."

I wasn't satisfied. I knocked on Professor Crandall's door. He was one of the 10 percent crème de la crème of MIT professors who give the institute its reputation. He wore a bow tie and half glasses and a suit, and his course, Methods in Engineering Analysis, was an MIT classic. A Turkish friend at the von Kármán Institute had first told me about him.

I repeated my question. "I'd like to see the connection between stability in the two oh two (System Dynamics) sense and in the two nine four (Dynamics) sense."

"Yes," he said softly, deliberately. "It's a continuum of thought. You see, if you draw your automobile going around a turn, and if you look at moving it away from its equilibrium position by a small amount as it goes around that curve, you'll arrive at a second-order differential equation for how it will return to that equilibrium position. The coefficients in that equation determine the natural frequency and damping of the system, and those are the same coefficients you use when designing a controller to, for example, prevent the vehicle from flipping over."

He pulled a piece of scrap paper from the desk drawer reserved for scrap paper and sketched the similarities. I asked other questions, and he presented at least two ways of looking at each.

He confirmed my hunch that a problem is like a machine inside a clear cube. When you look at one side of the cube you see what some of the machine looks like. But to understand it thoroughly, you have to pick up the cube and look at it from above, below, from all sides, shake it to see the connections.

T minus seven and counting

Snowstorm. Large flakes out the window from Atkinson 302's bedroom. I looked at the guidebook to the Fluids films from the first term. Every snowflake affects every other snowflake. Vortices carved horseshoes around trees; vortices shed off corners of buildings. Howard Gelman wore gym shorts, a T-shirt, black socks, and high-top Keds.

T minus six

Ming Tsang, Professor Keck's student from the People's Republic of China, ate lunch with me. He was studying for the qualifiers, too. On the way across Mass. Ave., Ming met one of his friends. "Disa man first Ph.D. at MIT from PRC," Ming said. "Ifah I pass qualifiers, I be number 30, 35."

"Gee, you guys should each have a T-shirt with your number on it," I said. They laughed.

Ming said, "You come to our study group tomorrow? I meet with some friends at 3-249, 7:00 P.M."

"Sounds good," I said.

These guys are smarter than 2 billion Chinese and I'm going to be competing against them. I just hope they have poor reading skills that will slow them down.

T minus five

There were two others at the review session with Ming. One would take the exams this month, the other in May. They both looked worried. If I failed, I'd find a job at about 30 grand a year and begin to build up equity. If they failed they'd be on the first 747 back to the world's largest prison.

One of the worried ones, Mr. Wang, said, "I want exam be over. I be study five week straight now, since two weeks before Christmas. Twelve hours every day. I did every problem in back of Fluid book, Thermo book, Control book, Mechanics books. Now I start review reading."

So that's what it takes. I bet these guys don't have motivational lapses or get depressed. They beat it with work.

Ming pulled out a one-inch stack of papers from his backpack. They were problems from previous qualifying exams, with solutions, above and beyond the packet of sample problems Charlotte Evans had given to me. Perfectly legal; the China network had produced good files. Ming ran the session; the four of us sat around a card table.

"How 'bou dissa one?" Ming said as he put the first problem on the center of the table. It was a car's valve and rocker-arm assembly, assembelee assembelee.

"I tinka we have to do Lagrangian formulation for two degree of freedom system," Mr. Wang said. The others agreed and who was I to disagree?

Next problem. Again a quick look at the problem, a few words of discussion, and a decision on the principle involved. Boom boom boom the pattern continued, and we finished the stack of forty problems in less than an hour. Lord help us if these guys ever learn to build cars and VCRs.

Mr. Yuen, the third one, suggested, "Les try dissa one for five minutes; pretend it's oral exam. Say we have to say something after five minutes."

The problem was to design a wavy ramp for beer barrels to roll down. It couldn't be a straight ramp because the barrels would go too fast by the time they reached the bottom. What things should be considered in the design of the ramp? Mr. Yuen called on me. "Whatta you think?"

"It looks to me as if the point is to figure out how many ripples to put in the ramp. That will affect the number of barrels you can send down the ramp, and it'll tell you whether or not the barrels will run into each other on the way down. The ripples should be designed so that the frequency of the beer barrels pushing on the structure is far away from the resonant frequency of the structure," I said.

"And you need to consider effect of beer rotating in the barrel," Mr. Yuen said. We discussed it further before breaking.

As we left the room, Ming encouraged me. He said, "I tinka you pass."

T minus four

Kwang, the Korean shipbuilding engineer from Hyundai with whom I'd studied in Professor Hill's Statics class, who wrote on every square inch of paper, front and back, because paper is scarce in Korea, was in the student center library. He was preparing for the qualifiers in ocean engineering.

"At this point I don't care what happens," he said. "Just as long as I keep my health."

Professors who would be examining me in the orals walked around the institute. They were there before—I recognized them from the department seminars and the faculty meetings and the stories I'd heard from the other students. But now it was as if I were a spy and I had a photo of the Russian spy who was assigned to kill me and I'd spotted him but he didn't know who I was yet. Paranoia strikes deep. Into your life it will creep.

I talked to Chet Yeung again. I told him about the songs I'd been thinking of.

He said, "You might try 'To Dream the Impossible Dream.' No, seriously, though, I know what you're going through. When I went through those examinations I often found myself staring out the window for hours at a time, wondering why I put myself through it."

T minus three

High idea flux (flow per unit area). I came to MIT wanting to see the physical principles around me, and today everything shouted its principle out at me: masses and springs and dampers in cars, beams bending underfoot in buildings, more vortices in smoke-stacks and jet airplane con-trails and corners of buildings. I studied not in a room, but in a box with dashed lines into which mass and energy entered and out of which it exited. I wanted to make the ideas orderly; I wanted to turn the analysis off and on on demand; but it was stuck in the on position.

I went to the music library to seek refuge. Beethoven's Seventh Symphony. The motor provided a torque and an angular acceleration to the rotational inertia of the turntable. Big chord. Small chord, oboe. Scale. Scale. A musical scale permuted and repeated elegantly. Powerfully. Simply. Goosebumps. Chord. Scale again. A computer will never make music like this.

T minus two

I picked up the examination briefing packet from Charlotte Evans: a gray envelope with my name typed on the white label; five sheets of paper inside listing the names of the contestants, twenty-nine others and me; the times of their exams; the tight timetable matrix for the oral exams so we'd have no time to cheat; the schedule for the thesis presentations on Tuesday. The topics were impressive: "Control of Dynamic Interaction between a Manipulator and Its World," "Corrosion Control in a Hostile Environment," "Technological Support for the Involvement of the Sight-Impaired in Sports," "Diesel Combustion in a Rapid Compression Machine."

I couldn't sleep that night. The vortices and masses and springs interacted and danced through me—they wouldn't go away. But I wasn't bored. I was thinking in Cartesian coordinates. I was.

T minus one

The day before. One last pass through my notebooks. At noon, I took Chet's advice and locked away my books. I wanted to make myself tired enough to sleep before the exams so I took a walk in the snow. Halfway across the Harvard Bridge, the institute was everywhere: I. M. Pei ('40, Architecture) had designed the John Hancock Building. David Wormley ('62, Mechanical Engineering) was part of the team that fixed it. On the Cambridge side of the Charles, the institute, steel blue-gray, with smokestack plumes behind, Ionic columns and neoclassical authority ahead, challenged me to meet its standard—absolute, unforgiving, unassailably the best.

January 21

The ski jumper pulled up over the lip and accelerated down the take-off ramp.

The written exam was on the fourth floor of Building 3, in the room across the hall from Tom Bligh's office. It was the room I'd built part of the two seventy design project in, with drafting tables and gears and gear catalogs on the tables around the perimeter. The exams were to start at 9:00 sharp; everyone was in place with twelve number two pencils and milk crates full of textbooks and notebooks. The guy sitting next to me had a backpack with breakfast and lunch in it, plus a thermos full of coffee.

The proctors were two guys who'd passed the qualifiers the year before. I found this distasteful. It was as if they were the majordomos, the chief slaves in the southern plantations who were accorded special privileges in exchange for bossing around the other slaves. They handed out the institute gray envelopes and at 9:00:00 we ripped them open.

Exam 1. System Dynamics and Controls. The exam was a pneumatic control problem. Pneumatic control uses various air chambers to open and close valves. They are simple if you've seen them before. They're so simple, in fact, that in the two MIT Controls classes, they were not even mentioned. Of course, if you really understand the concepts of controls, the fundamentals, you can pick out the important points in any kind of control system and solve the problem. I remembered what Carlos said about the qualifiers: "Let them know everything you know. They have to give an exam that only one person will be able to finish in an hour. Otherwise, people would start to walk out midway through the test and that wouldn't be fair to the slower ones. Just put down everything you know."

I wrote that pressure times area equals force for all the components; I tried to link the components by fulcrums and geometric constraints. I scraped for partial credit. I hoped the other tests would be more familiar.

Exam 2. Fluid Mechanics. I got a B in Shapiro's class that first term. I spent a year studying fluids in Belgium. This should be easy. "A hose discharges horizontally to a bucket with a hole in it as shown in the figure. Find the force required to hold the bucket up."

Piece of cake. At least seven out of ten points.

Lunch break from 11:00 to 1:00. The guy sitting next to me sat and reviewed and ate his lunch and drank his coffee. I went to the ice rink. The pressure under my skate was high enough to melt a thin film of water upon which the blade slid with nearly no friction. The remaining friction between the skate and the ice provided the center-seeking centripetal force to balance my body's tendency to keep going straight, and I turned.

Exam 3. Mechanics. "A vertical rod is given an impulse. Find the magnitude and direction of the impulse required to make the rod do one revolution and land on its end. See figure."

Again, this is nothing like anything that was ever mentioned in any test or any class I'd taken at MIT. But I know how to think now, right? Sort of. I polled the data base and went back to high school physics class and back to the photos on Doc Edgerton's wall in Building 4. If you throw a wrench, this thing called the center of mass goes along a trajectory as if it were a baseball. The wrench rotates around that center of mass. So maybe the trick to this problem is to give the rod a kick big enough so that the time required for the center of mass to rise and fall (as if it were a baseball being thrown up in the air) is equal to the time required for the sideways component of the impulse to make the rod do a revolution. Break the problem into two separate problems; solve for a common link at the end.

If I pass, I'll be able to go over the problem with the professor who wrote it and learn how close I was, because if I pass I'll be a member of the club. If I fail, I will never know whether I was even close, because the graded exams are not given back because (1) they don't want to give you any evidence if you decide to sue them for flunking you and (2) graduate students at MIT don't have a union. Estimated points, six.

Exam 4. Thermo. I wanted to understand the smokestack, and here it was. "(A) Calculate the exit velocity from a smokestack, 300 feet high, with a 2 degree taper. Inlet conditions are air at 1200 degrees F, at a pressure of 2 atmospheres. Make any reasonable assumptions."

Another piece of cake.

"(B) Now assume that the flow is steady or does not vary with time."

Wait a minute. I assumed it was steady in part A. Gyftopoulos must have written this test.

Redo part (A). Ten minutes left. Start part (B). Estimated points, seven.

Off the end of the take-off ramp the ski jumper from the Saudi Arabian Nordic team went. He was in the air now, for the weekend, floating, hoping he wouldn't fall forward and land on his face.

I shared the analogy with one of the majordomos.

He answered, "I think it's more like going through both sides of a hurricane. You went through one side today, and now you're in the calm eye for the weekend. On Monday and Tuesday you'll come out the other side."

Sunday afternoon. I asked Ming how his weekend was going.

"Oh, pretty good. I just finish memorizing textbooks for oral exam."

Monday morning

I did the practice runs in my three-piece suit and leather-soled shoes up and down the stairs. The perfect line was to start a little wide, then grab the vertical piece of the bannister as I ran in to take the turn close to the inside, like in the Indy 500. Any seconds saved in the movement from test to test might be the seconds of inspiration.

Mechanics, Fluids, Thermo went well. Hill, Weare, Shapiro, Lincoln, and Gyftopoulos were surprisingly civil.

And then there was Controls. The last forty minutes.

"How would you design a feedback control loop to make the surface x move at a specified constant speed, when gas is allowed to enter chamber a from a large reservoir? Do NOT assume incompressible flow."

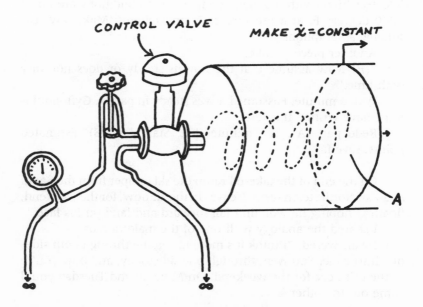

The good old balloon problem, but with a twist. Compressible flow. This brings Fluids and Thermo into Controls. This makes it doubly hard. Seventeen minutes left to prepare my presentation. No idea on the compressible part. What you need is a control valve and a motion transducer to tell you how fast the thing is moving.

This would be fine except the whole thing is highly nonlinear since the gas is compressible, so this problem doesn't fit within the framework of the Controls they've taught me.

Prepare to dive, Captain. Whoop whoop whoop whoop. Aooga Aooga. Battle stations.

I walked into the room where the three fat Inquisitors sat in judgment. I'd succeeded in not porking out during my studying;

I'd actually lost a few pounds. These guys were on their way to tenure, if they lived that long.

"Write your solution on the board," the first one said.

The board was not a regular blackboard attached to a wall, but a freestanding type that you could flip over. It was unstable when I wrote on it.

"Uh, I really don't know how to address the compressibility issue. I do have an idea for the incompressible case, though," I said.

"Do you expect us to give you any points for that?"

"Well, it would show some of what I know about this type of problem."

"Okay, go ahead."

I sketched the problem and what I remembered of the derivation I'd done for Greene's independent study. The blackboard flopped mercilessly as I wrote the symbols and equations, farther and farther down toward the floor. Any closer to the bottom of the board and the only way to write would be from my knees. I hesitated for a second and started to stand up.

"No. Keep writing down there. Write to the bottom of the board," the third Inquisitor said. On your knees, boy. Squeal. Squeal like a pig.

I don't need you, pal. I don't need your approval to make me complete. I stood up and said, "No. I prefer to stand. Like a man."

Late Wednesday afternoon I knocked on Rohsenow's door. He took me out to the bench in the hall outside his office. It was noisier there and therefore more private.

"Have a seat," he said. He opened the clipboard with the chart with everyone's scores on it. "You didn't do all that badly in Fluids; 7 written, 6 oral. And you got two 7s in Thermo, and 6s, one 5 and one 3 in the other areas. You add it all up plus your thesis points of 13 out of 20 and it comes to 60 out of 100. Now see when somebody's score is in that range we look at the distribution. If you'd had a couple of 10s and a couple of 2s, well, we might have let you pass. . . ."

"Will you let me try again in May?"

"Well, in a case like yours, we say, well, let's call it a ballgame."

Where's Stephanie? Where's Ari? Where's Mary? Where's

Nick? Who can I talk to now? Who can I cry to? The only shoulders are cold.

Rohsenow continued, "I always tell students in your position to think of it sort of as if you went through a rigorous application process and weren't selected."

"Ummmm. Ummmm. Okay, sir. I have to go, sir."

February 5, 1984

I put the completed thesis on Chet's desk. Submitted in Partial Fulfillment of the Requirements for the degree of Master of Science in Mechanical Engineering.

"So," Chet said as he signed the cover page, "you're a survivor."

Closure

"A hundred and one, a hundred and two, a hundred and three. . . ."

"May I help you?" the guy in the three-piece suit in the legal library said.

"Sure. I'm counting light bulbs," I answered. "Why don't you take that side of the room?"

"You're counting what?"

"Light bulbs."

"Why?"

"We're going to replace all the lights in this building with higher-efficiency ones and cut the power consumption in half and you won't go blind when we're done. But before we can order the new lights we have to know how many there are. If we want to stop the greenhouse effect we'll have to count every light bulb on the planet. It's a tough job, but somebody's gotta do it. What do you do for a living?"

"I sue people."

Yes, six, seven years out of MIT and I'm counting light bulbs. But that's not all I do. I count motors, too. And I'm starting to manage people who count light bulbs.

Schlumberger, the guys in Houston, didn't offer me a job after all, which may be just as well because I might have gotten stuck in Kuwait when the Iraqis rolled in. And I wouldn't have seen as much of my father in the last years of his life, or my mother or my sisters, who are still alive and well.

Renault, on the other hand, did offer me a job. They flew me to Paris a few months after Chet signed my thesis, and it was tough to turn them down. But a couple of kids selling lemonade by the side of the road during a bike ride in Lincoln kept me stateside. They just seemed so American, so optimistic, so nonexistential.

I started my energy career as a self-employed consultant in the Boston area, because as Johnny Venture said at the real estate seminar, I wanted to be Riiiiich! I lined up some interesting projects with people who'd offered me full-time jobs and helped out a couple of MIT staff members with their side businesses. For example, I installed the instruments that controlled four small hydroelectric plants, wrote a computer program to model the motion of an engine's piston rings, and supervised boiler repairs in Providence.

At this writing I work at an engineering firm that consults to commercial and industrial clients on saving money in air-conditioning systems, pumps, fans, heat, and, of course, light bulbs. I'm thinking of going off on my own again soon. Take my card, please.

But enough of me. What about the others? I recently met Chet at a conference on energy and the environment. We had a nice chat—he'd grown up and I'd grown up, and we talked almost as peers. He now has tenure. If anyone taught me how to solve problems, it was Chet, by example.

Gyftopoulos has not yet retired, and he remembered me when I spoke to him at the same conference.

I haven't seen Nick since I left MIT, even though he lives only four miles away. I've been meaning to call him and get together for a roll. If anyone taught me how to be a good person, it was Nick, by example.

Ben and my lab partner Scott are both Ph.D.'s working at General Motors. I hope to see them in a magazine someday, featured as "The Men behind the Work." The RCM is back in mothballs.

Doctor Ari retired after reaching the rank of colonel in the Israeli army. I last saw him in Manhattan—he'd lost twenty pounds or so and looked lean and kind and much healthier than he'd ever looked at MIT.

Shortly after Eldon graduated in 1986 his mother was afraid to leave him alone in the house—he was suffering from posttraumatic stress syndrome. He didn't make the space program, but he did work at Lockheed programming automatic pilots. At last report he was trying to break into robotics via computer science and wished he'd taken six double oh one.

Half of Dianne Mitchell went to Harvard Business School and wants to produce movies that gross $30 million in the first two weekends. The other half went to the '88 Olympics on the women's crew team and is now finishing a Ph.D. in computer science at MIT. She was a composite character, after all.

Stephanie is married and lives in Chicago.

And Mary. Well, in the male-dominated world of engineering, I try to rebuke sexism in myself and others. It may be a little late, but I told her I'd try to make it up to her someday.

I try to be innocent. I try to be a nice person. I try not to be an egotist. I try to think like a human being.

Appendix

Stop. Put down your pencil and wait for the proctor to pick up the test.

This final section presents more detail, chapter by chapter, on some of the technical points in the book—some definitions of terms, reference material, an amusing anecdote or two, and some horror stories. If it interests you, I suggest reading it a few days after finishing the book. I'm starting to write it nine months after writing what preceded; war has broken out in the Persian Gulf, and Patriot missiles (using technology developed by smart people from MIT, among others) are the heroes of the month of January 1991.

What follows is a list of people and products that have affiliations with MIT. More of this information is available from the MIT public affairs office and the walls of the Kendall Square subway station.

People with MIT Connections:

McDonnell, of McDonnell Douglas Aircraft Co.
Douglas, of same
I. M. Pei, architect
Skidmore, architect, founder of Skidmore, Owings & Merrill
Merrill, of same

Les Aspin, U.S. Congressman
Harvey Gantt, ran against Jesse Helms for Senate
Henry Cisneros, Mayor of San Antonio, Texas
Thomas Watson, assistant to Alexander Graham Bell
    ("Watson, come here. I want you" of first-phone-call fame)
William L. Underwood, of Underwood Deviled Ham, first food
    canner
Jay Forrester, developer of magnetic core memory for computers
    that was the big breakthrough in the '50s
William Shockley, co-discoverer of the transistor
Charles Stark Draper, inventor of inertial guidance systems that
    put a man on the moon
James Woods, actor, star of *The Hard Way*
Varga, former President of Colombia
David Baltimore, President of Rockefeller University and Nobel
    Biology Laureate
Robert Solow, Nobel Economics Laureate
Franco Modigliani, Nobel Economics Laureate
Paul Samuelson, Nobel Economics Laureate, author of the eco-
    nomics text that college students use
George Thomas, mathematician and author of the calculus text
    that college students use
Mr. Al-Kalhil, biographer of Saddam Hussein
Dr. Kendall, physicist and founder of Union of Concerned Scientists
Dr. Friedman, same as Kendall
Dr. Chivian, MIT staff psychiatrist and co-winner of Nobel Peace
    Prize for Union of Concerned Scientists
Salvator Uria, Nobel Biology Laureate
Har Khorana, Nobel Biology Laureate
Richard Feynman, Nobel Physics Laureate, popular writer and ex-
    plainer of why the O-rings in the space shuttle Challenger
    didn't work
Mitch Kapor, founder of Lotus Development Corp.
Vannevar Bush, presidential science adviser
Jerome Wiesner, presidential science adviser
James Killian, presidential science adviser
Guy Stever, presidential science adviser
John Sununu, White House Chief of Staff
Sam Chamberlin, etching artist
Louis Rosenberg, artist
John Taylor Arms, artist

Charles Woodbury, artist
Gyorgy Kepes, artist
Boston, rock band
Mr. Fisk, president of Exxon
Dr. Ballard, oceanographer and finder of the *Titanic*
Lester Thurow, famed economist and *Newsweek* contributor
Nathanial Herreshoff, and his son and grandson, America's Cup
    Yacht Designers
Pete Guerney, playwright
John Reed, president of Citycorp
Herbert Calmus, inventor of Technicolor
John Sheehan, inventor of penicillin
The Du Pont family likes to go to MIT
Alfred P. Sloan, founder of General Motors
Jerome Hunsaker, teacher of McDonnell, Douglas, et al
Philip Morrison, noted physicist and writer
Noam Chomsky, noted linguist and political writer
Buzz Aldrin, the second man to set foot on the moon
Ron McNair, astronaut and one of the seven who died in the
    Challenger disaster
Katherine McCormick, of the McCormick equipment family of
    Chicago, went to MIT and put up the money for the devel-
    opment of the birth control pill
Florence Luscomb, leader of the women's suffrage movement
Arthur Shurcliff, landscape architect, peer of Frederick Law
    Olmsted; Shurcliff designed the Boston Esplanade
Claude Shannon, initial inventor of artificial intelligence
Radar, though not strictly invented at MIT, was developed to its
    present state in a 5,000-person effort during World War II; it
    was the second biggest military project of the war
G. John Mili, famous *Life* magazine photographer
Cecil Green, founder of Texas Instruments

*Companies that are either founded by MIT people or have MIT
people as employees:*

E.G.&G. (Edgerton, Germeshausen and Grier)
Digital Equipment Co.
Data General
Analog Devices

Prime Computer
Apple Computer
Texas Instruments
Wang Labs (but Wang was from Harvard)
Polaroid (but Land was from Harvard)
IBM
AT&T
Silicon Valley start-ups
Kendall Square start-ups, e.g., Thinking Machines
General Computer
Thermo Electron
Dynatech
Du Pont
General Motors
Ford
Chrysler
Exxon
Shell
Schlumberger (oil exploration)
Ingersoll Rand (air compressors)
General Dynamics
Cummins Engine Company
Caterpillar Tractor Co.
Washington think tanks
Washington Beltway Bandits
Chevron

Products developed at MIT or with MIT-trained assistance:

Technicolor
Penicillin
Birth control pill
Radar
Computers
Cars
Airplanes
Cuisinarts
Buildings
Artificial intelligence
Parallel-processing computers

Lotus 123
Inertial guidance systems for airplanes
Bar codes on food at supermarket checkout
Canned food
Telephones
Transistors
Computer "core memory"

Chapter Notes

CHAPTER 1

The Canoeing on Waves Problem. For visual understanding of water waves, consult *Illustrated Experiments in Fluid Mechanics* (the National Committee on Fluid Mechanics Films book of film notes), (Cambridge, Mass.: MIT Press, 1972.) The film, described on p. 105 of the book, is entitled *Waves in Fluids*, and was produced by Arthur E. Bryson of Harvard University. Books that discuss water waves include *Introduction to Physical Oceanography*, by John A. Knaus, (Englewood Cliffs, N.J.: Prentice Hall, 1978); *Marine Hydrodynamics*, by J. N. Newman (Cambridge, Mass.: MIT Press, 1977), and *Sea Loads on Ships and Offshore Structures*, by O. M. Faltinsen (Cambridge, Mass.: Cambridge University Press, 1990).

The Hot Hard-Boiled Egg Problem. This is an unsteady heat conduction problem. "Unsteady" means that throughout the egg, the temperature at each point changes with time. If you take the egg out of the cold water, it will feel hot until the whole egg is cooled off. Unsteady heat conduction in various geometries is discussed in *Heat, Mass, and Momentum Transfer*, by Rohsenow and Choi (Englewood Cliffs, N.J.: Prentice Hall, 1961), pp. 110–19.

CHAPTER 2

Fluid Mechanics. The text *Fluid Mechanics*, by Potter and Foss (New York: John Wiley & Sons, 1975) was recommended as a reference when I took 2.25. Also recommended was *Physical Fluid Dynamics*, by D. J. Tritton (New York: Van Nostrand Reinhold, 1977).

Thermodynamics. For further elaboration on the thermodynamic principles and definitions of concepts described in the lectures by Gyftopoulos, refer to: *Principles of General Thermodynamics*, by Hatsopoulos and Keenan, (Malabar, Fla.: Krieger Publishing [originally published by John Wiley & Sons, 1965]); *Thermodynamics, Foundations and Applications* by Elias P. Gyftopoulos and Gian Paolo Beretta (New York: Macmillan, 1991); and the article in Encyclopaedia Britannica entitled "Thermodynamics, Principles of," by Hatsopoulos, Gyftopoulos, and Keenan. To save you a trip to the library, some terms are defined below. Definitions are drawn from lecture notes and/or class handouts for course 2.451, or where noted, from the *McGraw Hill Dictionary of Scientific and Technical Terms*, 2nd Edition.

State: The condition of a system at an instant in time, which encompasses all that can be said about the results of any measurements or observations that can be performed on the system at that instant in time.

System: Any identifiable collection of matter that can be separated from everything else by a well-defined surface so that the interaction between the "system" and everything else may be described by transfer processes across the surface.

Entropy: According to the *McGraw Hill Dictionary of Scientific and Technical Terms*, entropy is "a function of the state of a thermodynamic system whose change in any differential reversible process is equal to the heat absorbed by the system from its surroundings divided by the absolute temperature of the system. Also known as *thermal charge.*"

Energy: Again from *McGraw Hill*: "the capacity for doing work." Strictly speaking from a thermodynamics point of view, the *McGraw Hill* definition is not correct because energy may be classified as thermal energy and all other energy. Thermal energy has the distinction that not all of it is available for doing work. There is a limitation imposed by the Second Law of Thermodynamics. The 2.451 notes spent eight pages defining energy, so further reading is definitely in order.

Property: Any quantity the value of which depends on the state but not the history of the system; for a given state the value of a property can be determined by some type of measurement.

Enthalpy: From *McGraw Hill*: "The sum of the internal energy of a system plus the product of the system's volume multiplied by the pressure exerted on the system by its surroundings."

Stable equilibrium state: An equilibrium state that can only be altered by interactions that leave net effects in the environment.

Temperature: From *McGraw Hill*: "A property of an object which determines the direction of heat flow when the object is placed in thermal contact with another object; heat flows from a region of higher temperature to one of lower temperature.

Pressure: From *McGraw Hill*: "A type of stress which is exerted uniformly in all directions; its measure is the force per unit area."

Available Energy: A property of a system at a state, in reference to an environment of constant temperature and pressure; available energy is the maximum useful work that can be extracted from the combination of the system and the referenced environment.

Other terms in use in the general MIT environment are listed below.

Flush (verb): To reject unequivocally.

Flame (verb): To argue a point of view forcefully.

Cruisillate (cruise + oscillate, verb): To function very fast. Used in describing electronic chips.

Tool (verb): to study very hard; (noun) one who studies very hard.

Power Tool (verb): to study very hard; (noun) one who studies very hard.

Bogossify (bogus + ossify, verb): To fake, as in results for a laboratory project.

Bogosity (bogus + fugacity, noun): State of being bogus.

Bible (noun): Notebook for a course, 3 to 4 inches thick, including worked-out solution sets to problem sets, lecture notes, and past exams.

Grease (noun): A politically oriented person seeking institute-wide student elective office. *See* embezzler.

Subway Surfing: Riding on the Boston MBTA Red Line, standing up, without holding onto anything.

All-weeker: MIT's version of an all-nighter.

And while definitions are being offered, "Kvel" is Yiddish for a sense of extreme pride, as when a parent sees a child graduate from MIT.

Oil Burning in Closed Room Problem. I was right about the first half of the problem. If the room were perfectly insulated and sealed, there would be no change in energy and no change in mass.

The second part of the question was trickier: "What is the change in mass between the oil-air mixture and the products of combustion if the maximum energy is transferred to the environment?"

They wanted us to invoke Einstein's famous equation: $E = mc^2$. If all the heat of combustion were conducted through the walls of the room, the energy in the room would be reduced by the combustion, and thus the mass of the contents of the room would be reduced.

The problem is first to find the energy of combustion:

$$10 \text{ BBls} \times 6 \times 10^6 \text{ Btu/BBL} = 6 \times 10^7 \text{Btu} = \Delta E$$
$$\Delta M = \Delta E / C^2$$
$$= \frac{6 \times 10^7 \text{ Btu}}{(3.0 \times 10^8 \text{ m/sec})^2} \times \left(1054.7 \frac{\text{joule}}{\text{Btu}}\right) \times \left(\frac{1 \text{ KG-m}^2}{\text{sec}^2\text{-joule}}\right)$$
$$= 7.032 \times 10^{-7} \text{ kg}$$
$$= 7.032 \times 10^{-4} \text{ g}$$
$$= 0.7032 \text{ mg}$$

So the mass of the contents of the room did decline, by about seven-tenths of a milligram. I lost 3 points out of 50 on the problem set for missing that trick.

CHAPTER 3

The Gasoline and Egg Problem. The problem was to determine how many eggs would be required to feed the human to pump the water, and also to see how much gasoline would be required.

First, calculate the change in potential energy associated with lifting the water up from the bottom of the well.

$$\Delta E \text{ water} = \rho \times V \times g \times \Delta h, \text{ where}$$
$$P = \text{Density of water } (3.78 \text{ kg/gal})$$
$$V = \text{Volume of water } (10,000 \text{ gal})$$

g = Acceleration due to gravity (9.8 m/sec²)

Δh = 300 ft

ΔE water = (3.78 kg/gal) $\times$ (10,000 gal) $\times$ (9.8 m/sec²) $\times$

(300 ft) $\times$ (.3048m/ft) $\times$ $\left(\dfrac{1 \text{ joule-sec}^2}{\text{kg-m}^2}\right)$ = 3.39 $\times$ 10⁷ joules

To find the number of eggs required, we need to convert from kg-calories to joules, and to take into account the 25 percent efficiency of the human prime mover.

Number of eggs required =

$$3.39 \times 10^7 J \times \left(\frac{2.387 \times 10^{-4} \text{ k-cal}}{1 \text{ J}}\right) \times \left(\frac{1 \text{ EGG}}{80 \text{ kcal}}\right) \times \left(\frac{1}{.25}\right)$$

= 404.6 eggs.

The gasoline consumption can be calculated similarly:

$$3.39 \times 10^7 J \times \left(\frac{1 \text{ lbm}}{20,000 \text{ Btu}}\right) \times \left(\frac{1 \text{ Btu}}{1054.8 J}\right) \times \left(\frac{0.454 \text{ kg}}{\text{lbm}}\right) \times$$

$$\left(\frac{1 \text{ gal}}{2.65 \text{ kg}}\right) \times \frac{1}{.25}$$

= 1.10 gallon

The ratio of energy costs in this example is:

Eggs: 404.6 eggs $\times$ $0.10/egg = $40.46

Gasoline: 1.10 gallon $\times$ $3.00/gallon = $3.30

$40.46/$3.30 = 12.3

The cost of eggs as a fuel is 12.3 times the cost of gasoline. Next, we need to calculate the labor cost of the cyclist. Assuming this is a strong cyclist and can generate about ¼ horsepower continuously, or about 190 watts, the time required to pump all the water would be:

(3.39 $\times$ 10⁷ joule) / (190 joule/sec) = 178,420 sec, or 49.6 hours.

This cost comes to about $200, at $4 per hour.

Next, calculate the cost of the military might required to secure the oil fields in the Persian Gulf. At an incremental cost of

$1 billion per day, plus a cost of, say, $100,000 per life lost, times X lives lost. . . . Uh-oh. There I go being politically correct again. Shame shame shame shame shame. Of course, if this were written by illuminated manuscript rather than on a personal computer using 200 watts, under three 75 watt lights, with about 300 watts of other lighting on in the office to make me feel secure while working on a Saturday, well then, I might have more of a leg to stand on.

The Three Block Problem. The problem statement was: "Three identical blocks of metal are available. Initially they are at temperatures 300, 500, and 700 K (Kelvin). For each of the blocks, the relation between internal energy and temperature of stable equilibrium states is given by the relation:

"U = Uo + C * T, where C is the heat capacity and T is the temperature in degrees Kelvin. Let's say C = 10 joule/Degree K (the answer is independent of C).

"If interactions via cyclic machinery between blocks are allowed but interactions between the blocks and the environment are not, what is the maximum temperature that can be reached by one of the blocks?"

The hint that Professors Gyftopoulos and Beretta gave me was as follows:

At the end of the process, two blocks will have the same temperature, and one block will have the highest available temperature. If the two blocks did not have the same temperature, the cyclic machinery could be used to raise the temperature of the third block further. The highest temperature of the third block will be obtained if all processes are reversible (there is no entropy increase).

The scene in which this problem was described is meant in no way to reflect negatively on Professor Gyftopoulos, but rather to present an example of a student's being overwhelmed by the pressure and standards of excellence at MIT. There are great teachers at MIT, and Professor Gyftopoulos is one of them. On numerous occasions during his lectures I had goose bumps from both the way he clearly presented the material, and from the nature of the material and how it coincided with my energy-conservation interests, and from his enthusiasm.

Plate Cooling Problem. Again refer to Rohsenow and Choi, *Heat, Mass and Momentum Transfer*, pp. 143–53. Presented there is the case of a flat plate with a uniform temperature distribution. The uniform heat flux case is presented in *Handbook of Heat Transfer*, by W. M. Rohsenow and James P. Harnett (New York: McGraw-Hill, 1973), pp. 159–160.

Also note, on p. 117 of Rohsenow and Choi, an example of when the solution of a theoretical problem, such as the infinite flat plate, can be applied to a real system, the wall of a rocket motor combustion chamber. The wall is a cylindrical shell, with a wall thickness that is small compared to the diameter, and is calculated as an infinite flat plate.

CHAPTER 4

Sport Death. The design on the Senior House T-shirt is from the cover of *Fear and Loathing: On the Campaign Trail '72*, by Dr. Hunter S. Thompson (San Francisco: Straight Arrow Books, 1973). The Sport Death design is identical to the cover design, by Thomas W. Benton, with the exception that the Sport Death skull doesn't have swastikas in the eyes, and the Benton design doesn't have anything legible written in the teeth. In Dr. Thompson's introduction, on page 17, "Sport Death" is written in pencil in the margin in the MIT library's copy of the book, next to this (here slightly abridged) paragraph:

> People who claim to know jackrabbits will tell you they are primarily motivated by Fear, Stupidity, and Craziness. But I have spent enough time in jackrabbit country to know that most of them lead pretty dull lives; they are bored with their daily routines: eat . . . sleep, hop around a bush now and then. . . . No wonder some of them drift over the line into cheap thrills once in a while; there has to be a powerful adrenaline rush in crouching by the side of a road, waiting for the next set of headlights to come along, then streaking out of the bushes with split-second timing and making it across to the other side just inches in front of the speeding front wheels.

There will be more on Sport Death in the Chapter 11 notes.

Bernoulli Equation. See Potter and Foss, *Fluid Mechanics*, pp. 49–55. The Bernoulli equation, stated by Daniel Bernoulli in his 1738 book *Hydrodynamica*, is a special case of the general equations of fluid mechanics, the Navier-Stokes equations. It applies to steady (no variation with time), inviscid (not viscous), irrotational (no whirlpools), incompressible flow. Besides the carburetor, it also applies to things like curveballs, perfume aspirators, and airplane wings. The actual equation is:

$$P + \tfrac{1}{2}\,\rho v^2 + \rho gz = \text{CONSTANT}$$

where P is fluid pressure, ρ is fluid density, g is gravitational acceleration constant, z is the height of the fluid, and v is the fluid velocity.

In *Encyclopaedia Americana* it is noted that Daniel Bernoulli was Swiss, born in Groningen, Netherlands. He was a professor of anatomy at the University of Basel, Switzerland. Since he was not Italian as his name suggests, but rather Swiss, it is unlikely that he either (a) had a cousin with a jewelry shop in Florence or (b) received funding from the Medici or Sforza foundations. We did not know this at our study session, however, so the image made sense.

The Carburetor. A discussion of a real carburetor is in *The Internal Combustion Engine*, by C. F. Taylor, Vol. 2, pp. 193ff. The difference between the real carburetors described in that book and what is described in here is that in real carburetors, the air is considered compressible, whereas we assumed the air was incompressible. For a simple description of a carburetor, see *The Way Things Work*, by David Macaulay (Boston: Houghton Mifflin, 1988), p. 148.

The main point of the Bernoulli equation in this case is that when the fluid speeds up, its static pressure (the pressure you would read if you put a barometer on the wall of the tube) goes down. Since the flow speeds up in the contraction, the static pressure does go down, below atmospheric pressure, and the liquid, at atmospheric pressure, is sucked in by the vacuum created by the sped up air.

Just looking at the air side, the equations are:
Continuity:

$$V_1 * A_1 = V_2 * A_2$$

Bernoulli:

$$P_1 + \tfrac{1}{2}\,\rho a V_1^2 + \rho gz_1 = P_2 + \tfrac{1}{2}\,\rho a V_2^2 + \rho gz_2$$

The Tea Leaf Problem. For more on this, refer to *Illustrated Experiments in Fluid Mechanics,* p. 97. The film, entitled *Secondary Flow,* was produced by Professor Edward Taylor of MIT.

The Firehouse Problem. The question was: "How many firemen will it take to hold on to a fire hose shooting out 800 gallons per minute at 100 feet per second, if each is capable of providing a horizontal force of 125 pounds?"

The force required to restrain the hose will be equal to the mass flow rate times the velocity going out of the hose. First, convert everything to metric units:

The density of water is 8.3453 pounds per gallon
8.3453 lbs/gal × (.4536 kg/lb.) = 3.785 kg/gal
(100 feet/sec) / (3.281 ft/m) = 30.48 m/sec
The mass flow rate is:
800 gal/min × 3.785 kg/gal = 3028 kg/min
(3028 kg/min) / (60 sec/min) = 50.47 kg/sec
50.47 kg/sec × 30.48 meters/sec = 1538 kg-m/sec^2
= 1538 Newtons
1538 Newtons / (4.45 lb.-force/Newton) = 345.7 lb-force
345.6 lb / (125 lb/ fireman) = 2.77 firemen. But since firemen come in integer units, it will take 3 firemen to restrain this hose.

CHAPTER 5

The Tube in the River Problem. You could extract power from a flowing river without building a dam by constructing an underwater turbine resembling a windmill. This would be able to extract 16/27, or 59 percent of the energy flowing through the circular area swept by the turbine blades. For a discussion of this limit for regular windmills, see *Wind Power and Other Energy Options,* by David Rittenhouse Inglis, (Ann Arbor: University of Michigan Press, 1978), p. 248. The maximum power that could be derived from an underwater turbine would be:

$$P = 16/27 \times (\rho \times A \times V_1{}^3)/2$$
where ρ is water density,
A is the area swept by the underwater turbine blades, and
V_1 is the incoming velocity of the river water.

CHAPTER 6

Radiation Heat Transfer. Refer to Rohsenow and Choi, *Heat, Mass and Momentum Transfer,* Ch. 13. Also refer to *Thermal Radiation Heat Transfer,* 2nd ed., by Siegel and Howell (New York: Hemisphere Publishing, 1981).

CHAPTER 7

Here are a couple of afterthoughts that didn't really fit in the flow of the book. First, I derived a lot of support and hands-on education from various technicians and machinists at MIT. Nick is a composite of all of these people.

Second, when I was putting the experiment together, friendly salesmen's voices on the other end of the line would help me work my way through some of the design problems. And so it seems to be in the consulting engineering world I work in now. I, the engineer, am educated by the vendors, who may or may not be engineers, but who have been thoroughly briefed on how their products fit within larger systems.

Finally, I became a lot less scared of the word *design* when I translated it to, in the context of my experiment, "figuring out where to put things," and/or "figuring out how big things should be."

Some definitions pertaining to my experiment:

Test Matrix. The set of experiments used to enhance one's knowledge about a process. For example, if you think two variables, such as initial air temperature in the cylinder and amount of air motion, affect a third result, such as the time it takes the diesel fuel to ignite, you could construct something that looks like a tic-tac-toe board as shown below:

	Air Motion 1	Air Motion 2	Air Motion 3
Temperature 1	Time 1,1	Time 1,2	Time 1,3
Temperature 2	Time 2,1	Time 2,2	Time 2,3
Temperature 3	Time 3,1	Time 3,2	Time 3,3

The delay times are the outputs of the experimentally varied inputs, air motion, and temperature.

Turbulence Level. Also known as turbulence intensity, this is defined in *Internal Combustion Engine Fundamentals,* by J. B. Heywood (New

York: McGraw-Hill, 1988), p. 331, as "the root mean square value of the fluctuating component of the instantaneous fluid velocity in a turbulent flow." Turbulence intensity is a measure of how chaotic a flow is; rapids in a river have higher turbulence intensity than smooth, straight stretches.

Swirl Rates. The rate at which air spins within the engine's cylinder.

Parametric Influences. Referring to the test matrix above, the parameters are temperature and air motion. These parameters are varied on the input of the experiment, to see the influence on the output of the experiment, in this case the ignition delay time.

Ignition Delay. The time between the start of fuel injection and the start of combustion of the fuel in a diesel engine.

Engines. For more discussion of how engines work, consult *The Way Things Work*, by David Macaulay, pp. 164–65. Or for more technical discussion, consult *The Internal Combustion Engine in Theory and Practice* by C. F. Taylor (Cambridge, Mass.: MIT Press, 1960 and 1966 [Vol. 1], 1968 [Vol. 2]), or *Internal Combustion Engine Fundamentals*, by J. B. Heywood. Also, *Internal Fire*, by Lyle Cummins (as in Cummins Engine Company), is available from the Society of Automotive Engineers (mail $34 to Department 2414; SAE; 400 Commonwealth Drive; Warrendale, PA 15096).

Pulleys. Again, see *The Way Things Work*, pp. 58–65.

CHAPTER 8

Steam Engine. See again *The Way Things Work*, pp. 166–67. Basically, a heat source, either a coal, gas, or oil fire, a nuclear fission, or focused sunlight, boils water as in a teakettle. The steam pressure increases as it's heated, and the high-pressure steam pushes on steam turbine blades. As the steam pushes on the turbine blades it cools and drops in pressure and is sucked into the condenser, where it is cooled by water from the nearby lake or ocean or cooling tower. The water then is pumped back into the boiler, where it again becomes steam. This was all developed in the late 1700s. At first, they didn't have separate condensers, and then in 1765 Watt figured out they'd save a lot of fuel if they added those. And then about 1800 Trevithick added the innovation of high-pressure steam, so more power could be packed into a smaller engine.

"Pong" video game invention. According to the goalie on my soccer team, who took 6.111, the digital electronics lab, in 1974, this game was invented as a class project when he took the class. He has no more data on what happened to the invention after the class.

Balloon Problem. The balloon problem presented in the main text is simplified to a case with incompressible flow and with no energy losses associated with the flow through the orifice. The equations for this simplified example are presented below:

P_t = Air pressure in tank
P_b = Air pressure in balloon
A_1 = Area of hole to fill balloon from tank
A_2 = Balloon shell area
k = Spring constant (stretchiness) of balloon skin

Bernoulli: $P_t + \frac{1}{2}\,\rho v_t^2 = P_b + \frac{1}{2}\,\rho v_1^2$
But $v_t = 0$, so
(1) $P_t - P_b = \frac{1}{2}\rho v_1^2$
Continuity: (2) $v_1 A_1 = v_2 A_2$
Force Balance
on Balloon Skin:
(3) $(P_b - P_a) \times A_2 - kx = 0$

v_1 = Speed of air going into balloon from tank
$x = v_2$ = Speed of balloon shell
$v_t = 0$ = Speed of air in tank
P_a = Atmospheric pressure
x = Position of balloon shell

CHAPTER 9

The example of the bicycle race breakaway as it relates to a system with better information flow and hence lower entropy and higher efficiency alludes to the application of information theory to thermodynamics. For further reading on this subject, refer to *Thermostatics and Thermodynamics: An Introduction to Energy, Information, and States of Matter, with Engineering Applications*, by Myron Tribus, (Princeton, N.J.: Van Nostrand, 1961).

CHAPTER 10

First Amusing Anecdote. Norbert Weiner, MIT genius from earlier in the century, was teaching a calculus class when one of the students asked him to do one of the homework problems on the board. Professor Weiner looked at the problem in the textbook, did it in his head, and wrote the answer on the board. The intrepid student then asked, "Could you do that another way?" Professor

Weiner again looked at the problem statement in the book, did it in his head another way, and wrote the same answer on the board.

CHAPTER 11

More on Sport Death. This took a little digging. The term *Sport Death* was imported to Senior House and MIT by a geology student from Arizona, who had picked it up from rock climbers and parachutists at Yosemite and other rock-climbing sites out West. The T-shirt appeared in the academic year '76–'77, when several students on Runkle 4th and 5th had the idea. They were in fact reading the Hunter Thompson book at the time (*Fear and Loathing on the Campaign Trail '72*) and the reference to Sport Death penciled in the margin of the library copy of the book was in fact the connection that brought the two images together on the shirt. The painting on the fourth floor of Runkle was painted some time after the T-shirt appeared.

Some of the Senior House alums of ten or so years ago who I talked to had interesting things to say about MIT as well, and some of their comments follow:

The real story is over at Baker House. That's where they die of loneliness. And then beyond that the real story is that these dweebs who were pathetic as students stay pathetic as maladjusted adults. The men marry the first women they can, and since they never learned any social or human skills, they find themselves stuck in low-level management jobs. Harvard's just as bad, but you have to remember what these people were doing while they were going through puberty. The kids at Harvard got in there by being editor of the school newspaper and being on the student council and stuff like that, while most of the people at MIT were just studying their science and math all the time, so their grades and SAT's would be good enough to get them into MIT.

And from the alumna who told me the Sport Death story:

Two of my friends there killed themselves. That's one of the reasons some of us started Nightline, the phone service that you could call to have someone to talk to in times of desperation. I think it happens for a couple of reasons, beyond the loneliness and the intense work atmosphere. A lot of students are pushing that fine line between genius and insanity, and some go back and forth across that line. In the case of Senior House, maybe the drugs exacerbated the problem in some cases. The key is that when many of these people were in high school they weren't that well adjusted, and when they come to the abnormal environment of MIT there's no great opportunity to become well adjusted, and then when they leave they're still maladjusted. When I was there there was also the added issue that there were eight men for every woman, so when a woman student left MIT, she'd have to cope with not as much attention as she had at MIT. Plus you come here and you're used to being the best in high school and you're just average, or below. I was the only piano player in my high school, and I came here and everyone plays. . . . I like your title. I think that sums it up well. I used to call it "Metal Guru," after the song by T. Rex. I think it has that same cold metallic sense.

And from the primary Sport Death T-shirt source: "Everybody at MIT has something going on. If they're into something they're way into it . . . they're so wired up. Nobody's lethargic; they're really involved in what they're doing."

Graduate Student Horror Stories. This is as good a place as any for this. I bumped into a friend at MIT on February 9, 1991. His name will be Alfred Weil. He has been working on his Ph.D. for seven years, beyond his master's degree.

"Put the picture of the boxes in. I want you to put the picture of the boxes in."

"What's the big deal about the boxes?" I asked while I looked at the wooden crates in the photo.

"I built them. Every nail in them was hammered in by my hands. Is this the work of a Ph.D.? Let me show you my stack of drawings. Seven years I built every piece of equipment in this laboratory. It was an empty room when I started, and the professor says, 'We would like to study the effect of such and such on such and such.' That was it. Finally the thing is built, after seven years of work, and I complain that I've not done enough real science, and the guy, knowing he has a good slave here in his dungeon says, 'You can stay as long as you want.'

Three years ago I complained all I was doing was technician work and they said, 'You can quit.' They put you in a position where the only rational thing to do is to quit. If you complain that you're doing meaningless drudgery, slave labor, they tell you you're not good enough. It wasn't that it was hard, it's that it wasn't appropriate to a Ph.D. effort. Another guy I know complained, and his adviser said to him, 'You're the pacing item.' Like you're a machine.

"See, the public perception of MIT is like a peak detector. They only see the Nobel prizes, the discoveries coming out of this place, the books, the products. But those are the spikes, here, high above zero. Where most of the people at this place are here wasting their lives below zero.

"It's very non-homogeneous, the graduate education here. It all depends on who your adviser is. Some people I know, after they passed the qualifiers, it was smooth sailing from then on. But others . . .

"There was one guy, he spent three years on his master's, then he passed the qualifiers, but in his department they have generals at the end, and after six years of being a slave he fails his generals. Then he goes away for a year, comes back, and takes them again, after he petitioned the dean. They let him pass, and then they say, 'You need to prove your ability to do research on another project.' So the six years he spent building the experiment is shot. It's like they passed him but they didn't pass him.

"And another graduate student got electrocuted, and this technician I know told me that the guy's adviser told him, 'You have to sacrifice a student to science now and then.' This, of course, was taken out of context, and was probably the professor's way of dealing with any feelings of guilt he might have had, but it was said.

"I'd sum it up like this," Alfred continued. "They lure talented but gullible people in here with MIT's reputation, and they use them."

Alfred's case may not be representative, but it does exist.

Poisson Distribution. A Poisson Distribution is defined as follows: If the average arrival rate is v, the probability of having m arrivals in time t is:

$P(m,t) = (v \times t)^m \times e^{-vt} / m!$

It was 6:55 when Howard made his calculation, so 15 minutes is the total time, 9 is the total number of arrivals, and v, the average rate of arrival, is 9/15, or 0.6. The probability of a total of 3 (m) people arriving in 10 (t) minutes is:

$P(3,10) = 6^3 \times e^{-6} / (3 \times 2 \times 1) = 0.0892$

C H A P T E R   12

An historical note on 2.70: It was started in the early seventies by Woodie Flowers, professor in the design group of the mechanical engineering department.

C H A P T E R   13

For more about the Schwarzschild radius and black holes, consult *A Brief History of Time* by Steven Hawking (New York: Bantam, 1988). For more about the twin paradox in relativity, consult *The Special Theory of Relativity*, by H. Muirhead, (New York: John Wiley & Sons, 1973), p. 39, or *Relativity*, by Ray Skinner, (Waltham, Mass.: Blaisdell Publishing, 1969), p. 94.

C H A P T E R   14

Toy Bird. The bird toy is called the "Drinking Happy Bird," made in Taiwan (MIT) by ARORA. At this writing it is available at the Museum Store of the Boston Museum of Science, and at the Children's Story Toystore, 434 Harvard St., Brookline, MA (617-232-6182).

Perpetual Motion Machines (general). For further reading, consult the article: "Perpetual Motion Machines," by S. W. Angrist, *Scientific American* (1968), 218:114–22; and the article entitled "Perpetual Motion Machines" in *Encyclopaedia Britannica*.

Friction Calculation. From a knowledge of how long it takes the wheel to come to a stop once the energy source that keeps it going is off, it is possible to calculate approximately the power required to keep the wheel moving against the friction that makes it stop.

The wheel rotated at about 1 revolution every 4 seconds. Thus its frequency, f, was 0.25 sec^{-1}, and its angular velocity, omega, was:

W = 2 x π × f = 0.5 × π = 1.57 radians per second.

The bicycle wheel can be considered as a hoop rotating about its axle, and its moment of inertia (I) is simply:
M × R^2
M × R^2, where M is the mass of the rim, and R is the radius of the wheel.

A wheel might have a rim mass of about 1 kg. A 27-inch diameter wheel has a radius of 13.5 inches, or 0.343 meters. Its moment of inertia is then:

1 kg × $(0.343 \text{ m})^2$ = 0.1176 kg-m^2

It took about 30 seconds for the wheel to come to a stop. An estimate of the average power to keep it going can be made by dividing the energy stored in the motion of the wheel by the time it takes to dissipate that energy. The energy stored in the wheel was:

$\frac{1}{2}$ × I × ω^2 = 0.5 × 0.1176 × $(1.57)^2$ = 0.145 joules
0.145 joules / 30 sec = 0.005 watts

For the thing to run three weeks, as Dr. Jones claimed, it would need a battery capable of storing:

0.005 watts x 3600 sec/hr × 24 hr/day × 21 days = 9,072 joules
= 0.0025 kilowatt-hours

According to *Encyclopaedia Americana*, a typical D-cell battery (also known as a Leclanche dry cell) carries about 0.045 kilowatt-hours per pound. Three D-cell batteries weigh about a pound, so one battery should carry about 0.015 kWh, so one D-cell battery would be more than adequate to power the machine.

The battery was discovered by Luigi Galvani (as in galvanize, galvanic action), professor of anatomy at the University of Bologna, in 1791, when he accidentally brought two dissimilar metals into contact with a moist substance. Allesandro Volta (as in voltage), professor of natural philosophy at the neighboring University of Pavia, developed the first storage battery, the "voltaic pile," in

1800. Professor Volta spent much time in Como, the lovely town on Lake Como, in the foothills of the Alps.

For more on system dynamics of rotational systems, consult *Introduction to System Dynamics*, by Shearer, Murphy and Richardson (Reading, Mass.: Addison-Wesley, 1971).

Wind Force on Wheel. If the copper tubes had air going through them, to shear along the side of the rim, power would be delivered to the rim, as calculated below.

Power = $\frac{1}{2} \times \rho \times v^3 \times A$
where ρ = density of air, about 1.2 kg/m^3
        v = air velocity, estimated at 2 meters per second
        A = cross-sectional area of copper tube, available to deliver

flow : $A = \pi \times r^2 = 3.14 \times (2.5 \times 10^{-3} \text{ m})^2$
                    $= 1.96 \times 10^{-5} \text{m}^2$

Power = $\frac{1}{2} \times 1.2 \times 8 \times 1.96 \times 10^{-5} = 9.4 \times 10^{-5}$ watts, per tube

or about 2×10^{-4} watts in total. The friction power we just calculated above as about 0.005 watts, so the jets would not be able to deliver enough power to overcome the friction. If there were jets, they wouldn't turn the wheel.

Moving Plate Capacitors. For a discussion of these, consult *Dynamics of Mechanical and Electromechanical Systems*, by Crandall, Karnopp, Kurtz, and Pridmore-Brown (Malabar, Fla.: Krieger Publishing [originally McGraw-Hill, 1968]), Ch. 6.

Motor principle. For more on how electric motors work, consult *The Way Things Work*, pp. 300–301.

CHAPTER 15

Hacking (general). For more on this subject, see *The Journal of the Institute for Hacks, TomFoolery and Pranks*, by Brian Liebowitz (Cambridge, Mass.: MIT Museum, 1990). The live cow story may be apocryphal.

Resonant Frequency. For more about this, consult Shearer, Murphy, and Richardson, *Introduction to System Dynamics*, or any elementary physics textbook. In Halliday and Resnick, *Fundamentals of Physics*, resonance is defined as follows: "Whenever a system capable of oscillating is acted on by a periodic series of impulses having a frequency equal or nearly equal to one of the natural frequencies of oscillation of the system, the system is set into oscillation with a relatively large amplitude." This has happened with bridges occasionally, and there is a famous film clip of the Takoma Narrows (Washington state) bridge resonating and ultimately collapsing as a result of wind-induced oscillations.

The term *resonance* has also been stolen by the literary community, as that feeling of goose bumps when everything in the book comes together and you finally figure out what the author is trying to say.

CHAPTER 16

For more on the strobe light and how to use it, consult *Electronic Flash, Strobe*, by Harold E. Edgerton (Cambridge, Mass.: MIT Press, 1979), 2nd ed.

Second Amusing Anecdote. Ari, the Israeli army officer, and I attended an open mechanical engineering department meeting in the spring of 1983. Professor Rohsenow conducted the meeting, and the topic steered toward how the government was cutting back on research funding.

Rohsenow said, "Well, if you assume that private industry will take up the slack with the money that they don't pay the government in taxes, we should be fine."

Professor Weare asked, "Excuse me, but how can you make that assumption?"

"I'm a Republican," Rohsenow answered.

CHAPTER 17

For more on LISP, consult *Structure and Interpretation of Computer Programs*, by Abelson and Sussman (McGraw-Hill and MIT Press, 1985), and *LISP*, by Patrick H. Winston, Berthold Klaus, and Paul Horn (Reading, Mass.: Addison-Wesley, 1981). For reading on artificial intelligence, consult *Artificial Intelligence*, by Patrick Winston (Addison-Wesley, 1984). Also *Gödel, Escher, Bach*, by Douglas R. Hofstadter (New York: Vintage Books, 1989), is supposed to be really good along these lines, although I haven't read it. Which is not to imply that I've read any of the other books referred to herein.

Bicycles. If you're ever near Dinant, Belgium (incidentally the birth-place of Adolph Sax, inventor of the saxophone), go to Musée de la Petite Reine, in the village of Falmignoul. It was there in 1980, anyway. You might want to call ahead (Belgium: 082-74.44.05) or write. They have samples of the many different types of bicycles invented during the nineteenth century. The address is: Musée de la Petite Reine; Falmignoul, Province de Namur; Belgium. The museum was created by Mr. Ernest Wouters.

CHAPTER 18

Please note, the thesis results presented in this chapter are meant to illustrate the process of analyzing and discussing experimental data. The work I did fed into later work by E. Balles and M. Theobald. That work may be located by referencing Society of Automotive Engineers papers published by Professor J. B. Heywood.

The Harvard Bridge. The MIT Museum Shop has a file on this. It's not called the Technology Bridge because when it was built in the late 1800s, MIT was still in Boston. Technically it was named after John Harvard, not Harvard College, and since it had structural problems at various points in its history, culminating in its re-placement in the late 1980s, MIT was not all that eager to have the bridge's name changed to the Technology Bridge.

Wheatstone Bridge. For more detail on how these work, see *Instrumentation* by Kirk and Rimboi (Alsip, Ill.: American Technical Publishers, 1975), p. 117.

In a hot-wire circuit, the imbalance in resistances causes a voltage difference between two points of the bridge. That voltage difference then goes into an amplifier, which makes the voltage across the total bridge go up or down, to maintain the hot-wire anemometer at a constant temperature, and hence a constant resistance. So if the flow slows down, the hot wire gets hotter, and the amplified voltage goes down. Conversely, if the flow speeds up, the wire cools and the voltage quickly goes up to keep the wire hot. The amplified voltage is what you read on the oscilloscope screen. Thanks to Alfred Weil for correcting my explanation.

Spark Plug. See *The Way Things Work*, pp. 308–309. Also see *Internal Combustion Engines*, by Edward F. Obert (Scranton, Pa.: International Textbook, 1968), p. 532ff. The diagram is from that book.

CHAPTER 19

See Psalm 91.

CHAPTER 20

Final quotation:

> Let knowledge grow from more to more.
> But more of reverence in us dwell.
> That mind and soul, according well
> May make one music as before
> But vaster.

—From *In Memorium*, by Alfred Lord Tennyson

Index